DAVID ROBERTS R.A.
THE HOLY LAND

DAVID ROBERTS R.A.
THE HOLY LAND

5 PARTS

1. JERUSALEM

This edition of
The Holy Land was originally published in 1982
by Terra Sancta Arts.

This edition published 1989 by Studio Editions
an imprint of Bestseller Publications Ltd.
Princess House, 50 Eastcastle Street
London W1N 7AP, England

ISBN 1 85170 260 1

Editor: Nachman Ran

Sources of the originals: The illustrations and texts have been
taken from the First Edition of the coloured and mounted
lithographs in 3 volumes, prepared by Louis Haghe and
published by F.G. Moon, London, under the title: "The Holy
Land, Syria, Idumea, Egypt, Nubia," in the years 1842-1849,
preserved at The Victoria & Albert Museum, London.
Grateful acknowledgement is given to the Victoria & Albert
Museum's Library and its Staff for their permission and
assistance in the photographing of the First Edition of David
Roberts R.A. Lithographs.

We extend our thanks to the National Library of Scotland,
Edinburgh, for their permission to reproduce the Facsimile pages
from David Roberts Private Journal to the East.

The Volumes/Parts in the Series of
David Roberts Lithographs

THE HOLY LAND

Text and Lithographs by Courtesy of the
Victoria & Albert Museum's Library,
London

Volume 1 / Part 1: Jerusalem
25 Coloured Facsimile Lithographs
25 Coloured photos of the Sites
Historical descriptions by Rev. G. Crolly, L.L.D.
The Journal of David Roberts
Preface by Mr. Teddy Kollek, Mayor of Jerusalem

Volume 2 / Part 2 : Galilee & Lebanon
27 Coloured Facsimile Lithographs
27 Coloured photos from the Sites
Historical descriptions by Rev. G. Crolly, L.L.D.
The Journal of David Roberts
Introduction by Prof. M. Har-El

Volume 3 / Part 3 : Judea & The Jordan River
24 Coloured Facsimile Lithographs
24 Coloured photos from the Sites
The Journal of David Roberts
Introduction and Historical descriptions of the Sites
by Rev. G. Crolly, L.L.D.

Volume 4 / Part 4 : Samaria & Idumea (Petra)
25 Coloured Facsimile Lithographs
25 Coloured photos from the Sites
The Journal of David Roberts
Historical descriptions and Introduction
by Rev. G. Crolly, L.L.D.

Volume 5 / Part 5 : The Desert (Negev & Sinai)
22 Coloured Facsimile Lithographs
22 Coloured photos from the Sites
The Journal of David Roberts
Introduction by Prof. M. Har-El
List of Pictures painted by David Roberts
Map of the route of David Roberts

Awake, awake;
put on thy strength, O Zion;
put on thy beautiful garments,
O Jerusalem, the Holy City.....

Isaiah 52, 1

עורי עורי לבשי עזך ציון
לבשי בגדי תפארתך ירושלים עיר הקדש.

ישעיה נ״ב, ו

Contents

Note: The sequence of the Plates slightly differs from the First Edition, due to technical limitations.

JERUSALEM

DAVID ROBERTS R.A.
THE HOLY LAND

25 Coloured Facsimile Lithographs
25 Coloured Photos of the Sites
Introduction and Historical descriptions of the
Sites by Rev. G. Crolly, L.L.D.
David Roberts's private Journal
Preface by Mr. Teddy Kollek, Mayor of
Jerusalem
Text and Lithographs by Courtesy of the
Victoria & Albert Museum's Library, London

Published by Studio Editions, London

David Roberts R. A.

QUEEN'S MOST EXCELLENT MAJESTY.

MADAM,

The cultivation of the Fine Arts has been regarded by all civilized nations as an ornament of the Diadem; but by England in the higher light, of an essential instrument of her intellectual supremacy.

Your Majesty's ancestors, distinguished as they were by the triumphs of fleets and armies, never lost sight of the milder, but not less permanent lustre, reflected on the throne and the people by the triumphs of the national mind.

Yet, while your Majesty's known taste and royal munificence have already given new animation to the arts, the present work solicits your approval by higher claims than mere elegance of design or skill of execution. Illustrative of scenes once hallowed by the steps of the prophet and the apostle, possessing in all ages the highest interest for the scholar and the philosopher, and now opening the most sacred contemplations and most glowing prospects to the philanthropist and the Christian, these volumes are dedicated to your Majesty, as the DEFENDER OF THE FAITH of a great Christian empire, by,

Madam,

Your Majesty's most faithful Subject

and dutiful Servant,

FRANCIS GRAHAM MOON.

Dedication of the Book to Queen Victoria (in facsimile)

David Roberts*

David Roberts was born at Stockbridge, near Edinburgh, October 24th, 1796; his early love of Art may in some measure be traced to a mother, to whom he was devotedly attached. She was a native to the ancient episcopal town of St. Andrew's and often spoke to him of the magnificent remains of the cathedral and monastic edifices of this once celebrated seat of learning. These conversations influenced his taste for Art towards that particular department which he may be said to have made his own, for there was scarcely an old castle or ruined chapel in or around his native town that he did not visit and sketch when a boy.

By the advice of Graham, director of the "Trustees Academy" at Edinburgh, and the master of Wilkie and Allan, young Roberts, at the early age of ten years, was apprenticed to a house-painter named Gavin Beugo, who probably gave the lad some little instruction in drawing; beyond this, we believe, he has never been indebted to a single individual, for helping him onwards in the art he has practised with so great honour to himself, and so instructively and delightfully to others.

Having served a long and wearisome apprenticeship of seven years to Beugo, a harsh and overbearing master, we hear of him in 1818, as assistant scenepainter at the Pantheon, a second-rate theatre in Edinburgh, under one Dearlove, of whom nothing is known. In the following year he became principal painter at the Theatre Royal, Glasgow, and in 1820 and 1821, at the Theatre Royal, Edinburgh. Before the latter year expired, his fame had reached the ears of the then lessee of Drury Lane, the celebrated Elliston, who offered him an engagement for three years, in conjunction with his friend Clarkson Stanfield; it is a singular circumstance that these two fellow-labourers should have lived each to become the most distinguished artist in his respective department, and both to attain the highest academical honours.

From this point of time, the history of Roberts as a painter in oil really commences, his first picture being exhibited at the British Institution in 1824. It was about this period that the Society of British Artists was instituted; both Stanfield and Roberts were among its original members: here, as well as at the British Institution and the Royal Academy, both were constant exhibitors. But all who remember the beautiful series of pictures, for they could scarcely be called scenes, which the two artists produced at Drury Lane and Covent Garden Theatres, till 1830, must have felt how greatly these pictorial works influenced public taste in what was beautiful in scenic art, compared with what had previously existed.

The first picture exhibited at the Academy by Roberts was a "View of Rouen Cathedral"; this was in 1826. Notwithstanding the incessant demands upon his time during the early period of his career, he found frequent opportunities for visiting the continent, for many of his exhibited pictures were subjects sketched in France, Germany and Belgium, while his own native land was not forgotten: every successive year, during the lifetime of his parents, did he visit them, and on these occasions he was accustomed to make excursions through various parts of Scotland containing remarkable ancient edifices, of which he made drawings. One of the results arising from these hometravels was a series of etchings on copper, by his own hand, of the antiquities of Scotland, which were carried to a considerable extent; but from circumstances over which he had unfortunately little control, they were abandoned and never again resumed.

As soon as he found himself firmly established in the estimation of the public, Roberts gradually relinquished painting for the theatres and restricted his labours within the limit of the studio. His friend Wilkie, advised him to explore Spain, as a country less known, and one offering a rich field for his pencil: this was in 1832. The same year, before quitting England, he completed a series of drawings for Sir E. Bulwer Lytton's "Pilgrims of the Rhine".

Roberts devoted the years 1832—33 to his spanish tour; and after visiting Burgos, Madrid, Toledo, Segovia, Cordova, Granada, Malaga, Gibraltar, Cadiz and Seville, there he settled down and painted several pictures in oil. On his return from Spain, he followed the series of beautiful annuals commenced by Prout, and continued by Harding, which were published by Jennings under the title "The Landscape Annual".

Roberts was elected associate to the Academy in the year 1838, four years after his friend Stanfield. But before the election of Roberts as a junior member of the Academy, he was making preparations for the most important event of his life, namely, a journey to Palestine, Egypt, Syria; this was an undertaking he had long contemplated, and it seems to have been entered upon solely from a love of artistic adventure: for although, as we have just remarked, he had not yet been admitted into the ranks of the Academy, his fame was

* Revised text which appeared in The Art Journal, 1858

not only well established, but he was on the most friendly terms with the leading men in it all the time: Wilkie, Turner, Callcot, Landseer, etc; and among the most liberal patrons of Art, his works has found place in the collections of Lord Nortwick, the Duke of Beadford, the Earl of Essex, the Marquis of Lansdowne, the late Sir Robert Peel etc.

Supplied with a letter of introduction from the Foreign-Office to Colonel Campbell, Consul-General for Egypt, Roberts started from England on his great and hazardous expedition in August, 1838, taking the route by Paris and Marseilles. He arrived in Egypt by the end of September, 1838.

In February, 1839, Roberts left Cairo in the company of two friends, Mr. J. Pell and Mr. J.W. Kinnear, (the latter of whom wrote an account of the journey — by the title "Cairo, Petra and Damascus") - to cross the desert by way of Suez, Mount Sinai and Petra.

Roberts parted from Kinnear in Gaza and reached Jerusalem at Easter, when pilgrims assemble in the sacred city to witness "the descent of the holy fire" — and to bathe in the river Jordan. Having visited the most remarkable places from "Dan to Beersheba", illustrative with Biblical history, he returned to England in the latter part of 1839 after an absence of about eleven months.

The fruits of this expedition are too well known to require pointing out — "Roberts' Holy Land" has a world-wide reputation; nothing of a similar character has ever been produced that can bear comparison with it. On the artist's return, he submitted his drawings to that "most enterprising and prince of all publishers" — Sir F.G. Moon, who arranged with him to bring out a work illustrative of Scripture history, giving him the sum of £3,000 for the copyright of the sketches, and for superintending their reproduction in lithography, a task intrusted to Mr. Louis Haghe. This sum of £3,000 seems at first sight a very large amount to receive, but when we consider the dangers experienced by the artist in collecting his materials, and that he and Haghe were occupied nearly eight years in preparing them for publication, the sum dwindles into a very insignificant amount. If Roberts acquired a large increase of fame by his labours, the publisher found the adventure most profitable. Roberts, after one year of his return from his journey to the Holy Land — was elected full member of the Royal Academy.

In the forthcoming years he visited many European countries, and the results of these travels and their paintings have been exhibited in leading Galleries. He was awarded with honours, especially at the International Exhibition held in Paris in the year 1855.

In 1860 he started painting a series of the Thames, which included: the Houses of Parliament, St. Paul's Cathedral and others. Most of his pictures have been commissioned or sold after their completion. (See list of his paintings at the end of our book.)

He died at the age of 68, on 25 November 1864, and is buried in Norwood Cemetery.

Preface

Jerusalem has always been and will forever continue to be the core of the dreams of the believers.

For centuries Jerusalem had been sketched, painted, photographed. Travel journals have been written about Jerusalem in every conceivable language. And yet when people envision Jerusalem, very often what they envision is Jerusalem painted by David Roberts, 140 years ago. He succeeded so ably in capturing the beauty of the city, its special quality, its special colours.

The pastel colours, that were added to the original two-coloured lithographs, add a special value to the description of the scenery, drawn in their delicate lines.

David Roberts' personal Journal accompanying his paintings gives a verbal expression to his impressions in the lithographs he painted.

In juxtaposition with photographs of these very sites today, the works of David Roberts takes on added dimensions. The centuries past and present join together in telling the story of Jerusalem.

David Roberts' work has been praised by the international community as the complete work of art on the Holy Land and Jerusalem, depicted through centuries as the Center of the World.

Teddy Kollek

Teddy Kollek
Mayor of Jerusalem

Introduction*

To visit the Holy Land, and make drawings of the scenes of sacred history and the antiquities of Egypt, had been, long before this journey was undertaken by Mr. Roberts, the brightest of his anticipation as an artist. He had already acquired so high a reputation for his skill and judgment in the treatment of architectural subjects, that the service of his pencil was sought, to make us acquainted with the structures of the Moors in Spain, and to make drawings from, and adapt for the use of the engraver, many of the sketches furnished by travellers in Palestine, of the buildings and objects of interest published in the "Illustrations of the Bible:" these studies, and his journey to Spain and Morocco for his Spanish scenery, excited in him an irrepressible desire to visit the East. The drawings of the French Commission in Egypt had been declared very incorrect, and De Laborde's Petra was charged also with inaccuracy. To go and draw for himself scenes and objects of such intense interest could alone satisfy him; the result has been his richly stored portfolios, from which the subjects for this work have been selected.

Having made himself thoroughly acquainted with all matters requisite for the journey, and such works as were published on the countries and objects he was about to visit, and having prepared himself with letters and introductions, especially from the Foreign Office to Colonel Campbell, the Consul-General in Egypt and Syria, he left London August 31st, 1838, and reached Alexandria on the 24th of September following. Every facility was kindly and readily given by Colonel Campbell for the accomplishment of our artist's objects. The Nile was at its height, and therefore visited at the most advantageous time. He ascended to Cairo, with introductions from Colonel Campbell, and there, by the aid of those to whom he had been recommended, Mr. Roberts was furnished with a guard to accompany him everywhere, and protect him from interruption or insult whilst sketching: he even obtained permission to enter every mosque he desired to visit, a privilege never before given to a Christian, but to which one condition was attached — that in the instruments he used in making his studies, for he was allowed to paint there, he was not to desecrate the mosque by the introduction and use of brushes made of *hog's bristles.*

From Cairo Mr. Roberts, with an Arab servant, ascended the Nile in a boat commanded by a captain with a crew of eight men, provisioned for three months.

He was entirely master of the party, and carried the British flag at the mast head. He thus ascended to the second cataract, Wady Halfa, and before he returned to Cairo, had made drawings of almost every edifice from the extremity of Nubia to the Mediterranean.

While at Cairo, he made the acquaintance of M. Linant, who had been De Laborde's companion in his visit to Petra; he kindly showed Mr. Roberts the original sketches which had been made in that excursion, and thus added stimulants, which were unnecessary, to his undertaking the interesting journey to Wady Mousa, or Petra. He immediately made preparations for crossing the desert by the route of the Israelites to Mount Sinai — by Akabah, and through the great valley of El Ghor to Petra, and thence to Hebron, instead of entering Palestine by El Arish and Gaza, as he had intended.

On the 8th of February, 1839, having been joined by Mr. Pell and Mr. Kinnear, (the latter of whom has since published an account of this journey,) they assumed the Arab dress, and, with their servants well armed, left Cairo: taking with them twenty-one camels, and escorted by nearly as many Bedouin Arabs, of the tribe of the Beni Sa'ids.

On the 27th they reached the Fortress of Akabah, on the Red Sea; here they parted with the Arab tribe hitherto their friends and guides, and put themselves under the escort of the tribe of Alloeens, who were to conduct them to Petra and thence to Hebron. On the 6th of March they reached Mount Hor, upon which rests the tomb of Aaron: at its base, deeply seated in its ravines and bounded by its precipitous sides and lofty peaks, lies the excavated city of Petra, the Idumea of the Greeks, the Edom of the prophet Jeremiah — the city of impregnable position, which gloried in its strength, but which strikes the traveller, who is fortunate enough to visit it, as an awful realization of the prophetic denunciations: "Thy terribleness hath deceived thee, and the pride of thine heart, O thou that dwellest in the clefts of the rock, that holdest the height of the hill: though thou shouldest make thy nest as high as the eagle, I will bring thee down from thence, saith the Lord."[1]

Mr. Roberts and his companions were the first who had been permitted to pitch their tents within Petra; is was the result of a long and violent altercation between the Arab tribe inhabiting Wady Mousa and the Alloeens, with whom an old grudge remained unsettled. At length

*From the First Edition, London, 1842.

[1] Jeremiah xlix. 16.

a sufficient amount was agreed upon as a peace-offering for a truce, and the occupation of an encampment within the city for five days without molestation; during this time our artist, fortunately, worked incessantly on his studies, for on the fifth night the little party was assailed and some of their arms were carried off; but it was suspected by our travellers, that the attack of the Arabs of Wady Mousa was connived at by their guides, who were impatient to return; the next morning they struck their tents, and bade farewell to Petra, the wonder of the desert.

On the 16th, the party having reached Hebron, and learnt that the plague had barred access to Jerusalem, proceeded to the coast, visiting Gaza, Askelon, and Jaffa; but being informed here that no recent case had occurred in the Holy City, and that the quarantine would shortly be removed, they set out for Jerusalem, and arrived there on the 29th of March, the day before Palm Sunday, a day held by the Christians in the East in great veneration. While at Jerusalem, Mr. Roberts received much kindness and assistance from the then governor, Achmet Aga, whom he accompanied with about four thousand Christian pilgrims to Jericho and the river Jordan. He afterwards visited the Dead Sea, the Lake of Tiberias, the sea coast and mountain range of Lebanon, and the ruins of Baalbec; such exertions, and the severe privations which he suffered on the journey, produced intermittent fever, which compelled him to abandon his projected excursions to Damascus and Palmyra. How entirely he had been devoted to the great objects he had proposed to himself before he left England, this work will abundantly prove. The extraordinary merit and interest of his drawings, when seen after his return, created a sensation not easily forgotten; the fidelity of his accurate pencil, his skillful and rigid adherence to the truth of costume, his attention to just and characteristic effect, were acknowledged by all travellers and artists competent to judge. The demand for his work sprang out of the interest thus excited. Commissions from royalty and the chief patrons of art crowded upon him for pictures from the subjects he had studied in the East, and his contemporaries in art acknowledged his merits by the honour of electing him into the Royal Academy.

A Note from the Publisher:

The publishing of his great work "The Holy Land", caused David Roberts many unpleasant moments in dealing with some publishers, but at last he found Mr. Francis G. Moon, to whom he offered the work, as mentioned in his Journal:

"... I made him acquainted with all these circumstances, and he at once agreed to bring out the work in the manner I had proposed ... This was a great risk on the publishers' part: but by exhibiting the drawings in London and other principal towns, his subscription-list in May 1841 was nearly double Murray's estimated costs. ... Before the drawings were shown to the public, they were submitted to the Queen, to the Archbishops of York and Canterbury, and to the Bishop of London, who all subscribed for the work, the Queen graciously allowing it to be dedicated to her..."

The list of the subscribers can be found at the end of our book.

The work was received with great enthusiasm, as described by E.A. Abbey:

"... the first studies ever made to give the portraiture of scenes of historical and religious interest. They were faithful and labourious beyond any outlines from nature... In point of bulk and ambition, Roberts's "Holy Land" was one of the most important and elaborate venture of nineteenth-century publishing, and it was the apotheosis of the tinted lithograph..."

On the quality of the work, David Roberts himself gave his own appreciation of the lithographer, Louis Haghe, who "... not only duly surpassed himself, but all that has hitherto been done of a similar nature. He has rendered the views in a style clear, simple and unlaboured, with a masterly vigour and boldness which none but a painter like him could have transferred to stone...".

This book, of one hundred and twenty three coloured lithographs of the Holy Land are presented to the public as a facsimile reproduction from the First Edition of the printed and hand-coloured lithographs preserved at the Victoria and Albert Museum's Library, London.

We are publishing David Roberts's private Journal along with his lithographs, and a colour picture of today, taken at the spot where he made his sketches for his lithographs.

We hope that the re-publishing of this book, in 5 volumes / parts 140 years after the original was published, will give the reader the opportunity to enjoy the beauty and skill of the drawings of David Roberts, his love of the Fine Arts and the Holy Land.

Nachman Ran

May, 1982   Terra Sancta Arts Ltd.

The Lithographs

Entrance to the Holy Sepulchre (Title Page)

THIS Vignette represents the façade of the Church of the Holy Sepulchre, which is built over the spot where our Lord was presumed to have been buried. The streets leading to it are all traditionally distinguished by events connected with the crucifixion. From the Serai, the present residence of the governor, said to be on the site of Pontius Pilate's palace, a street, named the Strada Dolorosa, or "Street of Sorrow," represents, in part, the path trod by our Lord to Calvary; another street then intervenes, and brings the pilgrim in front of the Church. The ground there expands into a large open space, filled, at the chief festivals, with sellers of crucifixes, rosaries, carved shells, bracelets, and other matters of the same kind, which are carried away in remembrance of the sacred soil.

During Easter, the period of Mr. Roberts's visit, this court was used as a bazaar and was crowded with pilgrims and merchants. He thinks that the building must have been extremely beautiful previous to the fire of 1808, and regards it as still bearing a close resemblance to the rich architecture of St. Mark's at Venice. The entrance is by an arched porch with clusters of polished marble columns, principally of the beautiful verde antique, over which another tier of arches encloses the windows; the small building on the right is the Chapel of our Lady of Grief. The capitals of the pillars of the porch, with its frieze and cornices, are exquisitely carved, partly in the Greek style, and partly in what is termed the Gothic, forming as it were the link between the two, and showing that the arts at the time must have still been in a high state of excellence[1]. The narrow frieze over the doorway represents the triumphant entry of our Saviour into Jerusalem. One of the doors has been walled up; the existing one, formed of massive materials, has three locks, the keys of which are kept by the Turkish governor, and is opened only on certain days at fixed hours, in the presence of the three dragomen of the Latin, Greek, and Armenian convents. When the door is closed, the Greek monks, who are now in possession of the Holy Sepulchre, receive their supplies by means of a basket let down from one of the windows. At the season of Easter, and during some of the great ceremonies of the holy week, the façade is hung with rich tapestry.

[1]Roberts's Journal.

David Roberts Journal

The following texts are from David Roberts's private Journal and letters written during his wanderings in the Holy Land and neighbouring countries.
His Journal begins:

... I left London for France on the 31st August 1838, and passed a few days in Paris, where I was very kindly received by my friend Count Jennison, the Bavarian Ambassador. My course lay down the Rhone and the Seine, passing through Lyons, Avignon and Arles, to Marseilles, which having left in a steamer, we coasted fair Italy, passed half-a-day at Citta Vecchia, and in about six days reached Malta.

Here I was transferred from one steamer to another, and in about three days we reached Lysa, one of the Greek islands. Here we again changed steamers, and on reaching Alexandria, on the 24th September, I was kindly received by Colonel Campbell.

Note: The Artist continued in his Journal to describe his journey in Egypt prior to his entry into the Holy Land.

David Roberts began his journey to the Holy Land from Suez through Sinai, Petra, Jerusalem and from there to the north, reaching Baalbec. He returned to England via Egypt, after 11 months.
This route is described in the attached map in Vol. 5/Part 5, pgs. 70-71.

The original, First Edition book — without the Journal — begins with the Lithographs of Jerusalem, as reproduced here. The Journal was written in chronological order. Therefore, we have added an indication in the Journal of the corresponding Plates, mentioned in his descriptions.

David Roberts R.A.

Above: The Artist's Signature.

The text on the opposite page describes the following double-spread Plate.

Plate 1: Entrance to the Holy Sepulchre (Title Page)

The

HOLY LAND,

Syria, Idumea, Arabia, Egypt & Nubia.

FROM DRAWINGS MADE ON THE SPOT BY

David Roberts, R.A.

WITH HISTORICAL DESCRIPTIONS BY

THE REV.^D GEORGE CROLY, L.L.D.

LITHOGRAPHED BY

LOUIS HAGHE.

VOL I.

LONDON, F. G. MOON, 20 THREADNEEDLE STREET.

PUBLISHER IN ORDINARY TO HER MAJESTY.

MDCCCXLII.

PLATE 1: ENTRANCE TO THE HOLY SEPULCHRE

Citadel of Jerusalem, without the walls

The Tower of David

THE citadel of modern Jerusalem, an irregular assemblage of square towers, lies on the north-western part of Sion, to the south of the Yaffa gate. It has on the outer side a deep fosse. A solid sloping bulwark, rising from the bottom of the fosse, at an angle of about forty-five degrees, protects the towers. This bulwark bears evident marks of remote antiquity, and by Robinson[1] is thought to be of the time of Hadrian. At the capture by the Crusaders (A.D. 1099), this was the strongest part of the city, and here the garrison made their last stand. When the walls were thrown down by the Moslems (A.D. 1219), this fortress was preserved, and bore the name of the Tower or Citadel of David until the sixteenth century, when it was occasionally called the Castle of the Pisans, from having been once rebuilt by citizens of that republic[2].

The north-eastern tower, now especially called the Tower of David, attracts notice by its size and antiquity; for though the upper part is modern, the lower is formed of vast stones, wrought in the manner of the ancient masonry, and, in all probability, a remnant of the Tower Hippicus, built by Herod, and left standing by Titus when he destroyed the other defences.[3] Some of the stones are twelve feet long by three feet five inches broad. The height of the ancient position is about fifty feet.[4]

[1] Biblical Researches, vol. i. 454   [2] *Pisanorum Castrum*. Adrichonius, 156, quoted by Robinson.   [3] Josephus, Jewish War, vii. l.l.   [4] Roberts's Journal.

From the Journal

21st January, 1839

Having agreed today with a Mr. Walne to furnish me with four camels for Syria, after packing and arranging my sketches, I waited on that gentleman, and was informed by him that the plague had been in Jerusalem for three months; and as a cordon was drawn round the city, I should be subjected to quarantine if I attempted to visit it. This annoyed me very much. To visit Syria without seeing Jerusalem would be as bad as to visit England without seeing London. Colonel Campbell advises me to wait till the 24th, when he will have letters as to the real state of matters.

26th January, 1839

Still no news from Syria. Lost all day waiting at the consulate. In the evening, at Mr. Pell's, made a sketch of some dancing-girls.

27th January, 1839

Still no news. Mr. Pell is trying to persuade me to go with him to Petra, but this would take two months, a much longer time than I can afford.

28th January, 1839

News arrived. There is no cordon round Jerusalem, and no quarantine on entering Syria by Beyrout.

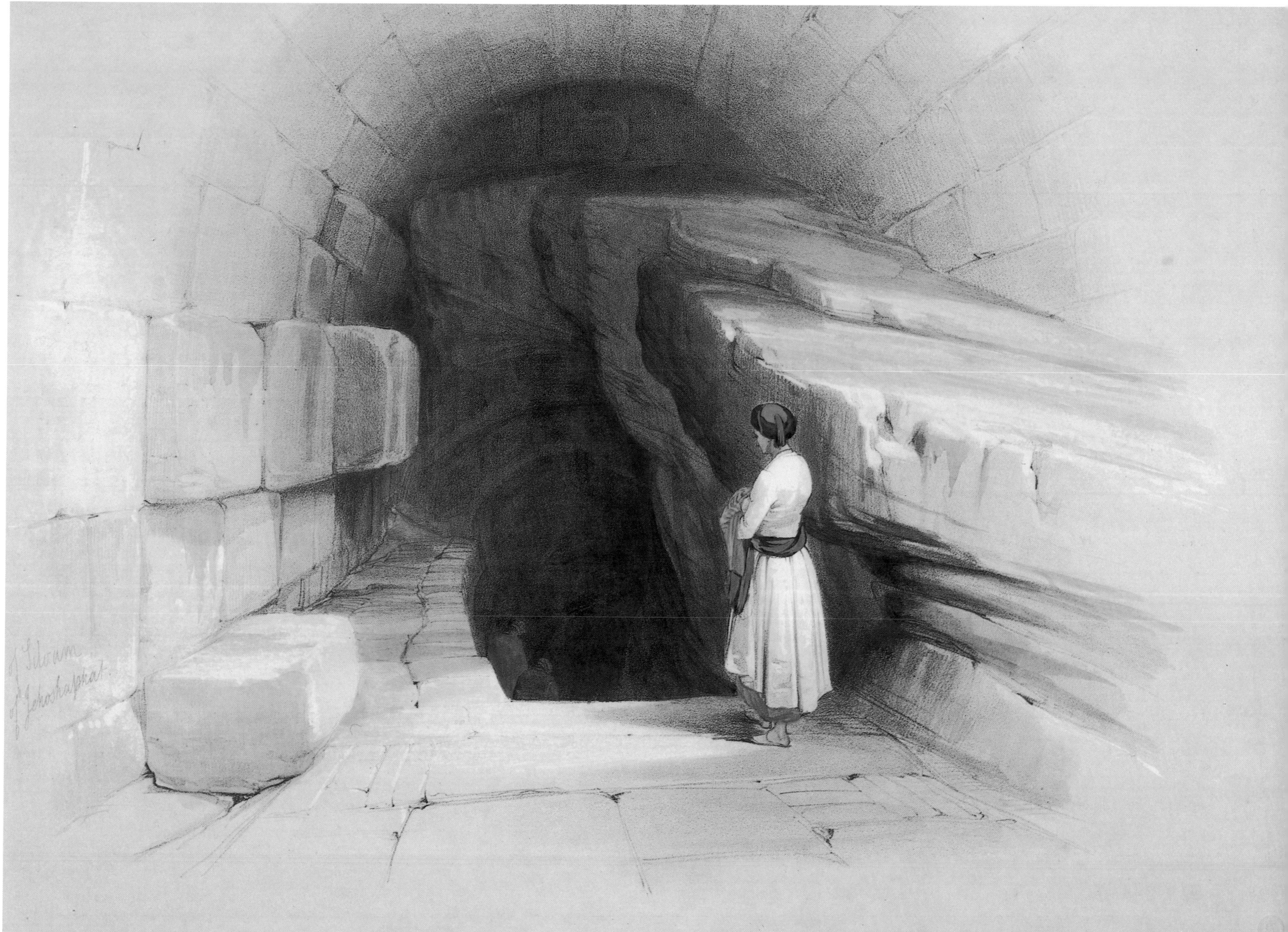
of Siloam
of Jehoshaphat.

The Upper Fountain of Siloam

SILOAM consists of two basins or fountains, the upper one of which is a fissure in the solid rock. A flight of steps leads down on the inside to the water, and close at hand, on the outside, is the reservoir.[1] This seems to be generally acknowledged as
"Siloa's brook that flowed Fast by the oracle of God."

The drawing of the water from Siloam in the Feast of Tabernacles (though no direction on the subject is to be found in the Mosaic Law) became a remarkable ceremonial in the latter ages of Judea.

The priest with his attendants received it from the fountain in a golden vessel, and then, returning to the Temple, mingled it with wine, and poured it on the altar. The origin of the custom has been the subject of much discussion among the rabbis, but it is generally supposed to have originated in the verse of Isaiah (xii. 3), "With joy shall ye draw water out of the wells of salvation." Much exhibition of popular rejoicing, with sounding of trumpets and horns, accompanied this ceremony. The whole Feast of Tabernacles was peculiarly a display of popular exultation, as it occurred in the finest season of the year, after the gathering of all the harvests; was under tents and bowers, reminding the people of the happiest scenes of the national life; and was typical of the period when earth is to be paradise again, and Israel is to be restored for ever. The water from Siloam was drawn on every day of the seven during which the feast continued. But the most solemn outpouring was on the last, the chief day of this memorable celebration. Our Lord refers to it, as prefiguring the outpouring of the Holy Spirit. (John, vii. 39).

[1] Robinson, Biblical Researches, vol. i. p. 497.

From the Journal

29th January, 1839

I have agreed to go to Syria with Mr. Pell, by way of Mount Sinai, Petra, Hebron, and Jerusalem. Mr. Pell promises to be ready in eight days, and I shall fill up the time here in making a panorama of Cairo for my friend Burford. Colonel Campbell is to give me introductory letters to the consuls at Jerusalem and Damascus.'

The following extracts are from a letter to his daughter:

Cairo, 31st January, 1839

My dearest Christine, — This is the first letter I have written you this year. May it find my dear child enjoying every happiness. Present my kind regards to Mrs. Cooke and her family. Tell Edward to go on and prosper. I suppose that this year he will be strong at the Institution, and XXX at the Royal Academy. I fear one of the associates will be missing this year, but hope next year he may appear stronger than ever. I have such glorious subjects here that I have scarcely felt the time pass, and could find ample employment for years to come. The mosques are said to number about four hundred, and looking on them from the citadel they seem numberless. An amateur artist said the other day, that 'Prout would never get out of this city, for there were no trees to bother him, but narrow, crowded streets, with the most grotesque-shaped houses in the world.'

Church of the Holy Sepulchre

The Exterior of the Holy Sepulchre

THE first and most interesting object within the walls of the Holy City, the spot to which every pilgrim first directs his steps, is the Holy Sepulchre: but the traveller finds his expectation strangely disappointed when, approaching the hallowed tomb, he sees around him the tottering houses of a ruined city, and is conducted to the door of a gigantic church.

Though the handsome cupola is visible from most parts of the town, yet, there being no peristyle, the access to this, the principal monument of the piety of the Empress Helena, is difficult, being nearly surrounded by buildings which at various periods have been allowed to be run up against it. It can be entered only from the south.

With the exception of the facade (represented in the vignette title-page), there is nothing remarkable in the external architecture or decoration of this mass of buildings, which is necessarily irregular from an attempt to bring under one roof the events of the Gospel history — the Golgotha and the Tomb, now shown in the Church of the Holy Sepulchre.

The ruined tower to the left was anciently the belfry.

These narrow, crowded streets render it very difficult to make drawings, for in addition to the curiosity of the Arabs, who, although they are picturesque in appearance, are ugly customers to jostle. I wish I could transport you for an hour into one of the bazaars. Such a scene! All the Eastern nations gathered together. Turks and Greeks in their picturesque costumes. The wild Arab, who never slept within walls; every tribe different in dress, and all armed. Then the motley groups of the lazzaroni lounging about; long strings of women sitting astride on mules or donkeys, all closely muffled up, going from one harem to another, attended by male and female black and white slaves on foot. Then the extraordinary variety of articles for sale, the gravity of the shopkeeper and his customer, each smoking a pipe in front of the shop. The ladies smoke as well as the gentlemen, but the chabouks of the former are more costly. But I must leave you now in the bazaar, and when I come home you will learn more about Cairo from my journal, which I have kept regularly.

I set out with two gentlemen, on the 6th of February, for Syria, the most interesting country on the face of the earth, the scene of our Saviour's sufferings.

The Church of the Purification

AN inquiry has been long on foot among the intelligent investigators of the Holy Land, for the site of the great Church built by Justinian, in honour of the Virgin Mary, in the sixth century. Procopius, in his description of the imperial works,[1] states it to have been erected on the loftiest hill of the city; adding, that as there was not space enough for its intended magnitude, the architect was compelled to raise a wall with arched vaults from the valley to support the south-east part of the edifice. The only fabric whose site corresponds with this description is the Mosque El-Aksa, at the southern extremity of the inclosure of the Harem-esh-Sherif. It stands adjacent to the southern wall, where the latter is about one hundred feet above the foundation of the parallel city wall. The mosque is 280 feet in length from north to south by 190 broad. It is universally regarded by the Oriental and Western Christians as an ancient Christian Church, once dedicated to the Virgin, and the latter give it the name of the Church of the Purification, or Presentation [2]. The interior retains exactly the appearance of an ancient *Basilica* [3].

In researches like these, the reader must be warned of the extreme difficulty of verifying points of topography much more important than the sites of imperial labours. Until the beginning of the fourth century, Jerusalem was in Roman hands, deprived of all rights but those which cannot be refused even to the slave, and almost forgotten by the world. The establishment of Christianity on the imperial throne once more turned the general eye to Jerusalem, yet less as the seat of Jewish grandeur than as the memorial of Christian sacrifice. Invention became busy, and perhaps unscrupulous. Whatever the mother of the Emperor sought for, she was sure to find. Where the site was unknown to authentic record, tradition was ready, or where even tradition failed, all difficulty vanished before a dream. Thus Helena ascertained all the chief localities of the life of our Lord in Jerusalem. During the three following centuries Jerusalem became a place of pilgrimage to the pious, the curious, and the superstitious. The pilgrims adopted the legends of the past, or made legends of their own; until every spot of the sacred region was partitioned among rival fables. But this visionary age received a sudden and formidable check; the Saracen came, overspreading the land like a flood, and the pilgrim and the fable perished together. The Crusades were a bold and brilliant effort to restore the fallen honours of Jerusalem; but, while the Saracen scimitar was still glittering from the Nile to Lebanon, the knights were too amply employed in guarding their feeble sovereignty, to revive controversies, which probably their martial habits taught them to disdain.

On the revival of letters in Europe, Jerusalem became once more that object of interest, which it has continued to the present day. But the eager acquiescence with which the first travellers listened to the authority of the Conventuals, was suddenly changed into almost total doubt; and a species of calm scepticism as to every locality became the tone of the European traveller [4]. This, too, has had its period, and a more rational spirit has succeeded. But Jerusalem is already assuming in the European eye a higher rank than belongs to historic recollections. For to what other spot of earth was language like this ever spoken?

"It shall come to pass in the last days, that the mountain of the Lord's house shall be established in the top of the mountains."

"And many people shall go and say, Come ye, and let us go up to the mountain of the Lord, to the house of the God of Jacob ... for out of Sion shall go forth the law, and the word of the Lord from Jerusalem.

"O house of Jacob, come ye, and let us walk in the light of the Lord [5]".

[1] Procop. de Ædificiis Justin, v. 6.   [2] The title of the Purification is rejected by Quaresmius.   [3] Bononi, quoted in Bib. Researches, vol. i. p. 439.   [4] Rauwolf, Korte, and Cotovicus were among the chief doubters; until the visit of Clarke, who doubts everything. Robinson, who has been adopted as our chief authority in these descriptions, evidently deserves respect for his judgment, diligence, and learning.   [5] Isiah, ii. 2, 3, 5.

Plate 5: The Church of the Purification

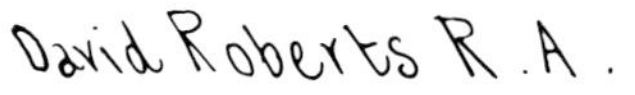

David Roberts R.A.

Above: The Artist's Signature.

The text on the opposite page describes the following double-spread Plate.

David Roberts, April 1839. אמבת ארץ ישראל; Courtesy of the Victoria & Albert Museum's Library, London

© Terra Sancta Arts —

The Damascus Gate

THE walls of Jerusalem are chiefly modern and Saracenic, but are built evidently on the site of more ancient walls, raised in the time of the Crusaders, and those not improbably, formed of the material of other still more ancient. They consist wholly of hewn stones, in general not of remarkable size, and laid in mortar.

An Arabic inscription over the Yaffa Gate, gives the rebuilding to Sultan Suleiman, in the year of the Hegira 948 (A.D. 1542). The walls are still stately, and at a distance, picturesque; they have towers and battlements, the latter crowning a breastwork with loopholes. A broad walk passes along the top of the wall, protected by the breastwork, and reached by flights of steps from within. Their height varies according to the inequalities of the ground outside from twenty to fifty feet.

Jerusalem has four open gates and four walled up: which seem in general to retain the places of still older ones, and, in some instances, to be older than the walls. Of the four open gates, facing the four points of the compass, that of which the view is given looks to the north, and is called by the natives Bab-el-Amud, or "Gate of the Pillar." The "Damascus Gate" is a name given by the Europeans, from its leading to Damascus and Nabulus by the great northern road. It is more ornamented than the others, and forms a striking object to the traveller[1].

[1] Roberts's Journal. Robinson, Biblical Researches vol. l. 386.

From the Journal

(Continued)

I am so completely transmogrified in appearance that my dear old mother would never know me. Before I could get admission to the mosques, I had to transfer my whiskers to my upper lip, and don the full Arab costume, since which I have been allowed to make sketches, both in oil and water colours, of the principal mosques, etc.

I have provided everything requisite for my journey. A tent (a very gay one, I assure you), skins for carrying water, pewter dishes, provisions of all sorts, not forgetting a brace of Turkish pistols, and a warm covering for night. Imagine me mounted on my camel, my black servant on another, and two men with my tent and luggage; the other two gentlemen similarly furnished and accoutred, surrounded by a host of the children of the desert—the wild Arabs; and you will have an idea of what an Eastern monarch I am. From Suez, we intend skirting the Red Sea, visiting Mount Sinai, Petra, Hebron, Jerusalem, Bethlehem, and all the more important places in the Holy Land. All this journey I hope to accomplish in about two months; and if God spares me in life and health, I expect to bring home with me the most interesting collection of sketches that has ever left the East. I told you I was getting on excellent terms with myself.

My health, thank God, never was better; and, thanks to Mahomet Ali, travelling now in Syria is as safe as in England. Colonel Campbell has procured me a firman, which empowers me to have soldiers should I think it necessary.

Tomb of St. James

THIS is one of four sepulchres in the Valley of Jehoshaphat, on the east side of the Kedron. It is an excavated tomb with an ornamental portal. The façade exhibits two Doric columns, fronting the west, and raised about fifteen feet above the ground in the same ledge of rock. The cavern is fifteen feet high by ten broad, and extends back about fifty feet. The monkish opinion is, that into this cavern the Apostle James retired during the interval between the Crucifixion and the Resurrection.

The other tombs are named from Jehoshaphat, Absalom, and Zechariah. There is no authority for those names. The mixture of the Greek style with the massive Egyptian, shows that they belong to a late period of art, and especially of art as adopted in the Oriental provinces of the Roman empire. They may be even of the age of Hadrian.[1]

[1] Robinson, Biblical Researches, vol i. p. 517.

Among others, remember me to Mr. Mark, and to all the Marks; and tell the consul how much I have been indebted to him for his letter to Colonel Campbell. I intend getting a book into which I shall put flowers from every remarkable place in the Holy Land, which I know you will prize more highly than anything else I could bring you. My dear child, your affectionate father,

DAVID ROBERTS

30th and 31st January, 1839
1st and 2nd February, 1839

In these four days I have worked at and completed my panorama of Cairo, there being four and a half sheets — not bad work for the time; the subject is excellent.

3rd February, 1839

Arranged and packed my drawings. In the evening rode to Boulak and dined with Mr. Boostal, principal engineer to the Pasha. Dined in the Turkish fashion, dispensing with knives and forks. There were present Captain and Mrs. Lucas, on their way to India, Dr. Abbot, and Messrs. Pell, Alwyn, and Kinnear. Having got the password for the night, we all returned to Cairo together at 11 P.M. A new servant whom I had hired had been drunk all day, and was nowhere to be found, and had not Mr. Pell's servant been with me, who took me to his master's divan, I should have had to sleep all night in the street.

The Mosque of Omar, on the Ancient Site of the Temple

THIS fine monument of the style of building under the Caliphate stands on Mount Moriah. It is recorded by the Arab historian, Seid Eben Batrik, that when the Caliph Omar took Jerusalem, the conqueror inquired of the Patriarch Sophronius, which would be the most fitting site for a mosque. The patriarch, by a choice which is now difficult to understand, led him to the ruins of the Temple. Successive caliphs enlarged and adorned the mosque. At the capture of Jerusalem by the Crusaders it was consecrated as a Christian Church, but on falling into the hands of Saladin, it became a mosque again. The lively narrative of Dr. Richardson, who had contrived to evade Mahometan vigilance gives us the best notice of the structure. Enveloped in a black robe to avoid observation, and attended by an interpreter, he ascended the southern slope of Mount Moriah, and entered the Haram Schereef, (or "Noble Retirement for Devotion,") an inclosure of 1489 feet by 995 in the centre of which stands the Sakhara, (or "Shut Up,") the Mosque of Omar.

"After viewing the building, we then," the narrative proceeds, "hied out of the Gate of Paradise (Bab-el-Jennè), passed by the "Judgment Seat of Solomon," and descended into the inclosure. Here we put on our shoes, and walked through the trees, to a house adjoining the wall of the inclosure, in which is said to be the throne of Solomon. From this we ascended by a stair to the top of the wall, and sat upon the stone on which Mahomet is to sit at the day of judgment, to judge the re-embodied spirits assembled beneath him in the Valley of Jehoshaphat. Descending from this seat of tremendous anticipation, we walked along the front of El Aksa, the other mosque, which occupies the side of the inclosure."

A visit in daylight, in which he was accompanied by some Turks of rank, enabled him to enjoy a still more accurate view. The ground is verdurous, and scattered over with orange, olive, cypress, and other trees.

"In the sacred retirement of this spot, the followers of the prophet delight to saunter or repose, and arrayed in the gorgeous costume of the East, add much to the beauty and interest of the scene, which they seem unwilling to quit either in going to, or returning from the place of prayer. Round the edge of the Stoa-Sakhara, or platform of the mosque, are many small houses, for private prayer, and other purposes connected with the principal building; but the Sakhara itself is the chief ornament of the whole. It is a regular octagon of about sixty feet a side. It is entered by four gates, and the walls are faced to a certain height with marble; the sides are panelled, and the upper story of this elegant building is faced with small tiles eight or nine inches square, and painted white, yellow, green, and blue. On each side there are seven well-proportioned windows, except where the front interferes. The whole is extremely light and beautiful, and from the mixture of the soft colours above, and the blue and white tinge of the marble below," says the Doctor, "I was more delighted with it than any building I ever saw. It is now, however, much defaced, and, like most of the Mahometan structures in Palestine, is sinking into decay[1].

The front group consists of Greek Christians, pilgrims to Jerusalem and praying towards the Holy Sepulchre. They stand on a terrace of the dilapidated Church of St. Anna, which is built over the grotto shown as the birth-place of the Virgin. The Mount of Olives is partially seen on the left. In the same direction is the principal entrance to the mosque, which no Christian is allowed to pass. The view is taken from the terrace, looking down to the Pool of Bethesda; the lower portion of the walls is ancient, (the upper part Saracenic,) and may have formed part of the Tower of Antonia.

[1] Roberts's Journal. Robinson, Biblical Researches, vol. i. p. 415, & c.

Plate 8: The Mosque of Omar, on the Ancient Site of the Temple

David Roberts R.A.

Above: The Artist's Signature.

The text on the opposite page describes the following double-spread Plate.

Mosque of Omar, shewing the site of the Temple.

Jerusalem from the North

THE view from this point is regarded as the most striking and extensive of Jerusalem. The road, first descending into the Valley of Jehoshaphat, crosses the ridge which extends between Scopas and the Mount of Olives. The city is thus seen diagonally, and the view includes the Great Mosque and the deep valley, while, at the same time, the domes and minarets are seen with better effect than from the other summit of Olivet.[1]

Lamartine, the celebrated poet of France, has described with picturesque power this scene, with all its associations, the noblest and most affecting on the globe.

"After ascending a second mountain, higher and more naked than the first, the horizon expanded all at once, and gave a view of the whole space which strecthes between the last peaks of Judea, on which we stood, and the high mountain-chain of Arabia. Beyond the lesser hills beneath our feet, broken and split into grey and crumbling rocks, the eye distinguished nothing but a dazzling expanse, so similar to a vast sea, that the illusion was complete. But on the edge of this imaginary ocean, about a league from us, the sun glittered on a square tower, a lofty minaret, and the broad yellow walls of some buildings which crowned the summit of a low hill; it was JERUSALEM!

"It stood out sombrely and heavily from the blue depths of heaven and the black sides of the Mount of Olives. Beyond those lofty walls and domes a high and broad hill arose, upon a second outline, darker than that which bore the city, and bounding the horizon.

"Nearer to us, and immediately beneath our eye, was nothing but a stony wilderness, which serves as an approach to the *'City of Stones.'* Those immense imbedded stones, of a uniform rocky grey, extended, from the spot where we stood, to the gates.

"The last steps that are made before opening on Jerusalem, are hollowed through a dismal and irremovable avenue of those rocks, which rise ten feet above the head of the traveller, and permit only a sight of the sky immediately above.

"We were in this last mournful avenue, and had marched in it for a quarter of an hour, when the rocks, retiring on a sudden to the right and left, brought us face to face with the walls of Jerusalem.

" A space of a hundred paces was now alone between us and the gate of Bethlehem. This interval, barren and undulating, like the banks which surround fortified places in Europe, extended to the right into a narrow vale, sinking in a gentle slope. To the left were five old olive trunks, bent beneath the weight of age, which might be called *petrified,* like the sterile soil from which they sprang. The Gate, commanded by two towers with Gothic battlements, deserted and silent as the entrance of a ruined castle, lay open before us.

"We remained a few minutes in motionless contemplation. We burned with desire to pass it, but the plague was now in its most intense state in the city, and we did not enter; but turning to the left, we slowly descended, skirting the high walls built behind a deep ravine, in which we perceived, from time to time, the stone foundations of Herod's ancient inclosure. At every step we met Turkish burial-places with tombstones surmounted by a turban. Those cemeteries, which the plague was nightly peopling, were filled with groups of Turkish and Arab women, weeping for their husbands or fathers.

"Those groups, seated there the whole day to weep, were the only sign of human occupancy that appeared in our circuit round Jerusalem. No noise, no smoke arose; and some pigeons, flying from the fig-trees to the battlements, or from the battlements to the edges of the sacred pools, gave the only movement in this mournful scene[2]".

[1] Biblical Researches, vol. i. p. 108.   [2] Travels in the East.

The Tomb of Zechariah

THERE are four monumental structures in the Valley of Jehoshaphat, on the east side of the Kedron, and opposite to the south-east corner of the Grand Mosque. Those have received from monks and travellers the names of the Tombs of Jehoshaphat, St. James, Absalom, and Zechariah. The two latter are real monuments of rock, the two former are only excavated tombs with ornamented portals.

The Tomb of Zechariah is so called in allusion to him who was "slain between the temple and the altar." It is a square block, of about twenty feet on each side, the rock having been cut away round it, so as to form an area in which it stands isolated. The body of the tomb is about eighteen or twenty feet high, and apparently solid. The sides are decorated each with two columns, and two half columns, the latter adjacent to square pillars at the corners, and all having capitals of the Ionic order. Round the cornice is an ornament of acanthus leaves, about three feet high, and above this the top is formed by an obtuse pyramid ten or twelve feet in height. The whole monument has thus an elevation of about thirty feet, and, with all its ornaments, is wholly cut out of the solid rock.[1] It exhibits a singular mixture of the styles of Greece and Egypt; somewhat of the classic elegance of the former, with the massiveness of the latter.

[1] Robinson, Biblical Researches, vol. i. p. 518.

From the Journal

4th February, 1839

Engaged another servant, highly recommended. Wrote to Christine and Durrant. Bought a handsome silk shawl to be used as a turban, intending to travel in the Arab costume. Mr. Kinnear, son of the Edinburgh banker, is to travel with us and share my tent. Drew on Mr. Thurburn for £60, which, with what I have, makes £100 — enough, I hope, to clear my way. Thank God, I never was in better health.

5th February, 1839

All day engaged in packing and getting ready. Sent my drawings to Mr. Alwyn — in all four packages.

6th February, 1839

All day occupied in buying provisions for our journey through the desert. Wrote to my friend Mr. Brackenbury at Cadiz. Paid my servant a month's wages in advance, and was much pleased with him. Introduced to Hassan, the sheikh of the Bedouins, and his followers. They seem a wild family, but I like their countenances, and am much mistaken if they are not trustworthy. Things are now in ship-shape, and I feel I shall enjoy the journey.

7th February, 1839

Left Cairo for Mount Sinai, and slept in the desert.

8th and 9th February, 1839

On our way. Overtaken by a storm of rain on the evening of the 9th, and before we could get our tents pitched everything was in a mess.

The Pool of Bethesda

THE eagerness of the early monks to give scriptural names to every prominent feature of Jerusalem, has affixed the title of the "Pool of Bethesda" to the reservoir on the north of the great mosque.

In the opinion of Robinson, this reservoir merely formed a part of the fosse of the "Acropolis," or Fortress of Antonia. Its dimensions certainly seem altogether incompatible with the purposes of the Bethesda of Scripture, whether those were the bathing of the sick, or the washing of sheep preparatory to their sacrifice in the Temple; for its measures 360 feet in lentgh by 130 in breadth, and is 75 deep, even now, though there is evidently a great accumulation of earth at the bottom. There can be, however, no doubt of its having been used as a reservoir, for its sides have been cased with small stones, and those again have been covered with plaster; but this portion of the work wants the completeness of ancient skill [1].

The western end is built like the rest, except at the south west corner, where two lofty arched vaults extend under the houses which cover that quarter. The northern one of those arches is nineteen feet broad, and it has been penetrated to the extent of a hundred feet, and apparently extends further. The other is twelve feet in breadth, but both are heaped with earth. It is conjectured that the trench, of which this excavation forms a part, was filled up by Titus in the siege, when, in order to carry on his works for the assault of the Temple, he levelled the Fortress of Antonia.

Eusebius and Jerome speak of a *piscina probatica*, shown in their day as Bethesda, a double pool, one part filled by ruins, and the other tinged of a reddish dye, as if mixed with blood; but they give it no locality. The name in later times was applied, apparently, from the neighbourhood of the reservoir to the St. Stephen's Gate, which was mistaken for the sheep-gate.

The bottom is generally dry, though at the time of the artist's visit, in April, there was some water stagnating in it. It contains shrubs, and a few trees not tall enough to reach the level of the street.

The view is taken from the street leading to the great mosque. The characteristic feature of Jewish architecture is exhibited in the domes, which form the roof of every house, a result of the costliness of timber; but, from its wanting the lightness of the oriental dome, in general the effect is poor and monotonous. The tower on the right is the minaret standing in the inclosure of the mosque, and the ruins beneath are conceived to be the remnants of the Tower of Antonia [2].

[1] Biblical Researches, Vol. 1. p. 434.　　[2] Roberts's Journal.

David Roberts R.A.

Above: The Artist's Signature.

The text on the opposite page describes the
following double-spread Plate.

Plate 11: The Pool of Bethesda

PLATE II: THE POOL OF BETHESDA

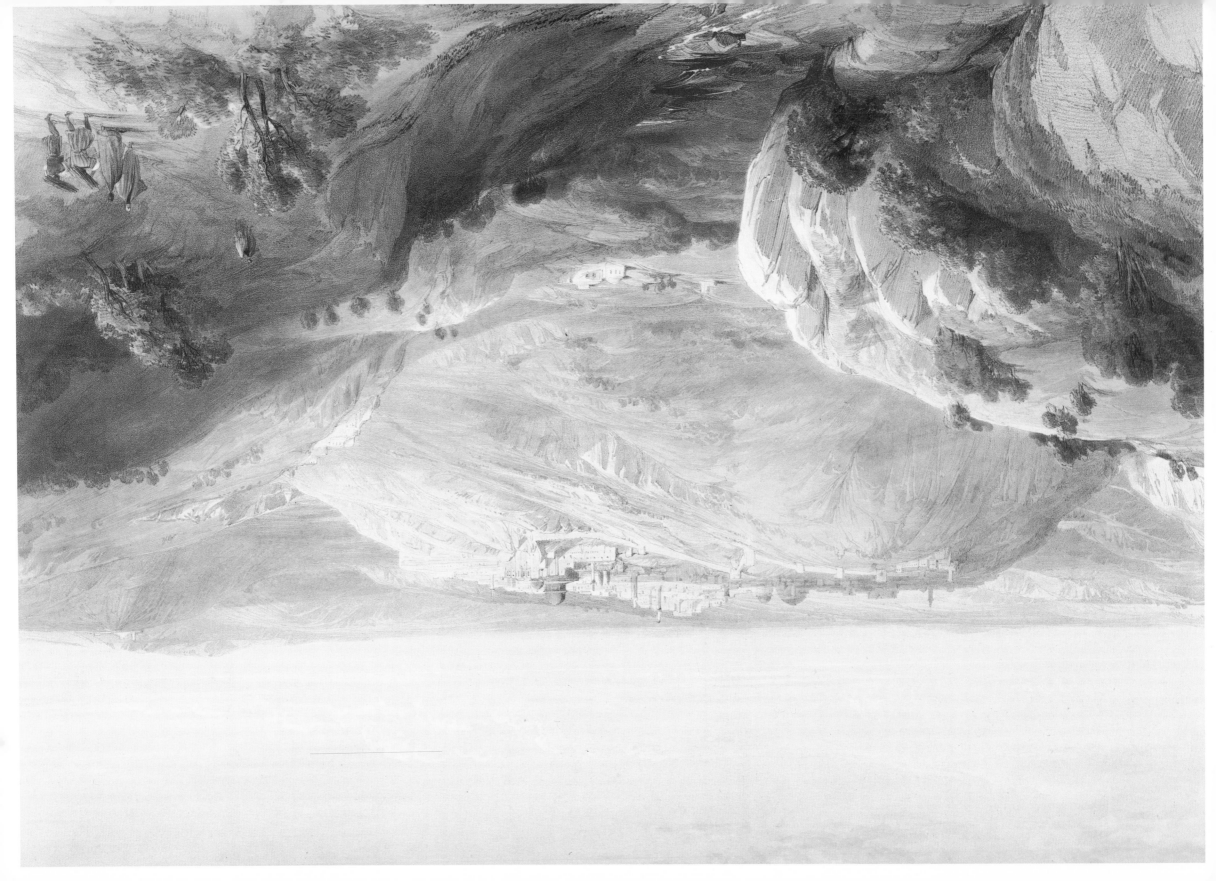

Jerusalem from the South

JERUSALEM was founded by Melchizedec,[1] in the forty-sixth year of Abraham, 2107 years before the nativity of our Lord, and 2177 before its siege by Titus. It was even then named Salem (peace), doubtless with prophetic reference to its future purposes, as the centre of pure religion in the world.

Yet, in an historical point of view, no name could seem more unsuited to its fortunes, for no other city of the earth has ever undergone so constant and so terrible a succession of sufferings.

After the general conquest of Canaan under Joshua, it fell into the hands of the Jebusites, by whom it was fortified, and from the strength of its position, it was probably impregnable to the rude science of those early times; but David[2] had the daring to attack, and the skill to master it, by entering through an aqueduct, from which he ascended, into the city. On its capture he made it the capital of the kingdom, and on the Hill of Zion erected a palace for himself with other buildings. Solomon next levelled the summit of Mount Moriah, and on it built the Temple. Our space prohibits the detail of the calamities which so soon overshadowed its splendours. Josephus sums them up in one expressive record: "Jerusalem was taken six times, but desolated only twice. The several captures were by Sesac, the Babylonians, Antiochus, Pompey, Herod, and Titus; its desolations were by the Babylonians and by the Romans under Titus."[3]

The horrors of the Roman siege, as narrated by Josephus, proverbially form the most overwhelming collection of the images of suffering by famine, popular fury, and national despair, that were ever combined, to make the fall of a people fearful to its own age and memorable to every age to come.

The siege, in all its parts, distinctly exhibits a supernatural influence, controlling human circumstances into the means of more consummate destruction. It was pressed at the Passover, the last period at which military prudence would have attempted the attack. But as almost the whole male population of middle age were assembled in the city, the havoc must have been thus only the more sweeping.

The singular tardiness, and even incertitude of design, exhibited by the Roman army in its first attempts, so inconsistent with the habitual daring and decision of the Roman system of war, unquestionably had the effect of deluding the city into a more continued resistance, and thus inflicting a more irrecoverable ruin.

The destruction of the Temple was wholly opposed to the policy of Rome, which prided itself on its indifference to the worship of its conquests; and it was even directly opposed to the commands of Titus, who naturally wished to preserve its plunder for his triumph, and who must have looked on the Temple as the noblest trophy ever won by a conqueror. But a mightier power was there, and all perished.

The prophecy of our Lord, "Verily, I say unto you, There shall not be left one stone upon another," was literally fulfilled: the Temple was utterly ruined and has never been restored.

In the sixth century Justinian built a superb church to the Virgin Mary, which stood on the site of the present Mosque El-Aksa. A hundred years after, the Caliph Omar took Jerusalem (A.D. 636), and was the founder of the mosque standing on the site of the Temple, and which still bears his name.

In 1099, the Crusaders took the city by storm. The mosque was then consecrated as a Christian church; but on the capture of this most unfortunate city again by the Saracens (A.D. 1187), the crescent was restored. Jerusalem has since fallen successively into the hands of the Turks and the Egyptians, and is now a Turkish possession. But the eyes of Europe have been directed to it in our day, with an interest unfelt since the age of the Crusades, and founded on higher principles than those of worldly ambition. At this hour, the whole Christian world, by a new and nobler impulse, "prays for the peace of Jerusalem."

[1] Joseph. B. Jud. vi. 10.   [2] 2 Sam. v. 6.   [3] Bell. Jud. vi. 10.

Jerusalem, from the Mount of Olives

OLIVET is a name connected with the most solemn remembrances of religion. The credulity of pilgrims or the artifices of monks may have done dishonour to the sanctity of Jerusalem; fiction has too often found sites for miracles, and legend has largely usurped the place of history; but nature remains; all the great features of the scene are unchangeable; and he who now explores the valleys or climbs the hills of this illustrious region, is secure that there, at least, he cannot be deceived. Every outline of those hills, every undulation of those valleys, has the matchless influence of reality. He feels, that he is traversing the very ground which was traversed by those great agents of Providence, whose memory has given a character and an impulse to every succeeding period of mankind; that he stands where they taught, and suffered, and triumphed; that he looks on the landscape on which they so often gazed; and that he sees the same grandeur and beauty, the same wild majesty or cultured loveliness, which so often lifted their hearts in strains of holy exultation to the God and Father of nature and man.

Olivet is memorable in the national annals as the first resting-place of David, when he fled from the rebellion of Absalom.

"And David went up by the ascent of Mount Olivet, and wept as he went up, and had his head covered and he went barefoot: and all the people that were with him covered every man his head, and they went up, weeping as they went up [1]."

But, to us, it has still more solemn recollections. No portion of Palestine was more hallowed by the frequency of our Lord's presence, and the events of his closing life, than the region of Olivet. To meditate, to pray, and to prophecy, He "went, as he was wont, to the Mount of Olives." From its slope He uttered the great prediction of the calamities of the siege, and the fall of the people; there He underwent that most fearful and profound sorrow which commenced his sufferings; there, finally, He met his disciples before he ascended to heaven; and there, if the prophecy is to be literally interpreted, the world shall yet see a still more awful and astonishing scene.

"His feet shall stand in that day upon the Mount of Olives, which is before Jerusalem on the east, and the Mount of Olives shall cleave in the midst thereof toward the east and toward the west, and there shall be a very great valley: and half of the mountain shall remove toward the north, and half of it toward the south. And ye shall flee to the valley of the mountains; ... and the Lord my God shall come, and all the saints with thee [2]."

At the foot of the mount, and between it and the brook Kedron, is the "Garden of Gethsemane." General consent adopts this as the scene of the "Agony." It is still an olive-ground, with many neglected trees widely scattered over the slope of the hill; but the spot especially sacred in the estimation of the pilgrims, is a space of fifty seven yards square, with a low stone inclosure; containing eight large olive trees, apparently of great antiquity. "They are," says a recent traveller, "still in a sort of ruined cultivation; the fences broken down and the trees decaying. Here no violence, or none that merits notice, has been done to the simplicity of the scene [3]."

The view is extensive beyond the city, commanding the plain of Jericho, and, on the east, the valley of the Jordan, and a portion of the Dead Sea. On the summit of the mount is an Arab village, with a stone building in its centre, which is said to mark the spot of the "Ascension." But our Lord ascended from Bethany.

[1] 2 Samuel xv. 30.   [2] Zechariah xiv. 4,5.   [3] Jowett's Researches, p. 253.

Stone of Unction Church of the Holy Sepulchre

The Stone of Unction

IN the description of the Church of the Holy Sepulchre, it was mentioned that the "Stone of Unction" was the first object of homage which meets the pilgrims on their entrance, and that it always attracts a large concourse, who exhibit the strong extravagances of foreign feeling and gesture. It is a long slab of polished white marble; but this is admitted to be only a covering for the true stone, to protect it from the casualties to which all relics were subject during the sway of the unbelievers. The Turks, however, looking upon the whole ceremonial as an advantageous source of revenue, and an inducement for strangers to visit the city, seldom interefere, but to prevent tumult; and whether their toleration results from contempt or policy, it is practically complete.

The monks say that the stone, of which this marble is the cover, is the one on which the body of our Lord was laid, when given to Joseph of Arimathea and Nicodemus, and by them anointed for sepulture. It has as largely shared the general decoration of this sumptuous dome, as it does the homage of the pilgrims. Having at each end three enormous wax candles upwards of twenty feet high, and with the light of a number of lamps poured upon it from above, it forms a striking centre for the first gathering of those picturesque and enthusiastic groups. The lamps are silver, and some of them of rich and curious workmanship, the gifts of the Greek, Latin, and Armenian convents, or of royal and noble devotees.

From the Journal

10th February, 1839

Came in sight of Suez and the Red Sea; country around, a desert — not a shrub or tree in the whole line of road, marked only by the mouldering skeletons of camels. Suez runs out into the sea, defended landward by a wall. On the opposite side of the gulf, the mountains are reflecting the rays of the setting sun, in a red glow of fire, contrasting powerfully with the deep blue sea, and surpassing all other scenes in moral grandeur, from the mighty events which took place there. Suez picturesque. Made a few sketches. Boats curious in form; sea limpid and pure. (See Plates 120, 121).

11th February, 1839

A row with our Arabs. Found out that the immense quantity of corn with which the camels were loaded, instead of being for their food during the journey, was intended chiefly for seed, the last years's crop having been a failure. Overtaken by a storm of sand so overpowering that about mid-day we pitched our tents close by the sea.

12th February, 1839

Delightful morning. On our right is the sea, with a high range of bold and picturesque mountains, with beetling headlands, stretching far into the distance. A few fishing-boats give animation to a scene that would otherwise be lifeless.

Church of the Holy Sepulchre,
Jerusalem.
April 10th 1839.

David Roberts

The Greek Chapel of the Holy Sepulchre

THE Church of the Holy Sepulchre was nearly destroyed by fire in the year 1808; long neglected by the Latin Christians, it was repaired by Russia, which carefully cultivates its connexion with the Asiatic Greeks; and in consequence of this expenditure, the Greek monks have been put in possession of the most venerated parts of the edifice.

In the engraving the view is directed to the screen, which, as in all the churches of the Greek ritual, separates the nave from the altar. Though sculpture is rigidly excluded, pictures and other embellishments are largely employed. This chapel is lavishly ornamented; and though it exhibits a barbaric mixture of styles, Greek, Gothic, and Saracenic, the general effect is rich in the extreme. The profusion of gilding, the gold and silver lamps continually burning, and the elaborate decoration of every part, render the first view overpowering.

Near the centre stands a small vase, to which the Greeks attach great reverence, regarding it as the central spot of the earth, and call it the "Navel of the World." Mr. Roberts's Journal thus describes the scene as it met his own eye:

"March 31, 1839 (Palm Sunday).—This is a great day at the Holy Sepulchre, and we witnessed the procession early in the morning. Perhaps after seeing the splendid sights of this kind in Spain, they were seen to disadvantage, still to me they were most interesting. The Latins took no part in the spectacle, being shut out on account of the plague, and holding no communication with the city.

"The first, therefore, in the ceremonial, were the Greeks. Entering from their convent by the grand entrance, they walked three times round the rotunda inclosing the Holy Sepulchre, chaunting the service, and each bearing a palm branch. Their banners and dresses were splendid. Their two bishops, wearing circular caps and sumptuous robes, were supported each by two dignitaries wearing similar robes, crimson velvet embroidered with gold. At the head of the procession was carried a representation of Christ on the Cross, which the pilgrims pressed forward to kiss. On entering the chapel, the chief bishop ascending the steps to the central opening of the screen, gave his benediction to the multitude, holy water was sprinkled, and flowers were strewed on the steps leading to the Holy Sepulchre. The two bishops then seating themselves on gilded thrones on either side of the chapel, distributed baskets of consecrated bread.

"Next followed the procession of the Armenians; their bishop wearing a mitre and a robe still more glittering than those of the Greeks, being covered with pearls and precious stones on a ground of crimson velvet. The Copts and Syrians joined this procession, being too few to form a separate one. The Copts carried a representation of Christ on the Cross and banners. But their appearance was poor, and their bishop bore but a staff of ivory, while those of the Greeks and Armenians were of chased gold set with gems."[1]

The point of time in the engraving is when the Armenian bishop has taken his place in front of the altar.

[1] Roberts's Journal.

The Lower Pool of Siloam

THE site of this memorable fountain is not determinable from any of its notices in Scripture,[1] but Josephus describes it as in the valley of the Tyropæon, on the south-east part of the ancient city, the precise situation in which we find the pool now bearing the name.[2] Jerome, about the close of the fourth century, describes it as "a fountain at the foot of Mount Sion, whose waters do not flow regularly, but on certain days and hours, and issue with great noise from caverns in the hard rock."[3] It is subsequently mentioned by a long succession of authorities, and Phocas (A.D. 1185) states it to have been "surrounded by arches and massive columns, with gardens below."

It is a small, deep reservoir, in the form of a parallelogram, into which the water flows from under the rocks, out of a smaller basin, or fissure in the rock, a few feet farther up. The reservoir is an artificial work, and the water comes to it through a subterranean channel from the Fountain of Mary, higher up in the Valley of Jehoshaphat. The ridge Ophel ends here, just over the Pool of Siloam, in a steep point of rock, forty or fifty feet high. Along its base the water is conducted from the pool in a small channel hewn in the rock, and led of, to water the gardens of fig and other fruit-trees lying in terraces, which extend to the bottom of the Valley of Jehoshaphat, a descent of forty or fifty feet.[4] Siloam is now used as a public fountain; but it seems to have been once sacred to the uses of the Temple. Its perpetual stream was the subject of allusion by our Lord, and it was made the visible instrument of one of those mighty acts which He wrought among the people.[5]

[1] Isaiah, viii. 6-Nehemiah, ii. 15. [2] Bel. Jud. v.4.1. [3] Hieron. Comm. in Esaiam, viii. 6. [4] Biblical Researches, vol. i. p. 493, 501, &c. [5] John, ix. 7-11.

From the Journal

(Continued)

Our camels, Arabs, tents, and baggage lie scattered about in the way an artist likes; but the mighty event said to have taken place here invests the scene with tenfold interest, for here the multitude of Israelites were miraculously preserved, while their pursuers were engulphed in the waters.

In two hours we reached the Wells of Moses, which are fifteen in number. They are surrounded by a few stunted palm-trees, and the waters are not sweet but bitter. What a picturesque group are our Bedouin Arabs at night, as they gather round the watch-fire! They would suit Wilkie or Allan delightfully; but thirty miles a-day, sitting on a camel, rather unfits me for sketching them. (See Plate 118).

13th February, 1839

Started as usual at 7, and at 4 in the afternoon pitched our tents near a spring of water at Wady Howara. Our route still near the shore of the Red Sea, — the mountains, though barren, picturesque in form.

14th February, 1839

As usual, start at daybreak, take a cup of coffee, walk two hours, spread our carpets on the sand. The remnants of our yesterday's dinner in our leather wallet, and a drink of water from our leather bottle, is our breakfast, relished with a gusto I have not experienced since boyhood. We are at the Wells of Marah, the water of which we thought delicious. We now leave the coast, and enter amid the mountains, of which today I made a coloured sketch. (See Plate 119).

Entrance to the Tomb of The Kings

THIS remarkable sepulchre, strongly resembling those of the Egyptian Thebes, is the finest relic of its kind in the neighbourhood of Jerusalem. Its present name has been given long ago by the Europeans, from a vague conception of its being the burial-place of some of the Jewish monarchs. From the elegance of its front and the general beauty of its sculpture, it has been compared with the sepulchres of Petra, and thence conjectured to have been the work of Herod, whose descent was Idumaean. But the weight of evidence inclines to its being the tomb of Helena, Queen of Adiabenè, who had become a convert to Judaism[1].

The sepulchre lies to the north of the Damascus Gate, and at a short distance from it, on the slope to the Valley of Jehoshaphat. The portal was originally twenty-seven feet long, but it is now much broken away. The sides of this portal were ornamented with columns or pilasters; and there were two intermediate columns, now broken down, which divided the front into nearly three equal parts. The rock above is richly sculptured in the later Roman style. The sepulchre consists of a large square pit sunk in the solid rock. In the western wall of this sunken court is a hall also excavated in the rock, thirty-nine feet long by seventeen wide and fifteen high. To this belongs the portal just mentioned. Within this hall is the entrance to an ante-chamber, and within this again are three large and two smaller chambers containing the fragments of marble sarcophagi[2].

From the Journal

15th February, 1839

Made three sketches, and travelled fifteen hours through the wilderness of Sinai, where the Israelites were condemned to wander for forty years. Nothing can exceed its sublimity desolation; and, although we have been eight days traversing the waste, we have only met one or two Arabs, on their way to Egypt.

16th February, 1839

Leaving Wady Ramleh, or the Sandy Valley, this morning, we sent our camels with our tents and baggage forward, and prepared to ascend the mountain called Jebel Gerabee, on the summit of which Laborde discovered the monumental stones of which he has given engravings. Our way lay in the bed of a mountain-torrent recently dried. Numerous flowers were springing; among others, a species of broom with white blossom, challenged comparison with the beautiful acacia. The naked rocks, riven into fantastic shapes, towered in mighty grandeur over us. After much fatiguing climbing, we reached the summit of the mountain; and, to my amazement, instead of a few stones, we found an Egyptian temple in good preservation, the walls covered with emblematic figures, hieroglyphics,and the cartouches of the early Egyptian kings, I made a sketch of this, and felt very much pleased at our discovery. (See Plate 116).

[1] Josephus, B. J. v. 4.2.   [2] Robinson, vol. i. p. 528.

CRYPT of the Holy Sepulchre

The Chapel of St. Helena

THE discovery of the Cross on which our Lord died, was one of the most memorable exploits of the mother of Constantine. From the Greek Chapel in the Great Church of the Holy Sepulchre, by thirty broad marble steps, a large underground chamber is reached, its roof supported by four short columns, and dimly lighted. In front of those steps is an altar, and, on one side, the seat on which St. Helena, instructed by a dream where the true Cross was hidden, sat and watched while the progress of discovery was going on. Fourteen steps deeper is another chamber, still more dimly lighted, and in its centre a marble slab, covering the pit where, deeper yet, the mysterious object of search was at last found.

But humiliating as are those legendary absurdities, the scenes which take place in connexion with them are not less humiliating. An intelligent traveller [1] supplies us with the substance of the following exhibition at the Holy Sepulchre (1821). The 21st of April is called the Day of Charity. By ten in the morning, an immense crowd were collected at the Church and round the Chapel of the Holy Sepulchre. In this assemblage was to be recognized every description of Christian Europe, with Copts, Maronites, Armenians, Syrian Arabs, &c. Their object was to see the kindling of the sacred fire in imitation of that which descended at the prayer of Elijah. "During the period when the miracle was preparing within the Shrine, what were the crowd doing? They selected this interval for performances worthy of an Italian Carnival. They ran and dragged each other round the Church, they mounted on each other's shoulders, they built themselves up into pyramids, they tumbled like mountebanks. The shouts and shrieks from so many voices, in so many languages, sharpened with oriental shrillness, were intolerable. The uproar was rendered more discordant by the violence of the Turkish soldiers in the attempt to tranquillise fanaticism by blows."

Two priests, a Greek and an Armenian, next entered the Shrine, and the door was closed after them and guarded by a body of soldiers. The crowd now rushed towards the walls of the Shrine, every one with a torch or taper ready to be lighted by the miraculous flame. But the miracle was delayed until the arrival of the Turkish governor. The gallery overlooking this ceremonial was filled by various groups; Turks, who laughed at it; Armenians, who believed in the miracle; Latins, who might be sceptical or not, as they pleased; and English, who naturally looked upon it with mingled feelings of contempt and compassion. At length the governor arrived, and the miracle had permission to display itself. Every light was put out, and the multitude were left in almost total darkness; but after some moments of anxiety a glimmer was seen through the orifices in the Shrine, it increased to a flame, and the multitude burst into a general exclamation. All now was enthusiasm, delight, and not a little danger. For the zealots fought fiercely for the honour of lighting their torches and tapers at the flame itself; but those who were not fortunate enough to reach it, took it from others, and, in a few minutes, the whole area was a blaze of thousands of lights. The two priests again made their appearance, each waving a torch of "celestial flame," and with those in their hands, they were hoisted on the shoulders of the devotees, and carried in triumph out of the Church.

When the display has been thus gone through, the crowd slowly retire, preserving the remainder of their tapers to melt them on strips of linen, which they intend to be sewed into their winding-sheets, as sure passports to Paradise. The whole performance, monstrous as it is, has been authenticated by every European writer who has been present during the Easter celebrations. To us, even its extravagances may furnish the important lesson of the general and dangerous tendency of human nature to superstition; of the strange facility with which minds, even acute and intelligent on other subjects, may abandon themselves to the grossest follies in religion; and of the wisdom of limiting our zeal to the simplicity of Scripture.

[1] The Rev. G. Waddington: "Condition of the Greek Church."

Fountain of Job, Valley of Hinnom.

The Fountain of Job

THIS is an ancient well, situated just below the junction of the Valley of Hinnom with that of Jehoshaphat. Tradition has been busy with its name, and the legend tells us, that this was the especial spot in which the sacred fire of the Temple was preserved during the captivity, until the restoration of the Temple by Nehemiah; the European monks, therefore, call it the Well of Nehemiah. The natives name it Byr Eyub, the Well of Job; but until the sixteenth century it was called En-Rogel. [1]

It is a very deep excavation, of an irregular quadrilateral form, walled up with large square stones, terminating above in an arch on one side, and apparently of great antiquity. There is a small rude building over it, furnished with one or two large reservoirs of stone. The well measures 125 feet in depth, and, in the rainy season, the water rises to the full height and overflows from the summit.

This well has perhaps the most distinct connexion with remote history of any relic of the city of David. It is mentioned in the Book of Joshua [2], in describing the border between the tribes of Judah and Benjamin. And when Adonijah was to be proclaimed king, he made a feast at En-Rogel, or in the phrase of Josephus, "outside the city, at the fount which is in the king's garden."[3] It is not mentioned by the historians of the crusades; it was then probably filled up.[4]

From the Journal

17th February, 1839

Mount Sinai burst upon our sight in all its grandeur; and here we met, for the first time, with an Arab encampment, surrounded by flocks of sheep and goats. (See Plate 111).

18th February, 1839

Started at 12 for the convent of St. Catherine, winding through a gloomy pass for about three hours. Night closed on us before we reached the convent. The effect of the setting sun gilding the high peaks of the pass, while the ravine was a mass of shadow, far surpassed anything I had ever seen. About 7 o'clock we reached the convent. The only entrance is by an opening in the wall at the height of 30 feet, having a strong iron door, which, after considerable reconnoitering on the part of the monks, was unbolted, a light was lowered by a rope, and some faggots were thrown down to burn. These were kindled, and we were drawn up by ropes, one by one, our elbows and knees receiving in transit many thumps and bumps. After being ushered through a long labyrinth of passages, we were received with great kindness by the superior. Supper of rice and dried dates was set before us, and never did a poor pilgrim sleep more soundly than I did under the hospitable roof of the monks of St. Catherine, Mount Sinai. (See Plates 106, 113).

[1] Cotovicus, in 1598, calls it *Puteus Ignis.*   [2] Josh. xv. 7,8; xviii. 16, 17.
[3] 1 Kings, i.9. Joseph. Antiq. vii 14. 4.   [4] Biblical Researches, v. i. 492.

Calvary

THE history of the building erected on the site of the Crucifixion, has given rise to long disquisitions, from the days of Eusebius to our own. But in limits like those of the present work, we must content ourselves with conclusions. In the year 326, Helena, the mother of the great Constantine, ordered the erection of Churches at Bethlehem and on the Mount of Olives, on the presumed sites of the Nativity and the Ascension.

The strong interest excited by the Nicene Council probably revived religious subjects in the mind of a monarch, till then engrossed with the government of the civilised world; and he determined to distinguish himself by giving such honour as imperial munificence could give, to the place of the Resurrection. The pagans had intentionally desecrated the spot, and had even hidden it beneath an idol temple[1]; Constantine commanded that a Church should be erected over the Holy Sepulchre. A great assemblage of Bishops was convened, first at Tyre and afterwards at Jerusalem, to do honour to the dedication[2]; but the Church then erected seems to have had but little resemblance to that of the present day. We may well regret its loss, for it is recorded to have been of "great length and breadth," and of "immense altitude, the interior covered with variegated marbles, the ceilings decorated with carved work, and the whole glittering with burnished gold[3]."

The fifth century was the age of pilgrimages, and the journey to the Holy Sepulchre became a constant exercise of piety. But it received a formidable check from the Persian invasion under Chosroes II., who, after overrunning Syria, stormed Jerusalem in June of the year 614, slaying many thousands of the clergy and pilgrims, destroying the Churches, and burning the Holy Sepulchre. The Patriarch Zacharias, with multitudes of the people, was carried into captivity[4]. On the turning of the tide of war, Chosroes was pursued into his own dominions by the Greeks under Heraclius, when the Persian monarch was put to death by his own son; the Patriarch, after fourteen years of exile, was restored.

After various calamities under the Saracens, the Church of the Holy Sepulchre, though twice burned in the interval, was again opened in the year 1048, to the general rejoicing of Christendom. An impression, that in the eleventh century the Day of Judgment was at hand, poured immense crowds of pilgrims of every rank and from every soil into Palestine; princes and nobles with retinues of armed followers, and sometimes with the royal luxury, filled the roads of Europe on their way to Jerusalem.

Jerusalem, in possession of the Crusaders for nearly the entire of the twelfth century, rose once more from its ruins. Calvary forms a portion of what is now termed the Holy Sepulchre. The spot is covered with a small chapel, in whose centre, under an altar, is shown an orifice encircled with gold, which is pointed out as that in which the Cross was fixed, while on each side are two similar orifices, for the crosses of the two malefactors. The chapel is lighted with rich and massive lamps, which burn night and day.

We have taken it for granted, that this is the actual site of the Crucifixion; notwithstanding the known fact, that the Cross was raised *outside* the city; for, it seems singularly improbable that Calvary, which was an established place of public execution, should have been forgotten in the lapse of less than three centuries. The city has considerably changed its position; and it is more likely that the walls should have been extended to Calvary, in some of those periods which were too disturbed for exact record, than that the mother of the Emperor, furnished with all the means of inquiry, and attended by the leading authorities, should have been totally deceived in the express object of her investigation. But Calvary was the spot first sought for; and the only reason discoverable, why the present site should have been fixed on in preference to all others, is, that it was the true one.

[1] Euseb. Vita Constan. iii. 26.33; quoted by Robinson.   [2] Euseb. Vita Constan. iv. 43. Sozomen. ii. 26. Tillemont, vii. 12.   [3] Cyril, Hieros. e. xiv. 6.   [4] Eutych. Annales, ii. 213.

Jerusalem. April 5th 1839.

Jerusalem, from the Road leading to Bethany

JERUSALEM lies near the summit of a broad mountain ridge. This ridge, which is everywhere not less than from twenty to twenty-five miles broad, is in fact a high irregular table land. The surface of the elevated promontory on which the city stands sinks somewhat steeply towards the east, terminating in the Valley of Jehoshaphat.

The breadth of the whole site of Jerusalem from the Valley of Hinnom to the Valley of Jehoshaphat is about 1020 yards, or half a geographical mile. The surrounding country is of the limestone formation. The region is dreary, and the soil seems sterile; yet the olive thrives, and corn is grown in the levels and valleys. The vine and fig-tree flourish no longer on the hills, but the latter grows in the sheltered spots, and is frequent near Bethlehem. The city is called by the Arabs, El-Kuds (the Holy); and also by Arabian writers, Beit El-Mukaddas (the Sanctuary).[1]

The spectator is presumed to be standing on the Mount of Olives, looking towards the Mosque of Omar, which stands on the central point of the view. On its left is the Mosque El Aksa.

The space within which those edifices stand, is inclosed by a wall of great thickness, formed, of stones of remarkable size, some of them thirty feet, and with great probability supposed to have formed part of the original wall of the platform, on which stood the temple built by Herod. This inclosure is the summit of Mount Moriah, on which no Christian or Jew was once permitted to set his foot (though of late years, the prohibition is occasionally relaxed).

Beyond, and rising above it, is Mount Sion, the site of the city of David. Its northern part is now the most dilapidated portion of Jerusalem, and is chiefly inhabited by Jews, in a state of poverty. On the summit are seen the towers of the citadel. To the left is the Armenian convent: still farther to the left, and outside the walls, is the Muslim Tomb of David; and near it a small Greek Church built on the spot assigned by tradition as the place where the "Last Supper" was solemnized. Farther on the right is Acra, the third hill, on whose ridge stands the Church of the Holy Sepulchre; the ridge is separated from Sion by the Tyropaeon. And still farther to the right, and also within the walls, is the fourth hill, now covered with hovels. The summit commands a fine view of the city; and the monks have chosen to assign it as the site of a palace of Herod Agrippa. Its position would certainly accord with the taste and policy of a race, who so strikingly united the pomp of royalty with the vigilance of despotism. Beyond this hill and the walls lies the Tomb of the Kings.

At the foot of the spectator is the Valley of Jehoshaphat, through which flows the brook Kedron. Immediatedly under the Gate of St. Stephen is a small church traditionally standing over the burial-place of the Virgin Mary. Close to it is the memorable Garden of Gethsemane. To the right of the garden is the Pillar of Absalom, and lower down are the disputed "pools of Siloam."

[1] Robinson, vol. I. p. 380.

PLATE 22: THE SHRINE OF THE HOLY SEPULCHR

The Shrine of the Holy Sepulchre

EASTER is the chief period of pilgrimages to Jerusalem, and the number of pilgrims frequently amounts to 20,000. The Church of the Holy Sepulchre is opened but on fixed days, and on those, at this season, the pressure is enormous. The first aspect of the exterior is striking. It is a vast and splendid monument, imposing, and rich for the time at which it was erected. It is true, that it is not the Church built by the mother of Constantine; but in its rebuilding by the Christian kings of Jerusalem, the ornaments of the Byzantine architecture have been preserved, and, with those of the Greek and Eastern, form a noble and most picturesque temple.

But the multitude offer a vivid and still more picturesque scene. There are displayed costumes and countenances from all parts of the world; the splendid robes and dark visages of the Asiatic, the powerful features of the Greek, the Italian monk, the Syrian mountaineer, the Christian of India, some countenances wild and barbarian, some brilliant and civilised; some which give the impression of every sterner practice and passion of desert life; others which a Titian or a Raphael might have taken as models of the saint or martyr, calm, lofty, and intellectual: a vast congregation gathered by one powerful impulse to do homage to the most awful place of recollection on the globe.

But the gate is at last opened, generally after a delay which produces many a murmur, and the multitude, with the rush and roar of a torrent, burst in. On entering the vestibule, the keeper of the porch, a Turk, is seen sitting, frequently with a group of Turks, on his richly-covered divan, smoking, and with coffee before him. But none pause there; the crowd pass on, struggling, pressing, and clamouring. But, at the instant of their entering the grand dome, all is hushed; in front of them lies the "Stone of Unction", the crowd fling themselves on their knees round it, weep, pray, and attempt to touch it with their foreheads; hands are seen everywhere clasped in prayer, or hiding their faces as if the object were too sacred to be gazed at; tears are rolling down cheeks, and sobs are heard that seem to come from hearts overwhelmed with reverence and sorrow.

The Church is a lofty circular building, surmounted with a dome, and surrounded by tall square pillars supporting a gallery. The general effect is bold and stately. Immediately under the dome stands the shrine, an oblong building, twenty feet long and twelve feet high, circular at the back, but square and finished with a platform in front, and with a cornice and cupola of marble. The style of this structure is fantastic and poor, the work of a nameless builder employed by the Greek monks in 1817. But who can regard such trivialities in the midst of such a scene? That building covers the Holy Sepulchre!

It is perfectly known that the site of our Lord's tomb, of the crucifixion, and all the other leading events of his glorious Passion, have formed the topics of learned dispute. But into those discussions we have no wish to enter. The heart, and the understanding too, may rest fully contented with the fact, that whether within or without this dome, here trod our Lord; within the circuit of the city standing at this hour were wrought his miracles; were heard those lips "which spake as never man spake;" were uttered those fearful denunciations which condemned Judah to bondage; and with not less authority, those infallible and illustrious promises which declare that she shall yet break her chain, and see her King in triumph, as she saw him in humiliation. Under such feelings, all minute doubts disappear; the mind takes no interest in minor localities; all Jerusalem is one magnificent locality. Through these streets the Saviour passed; on that height he taught in the courts of the Temple; from that Mount of Olives he looked upon the golden domes, and sculptured towers, and marble walls of Jerusalem! Those facts are known beyond all doubt; those are sufficient for the heart; and fallen as the City of David is, Chistendom bears in sacred memory, that "her stones were laid in holiness," and longs for the coming of the day when a splendour, not borrowed from sun or star, shall fill her courts with new-born glory.

The Entrance to the Citadel

IN the description of the vignette of the "Tower of David," we adverted to its history, as forming a part of the Tower of Hippicus; we now proceed to give an outline of the history of the city walls.

The ancient city was thirty-three stadia, or three and one third geographical miles in circumference. The southern wall included the whole of Sion. The eastern ran probably along the bottom of the Valley of Jehoshaphat, and the northern passed about fifty rods north of the present city. The present circumference is about two and one-eighth geographical miles.

The building of Ælia, by Hadrian, seems to have occupied briefly the site of the present city. But a large portion of Sion was probably then excluded, for Eusebius and Cyril, in the fourth century, speak of Sion as then fufilling the prophecy, and being as a "planted field;"[1] the wall being carried across the brow of the Valley of Jehoshaphat on the east, so as to include the hill Bezetha, instead of bending southward, as formerly, to the Tower of Antonia.

The walls of Hadrian seem to have remained until the Crusades. At this period the chief part of Sion was outside the walls. The Count of Toulouse pitched his camp between the city and the Church of Sion, "which was a bowshot distant from the walls."[2] In process of time, however, the walls fell into decay, and (A.D. 1178) contributions were demanded in Europe for rebuilding them. In 1187, the city was besieged by the Saracens under the famous Saladin, and captured after a courageous resistance. But the captors then began to tremble; the name of Richard Cœur de Lion threatened to shake the Saracen throne, and Saladin was indefatigable in fortifying Jerusalem. To excite the Moslem activity, he was constantly present at the labour, animated his troops by the sight of his chieftains engaging in it with their own hands, and even himself frequently brought stones to it on the pommel of his saddle. Six months of industry, thus encouraged and sustained, rendered the place nearly impregnable to the inartificial means of the times.[3] But, in 1219, the Sultan Melek of Damascus, dreading that it might be made a Christian fortress, ordered that all the walls and towers should be dismantled, except the Citadel and the inclosure of the Great Mosque; to the general chagrin of the inhabitants, many of whom abandoned it in consequence. In 1229, a treaty with the Emperor Frederick gave it up to Christian hands once more; with the stipulation, however, that the walls should not be rebuilt. But from some new alarm, in ten years after, the barons and knights began to restore the walls, and erect a strong fort on the west of the city. The breach of treaty, if breach it were, was suddenly and ferociously avenged by the assault of the Emir David, of Kerek, who entered the city with his troops, strangled the Christians, threw down the newly raised walls, and added to the havoc, the dismantling of the Tower of David.[4]

But in this city of endless vicissitude, a new treaty, in 1243, gave the possession to the Christians without reserve; to the boundless indignation of the Mahometan inhabitants. The new possessors immediately repaired the fortifications; yet, within a year, Jerusalem was again stormed. The Kharismian hordes were now the assailants, (A.D. 1244,) from which period it has remained in Mahometan hands. In 1542, the walls were once more rebuilt. The chief interest connected with the modern walls, is, that they generally exhibit evidence of their having been raised on the site of others, going back to the ages of the Roman conquest, of the Idumæan dynasty, or perhaps even of the reign of Solomon, the last, a time all whose recollections are hallowed to the Jew, and not less to the Christian.[5]

[1] Eusebius, D. Evang. viii. 3. p. 406 — Edit. Colon. Cyril, Hieros. Catec xvii. 18.
[2] Will. Tyr. viii. 5.   [3] Wilken. Gesch. B. iv.   [4] Wilken. B. vi.
[5] Biblical Researches, vol. i. p. 467.

David Roberts R.A.

Above: The Artist's Signature.

The text on the opposite page describes the
following double-spread Plate.

Plate 23: The Entrance to the Citadel

Citadel of Jerusalem.
April 19. 1839

Golden Gate of the Temple shewing Roman walls

The Golden Gate

THIS is a massive structure, a double gateway, projecting from the eastern wall into the area of the Harem-esh-Sherif (the Noble Sanctuary), in which stands the Great Mosque. Its floor is several feet below the level of the area. After the second revolt and total ruin of the Jewish people, Hadrian (A.D. 136) built a new city, which he called Ælia; and, for the purpose of offering the last insult to an unhappy nation, he raised a temple to Jupiter on the site of the Temple of Solomon. The style of the Golden Gate appears to refer it to this period; the external front and arches are unquestionably of Roman origin; and of the interior it is evident, that "a central row of noble Corinthian columns and a groined roof, had once formed a stately portico of Roman workmanship."[1]

The name "Porta Aurea" cannot be followed higher than the tenth century. This gate was found walled up in the time of the Crusades, but was then opened once a year, on Palm Sunday, from a tradition that through it our Lord made his entry into Jerusalem as king; a tradition probably arising from the stateliness of its architecture. By the Moslem, however, it is kept constantly walled up from a singular dread, that through it a king shall enter, who is to make himself master not only of Jerusalem, but of the globe. And that their vigilance, at least, may not be wanting to avert the conquest, they keep a sentinel constantly on duty in a tower flanking the gateway.[2]

[1] Bononi and Catherwood, referred to by Robinson, Biblical Researches, vol. i. p. 438.   [2] Stephens, p. 94.

From the Journal

19th February, 1839

The convent is a large square enclosure, the walls and flanking towers built of hewn granite. Inside, it looks like a small town, for beside the apartments and store-houses there is a chapel and a mosque. The former is said to be built on the site of the burning bush, the latter erected by Mahomet, who gave the monks a written protection from his followers. The Mahometans and Christians here perform their ablutions and go through their different forms of worship in perfect harmony, and this has, perhaps, preserved the place more than the prophet's letter of protection.

20th February, 1839

Today we ascended to the summit of Sinai, which took us two hours. Near the top are two small chapels. One covers the cave where Elijah passed the night, the other is dedicated to Elias. On the summit are other two, — one where Moses received the tables of the law, the other belongs to the Mahometans, and under it is pointed out the foot-mark of the camel that carried the prophet from Sinai to Mecca. The view from the top is the most sublime that can be imagined. (See Plate 112).

The Pillar of Absalom

IN the Valley of Jehoshaphat one of the most striking features is a group of four tombs, one of which has been traditionally named with reference to the Sacred record. "Now Absalom in his lifetime had taken and reared up for himself a Pillar, which is in the king's dale: for he said, I have no son to keep my name in remembrance: and he called the pillar after his own name: and it is called unto this day, Absalom's place ."[1]

Josephus mentions the "pillar"[2] as about three furlongs from the city, which corresponds sufficiently to the distance of the present structure. But Absalom died on the east of Jordan, and was probably buried on the field where he fell.[3]

This monument stands close by the lower bridge over the Kedron. It is a square isolated block, hewn out of the rocky ledge. The body of the block is twenty-four feet square, having on each face two columns and two half columns of the Ionic order, with pilasters at the corners, and an architrave exhibiting triglyphs and Doric ornaments. To the top of the architrave the elevation is about twenty feet. Above this the work is masonry, consisting of a large layer, with a smaller one above it, and the whole surmounted with a small dome with a spire, gracefully expanding at the summit like the bell of a flower.[4] The tomb contains a small chamber. The entire height is about forty feet. The effect of the work is picturesque, and is of the same taste, if not of the same age, as those at Petra, in which the peculiarity exists, that the outer pillars join the pilasters at the angles. The numerous excavations along the whole line of rock appear, like those at Petra, to have been more probably dwellings than tombs.[5] The Mahometans, Jews, and Christians, as they pass, throw stones into the aperture of the tomb, as a mark of abhorrence for the memory of the rebellious son.

From the Journal

21st February, 1839

By permission of the superior, I made a drawing today of the chapel of St. Catherine, which, including the smaller chapel of the Burning Bush, is about eighty feet in length. It is supported by two rows of pillars, the capitals of which are similar to what in England we call Norman. The walls are covered with ancient paintings of scriptural subjects. A richly-decorated crucifix surmounts a screen of carved work, with two folding-doors opening into the high altar. In front are six enormous candelabra, and suspended from the ceiling are numerous silver lamps. The altars behind the screen are covered with various shrines and crucifixes of the most exquisite workmanship, and inlaid with precious stones. On the altar are several costly-bound copies of the Scriptures, and on the left is the shrine of St. Catherine, with an embroidered covering. Beyond this is the chapel of the Burning Bush, the most sacred of all, on entering which we had to take off our shoes.
(See Plate 108).

[1] 2 Samuel xviii. 18.   [2] Josephus, B. 20.   [3] 2 Samuel xviii. 17.   [4] Biblical Researches, vol. i. p. 519.   [5] Roberts's Journal.

LIST OF LITHOGRAPHS
IN THE SERIES OF
DAVID ROBERTS
"THE HOLY LAND"

terra sancta arts

אמנות ארץ ישראל

VOLUME 2/PART 2
GALILEE & LEBANON

VOLUME 4/PART 4
SAMARIA & IDUMEA (PETRA)

VOLUME 1/PART 1
JERUSALEM

VOLUME 3/PART 3
JUDEA & THE JORDAN RIVER

VOLUME 5/PART 5
THE DESERT (NEGEV & SINAI)

Note: The sequence of the Plates slightly differs from the First Edition, due to technical limitations.

2. GALILEE & LEBANON

The glory of Lebanon shall
come unto thee, the fir tree, the
pine tree, and the box together,
to beautify the place of my
sanctuary; and I will make the
place of my feet glorious.

Isaiah 60, 13

כבוד הלבנון אליך יבוא
ברוש תדהר ותאשור יחדו
לפאר מקום מקדשי ומקום רגלי אכבד.

ישעיה ס', 13

Contents   Page

Note: The sequence of the Plates slightly differs from the First Edition, due to technical limitations.

2

GALILEE & LEBANON

DAVID ROBERTS R.A.
THE HOLY LAND

27 Coloured Facsimile Lithographs
27 Coloured Photos of the Sites
Historical descriptions of the Sites
by Rev. G. Crolly, L.L.D.
David Roberts's private Journal
Introduction by Prof. M. Har-El
Text and Lithographs by Courtesy of the
Victoria & Albert Museum's Library, London

Introduction

"THE GOODLY MOUNTAIN AND THE LEBANON": The mountains of the Lebanon are among the highest on the eastern coast of the Mediterranean Sea with peaks rising to more than 3000 meters above sea level. Rainfall averages 1700 mm. annually, and traces of snow linger on the upper ridges for most of the year. Because the mountains of the Lebanon are the most snow covered in the entire eastern and central coast of the Mediterranean, it is suggested that the name Lebanon derives from their white coated summits (Leban meaning white in Hebrew). Another possible source for the name comes from the white limestone cliffs north of Rosh Hanikra, called Levanvan in the Talmud. From the summits of the Lebanon one can see Damascus and Geshur in the east, Hamat in the north and the Land of Israel in the south.

The Lebanon Range comprises two parallel ridges, the western-most known as "The Lebanon" in the Bible, and the eastern ridge called the "Anti Lebanon" (Joshua, 9,1) or the "Lebanon of the Sun Rising" (Joshua, 13,5). The Lebanon Range extends from the Leontes River in the south to the Kabir River in the north, a distance of 170 kilometers. From the Mediterranean in the west to the Damascus Valley in the east, the Lebanon Range is 70 kms. wide.

The mountains of The Lebanon and the Bekaa Valley are the most fertile areas in the entire eastern Mediterranean as a result of ample rainfall and proximity to the sea. The watershed of the Bekaa Valley, which rises to a height of 1200 meters above sea level, is located near Baal Gad or Baalbec. Grains and fruit trees are grown in the area.

Two rivers drain the Bekaa Valley: the Orontes, 360 km. long, which flows northward; and the Leontes, 130 km. long, which runs from east to west and is in the south of the region. The Lebanon mountains are among the most heavily forested in the region, covered with cedars and cypress trees, oaks, and the Biblical Tidhar and Tashur.

The Lebanon was inhabited on the western coast by the Tyreans and Sidonians, renowned for their sailing prowess, who lived in the cities of Byblos, Berytus, Tyre, Zarephat and Sidon. In the Bekaa Valley the Kingdom of Hamat was located where copper was mined and crops were grown under irrigation. The higher hill regions were inhabited by the Hivites, who were woodcutters.

THE UPPER GALILEE — THE LOOKOUT POINT OF THE WESTERN LAND OF ISRAEL: The Upper Galilee is the high hill range of the Western Land of Israel. Historically its boundaries have extended from the Leontes River in Lebanon to the Beit Kerem Valley. This region is the wettest among the mountain ranges of the Holy Land (except for the Carmel). From a geological standpoint the range is the most faulted, being broken down and by its proximity to the Hula Valley and the Jordan Rift. As a result of the uplifting and faulting the mountains relatively abound in natural springs.

In the east run two basaltic plateaus, Dalton and Alma. They are quite rainy, receiving 1100 mm. of rainfall annually, in addition to annual snowfalls. In this region one finds the steepest slopes and gorges as well as examples of extreme surface erosion.

Prof. M. Har-El

The Lithographs

Mount Tabor, from the Plain of Esdraelon

TABOR is a beautiful mountain, wholly of limestone, and rising about a thousand feet above the great Plain of Esdraelon. Among the Arabs it bears only the general name of Jebel-el-Tur. It stands out alone towards the S.E. from the high land around Nazareth, while the north-eastern arm of the Plain sweeps round its base, and extending far to the North, forms a broad table-land, bordering on the Valley of the Jordan and the Lake of Tiberias. Seen from the S.W. it has the appearance of the segment of a sphere, but from the W.N.W. that of a truncated cone. The summit is a little oblong plain or basin.[1]

"The present view," observes the Artist, "was taken while crossing the Plain, on the road from Jenin to Nazareth. It is the very opposite to the ruggedness and grandeur given to its form in the sketches which I had hitherto seen. Though a fine hill, it has long lost all claims to the picturesque; the labours of the ancient population having cleared and shaped it into its present form. In many instances this process may be still traced by the terraces remaining on the sides, though often, by time, undistinguishable in colour from the rocks on which they are raised. The general character of the hills of Palestine is roundness, arising from the same cause."[2]

The figures in the foreground are a caravan of Christian pilgrims, whom the Artist found resting during the mid-day, on their return from Damascus to Jerusalem.

[1] Biblical Researches, iii. 211, &c.   [2] Roberts's Journal.

From the Journal

22nd February, 1839

Went to the summit of Mount Horeb, and descended into the valley on the west. Made a drawing of the Rock of Moses, said to be that from which the water gushed forth to the thirsty multitude. Took leave of our friends the monks of St. Catherine's, of whose kindness it is impossible to speak too highly. Our baggage had been forwarded early in the morning, and in the afternoon we found our caravan encamped in a beautiful wady amidst the mountains. After a pleasant gossip, we retired early to rest, intending, if possible, to reach Akabah on the following day. (See Plate 107).

23rd February, 1839

Started by daybreak. Walked for two hours, then spread our carpets and breakfasted, on bread baked by the monks, cold meat, butter from Cairo, dates, olives, and water *diluted* with a little brandy to take off the bitter taste. After resting about an hour, smoking a pipe of the finest Turkish tobacco, we start as usual after the caravan, and halted about five in the afternoon, generally travelling about ten hours a day. Our route was over the mountains; our resting-place for the night in a beautiful plain.

Plate 26: Mount Tabor

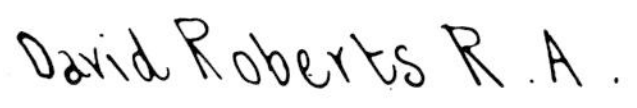

David Roberts R.A.

Above: The Artist's Signature.

The text on the opposite page describes the
following double-spread Plate.

"Mount Sinai, from the Plain of Sebaiyeh" אפסה ארץ סיני

David Roberts R.A.

Fountain of the Virgin Nazareth April 21st 1839

Fountain of the Virgin, Nazareth

AS this is the only fountain in Nazareth, it is held in great respect by the Christians, not merely as important to the supply of water to the town, but in the belief that to this fountain the Mother of our Lord *must* constantly have come.

"The figures introduced were all drawn on the spot, and convey an accurate representation of the female costume of Nazareth. Round the face, and hanging down on each side, they wear rows of gold and silver coins, which relieved by their jet-black locks, have a remarkably graceful and novel appearance to the European eye. The younger women were in general remarkably beautiful; and as they perceived in this instance that the strangers were Christians, they made no attempt to conceal their faces."[1]

The source is under the Greek Church of the Assumption, eight or tens rods farther north; and thence the little stream is conducted by a rude aqueduct of stone, over which an arch is turned, where it pours its scanty waters into a sculptured marble trough, perhaps once a sarcophagus. The Church is built over the source; as the spot where, the Greeks say, the Virgin was saluted by the Angel Gabriel. The aqueduct seems to have existed in Pococke's day. In the century before, travellers speak of a reservoir here, of which there is now no trace. In summer the Fountain dries up, and water must be brought from a distance.[2]

[1] Roberts's Journal. [2] Biblical Researches, iii. 188.

From the Journal

24th, Sunday, February, 1839

Leaving the granite mountains of Sinai, our course now lies, amidst high rocks of sandstone, over a level bed of sand, interspersed with bushes, principally of the wild thyme, of which the camels are very fond. The fragrance is delicious, and is almost the only scent in the desert. Passing a narrow ravine, we came upon an encampment of Arabs basking in the sun, with their donkeys browsing on the wild thyme, making altogether a very picturesque group. Passing into another plain, we struck into a defile with high mountains in the distance, but round and lumpy, quite unlike the bold and rugged pinnacles of Horeb and Sinai. The heat to-day has been excessive, but after two hours' walk through a wild and picturesque ravine, we descended to the shore of the Red Sea or Gulf of Akabah.

25th February, 1839

The sirocco or south wind set in to-day. It blew in a hurricane, with dense clouds of sand, so that we could not see our way six yards before us. At last, however, we came to a turn of the beach sheltered from the wind, where we pitched our tents for the evening. The shore was literally covered with shells of the most beautiful forms and colours, and we bought from a fisherman a basket of fish for 60 paras, or about 6d. The heat is oppressive, the thermometer being 85° on the sea-shore.

Convent of the Terra Santa, Nazareth

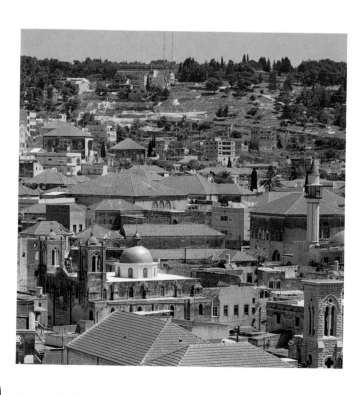

THIS Convent belongs to the Latin monks, and is a strong and spacious building, or rather collection of buildings, which, unlike the usual fate of the Convents in Palestine, has been repaired and restored within the last twelve years. The Convent had been originally built in 1620, on the site of a Church of remote antiquity. A century later, it had been, in some degree fortified, and by subsequent additions it now ranks as a respectable place of defence, at least against native assaults.[1]

M. Lamartine, who visited the Convent in 1832, gives its description most in detail. He arrived at the "high, yellow walls" at evening. A broad iron gate admitted him and his attendants into an outer court. Some Neapolitan and Spanish monks, who were winnowing wheat for the Convent, conducted them into an immense corridor, into which the cells of the monks and the chambers for the reception of strangers opened. In the morning they were shown the Church and the general buildings of the Convent. Fifteen or twenty Spanish monks resided in the Convent, occupied in attendance on its religious ceremonial, and in receiving strangers. One of the brotherhood, whom they name the Incumbent of Nazareth, is especially charged with the care of the Christian community in the town, amounting to about two thousand persons, who, as well as the monks, generally enjoy the full exercise of their religion.[2]

A little Maronite Church, on the S.W. extremity of Nazareth, has been regarded by recent travellers as marking the spot where the popular outrage was attempted against our Lord. It stands under a precipice, where the hill breaks off in a perpendicular wall of forty or fifty feet in height. The monks have been unsparing, and almost profane, in giving names to the various localities. A small Church to the N.W. of the Convent is asserted to be built where the "workshop of Joseph" stood. This was described by Maundrell and Pococke as in ruins, but was found by Dr. Clarke restored, and perfectly modern. To the west of this Church is a small arched building, which, we are told, "stands on the ground of the Synagogue," if it is not "the Synagogue itself," where our Lord applied the memorable prophecy of Isaiah to His own mighty mission.

"The Spirit of the Lord is upon me, because he hath anointed me to preach the Gospel to the poor; he hath sent me to heal the broken-hearted; to preach deliverance to the captives, and recovering of sight to the blind; to set at liberty them that are bruised; to preach the acceptable year of the Lord." It has been conceived by some writers, that it was His adoption of the prophecy in His own character which exasperated the people; but this is an obvious error, for the adoption, "This day is this Scripture fulfilled in your ears," was received with universal acknowledgement. "And all bare him witness, and wondered at the gracious words which proceeded out of his mouth." It was only when He predicted their rejection of Him, on the general ground of the jealousy and envy of human nature — "No prophet is accepted in his own country" — that they instantly proceeded to give demonstration to the truth of His words by the attempt to destroy Him, "and rose up, and thrust him out of the city, and led him to the brow of the hill *whereon their city* was built, that they might cast him down headlong."[3]

The site of Nazareth itself is admirable; and in the days when the land was fully peopled, when property was comparatively secure, as it was under the Roman authority, and when men dwelt "under their own vine and under their own fig-tree," the valley of Nazareth may have been one of the loveliest spots in Palestine, — a scene, whose luxuriance and retirement, the expanse of the noble Lake of Tiberias, and the grandeur of the mountain landscape, rendered it not unsuited to the earthly dwelling of our Lord. It is a circular basin, encompassed by mountains. Richardson describes it, "as if fifteen mountains met to form an enclosure for this delightful spot; they rise round it, like the edge of a shell, to guard it from intrusion. It is a rich and beautiful field in the midst of barren hills; it abounds in fig-trees, small gardens, and hedges of the prickly pear; and the dense rich grass affords an abundant pasture." The village stands on the slope of the west side of the valley; the Convent at the east end, on high ground. In the village there is but one Mosque, which, however, forms a prominent feature in the View.

[1] Roberts's Journal.   [2] Lamartine's Travels.   [3] Luke, iv. 18-29.

General View of Nazareth

THE man must be insensible to the highest recollections of our being who can look on Nazareth without reverence for the might and mercy that once dwelt there. Generations pass away, and the noblest monuments of the hand of man follow them; but the hills, the valley, and the stream exist, on which the eye of the Lord of all gazed; the soil on which His sacred footsteps trod; the magnificent landscape in the midst of which He lived, working miracles, subduing the stubborn hearts of the multitude, and pronouncing to the Earth that "The Kingdom was at hand."

The view from the hill above Nazareth is one of the most striking in Palestine. Beneath it lies the chief part of the noble Plain of Esdraelon. To the left is seen the summit of Mount Tabor, over intervening hills; with portions of the Little Hermon, Gilboa, and the opposite mountains of Samaria. The long line of Carmel is visible, stretching to the sea, with the Convent of Elias on its northern promontory, and the town of Caifa at its foot. In the West spreads the Mediterranean, always lovely, and reflecting every colour of the morning and evening sky. On the North opens out a verdant and beautiful plain, now called El-Buttauf. Beyond this plain, long ridges of hills, extending East and West, are overtopped by the mountains of Safed, crowned with that city. Towards the right is "a sea of hills and mountains," backed by the still higher ridge beyond the Lake of Tiberias, and on the N.E. by "the majestic Hermon, with its icy crown."[1]

The town of Nazareth (in Arabic En-Nasirah) lies on the western side of a narrow, oblong-basin, extending from S.S.W. to N.N.E. twenty minutes in length and ten in breadth. The houses stand on the lower slope of the western hill, which rises steep and high above them: the dwellings are in general well built, and of stone; they have flat, terraced roofs, without the domes so common in Southern Palestine. The population is about three thousand souls, of which the Mahometans compose 120 families; the rest are Greek, Latin, and Maronite.[2]

The Monks have been as active, and as unfortunate, as usual, in assigning Scriptural events to localities in Nazareth and the adjoining country. The "Mount of Precipitation" — "the brow of the hill," to which the people led Jesus, "that they might cast him down headlong," as narrated by St. Luke — is fixed by them at a precipice overlooking the Plain of Esdraelon, and nearly two miles from the town. But the improbability that a violent populace would have been content to lead the object of their indignation to so great a distance, when they might have cast him down from any of the surrounding cliffs, has induced the monks to move their imaginary Nazareth to the same hill.

As no mention of miracle is made by the Evangelist in the rescue of our Lord, it has been doubted whether any divine interposition was wrought. Yet it is difficult to conceive by what human means He could have escaped from the hands of a people who had been infuriated to the degree of forcing Him to the edge of the precipice. "He, passing through the midst of them, went his way," seems the language of innate power. We hear of no argument or remonstrance from our Lord. He allows the popular rage to act, up to the precise moment when it appeared irresistible; and then convinces His enemies at once of His divine authority and of their crime, by calmly returning through them, now consciously unable to arrest His steps, and leaving them behind, in astonishment and awe. It is also observable, that the twofold clearance of the Temple, at the beginning and the close of our Lord's ministry, is an example of silence on the subject of miracle, though both must have been acts of miraculous will; for what individual means could have driven out the whole multitude of money-changers, and the sturdy peasantry and cattle-dealers of Judea, from the court of the Temple? or what other rebuker would not have been trampled or slain by that furious multitude?

[1] Biblical Researches, iii. 183.   [2] Narrative of a Mission to the Jews, ii. 72.

Plate 29: General View of Nazareth

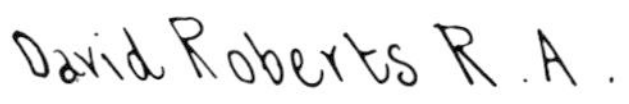

David Roberts R.A.

Above: The Artist's Signature.

The text on the opposite page describes the following double-spread Plate.

PLATE 30: THE SHRINE OF THE ANNUNCIATION

The Shrine of the Annunciation

BENEATH the Church of the Annunciation, and entered by a few steps descending in the rear of the High Altar, is a Grotto, with a marble Altar, lighted by silver lamps, the gifts of princes, and which are kept continually burning. The Altar is pronounced to stand on the exact spot where the Annunciation took place, according to the Latins, who establish *their* true place by a miracle. In the Grotto are two pillars, said to have been erected by the Empress Helena, in consequence of a dream, in which the real places were revealed to her, where the Virgin stood, and where the angel gave the Salutation. One of these pillars has been broken, the act of a Turk, a Pasha, looking for treasure, who was instantly punished with blindness for the desecration. But though the column is separated, about eighteen inches from the ground, the upper portion is till erect, miraculously sustained, as the Monks assert; but Dr. Clarke detected that the capital and shaft of grey granite are fastened to the roof of the Grotto; and, unluckily for the honest reputation of the pillars, he observed also, that the portion which rested on the ground is not granite, but Cipolino marble. However, the celebrity of those pillars is so widely extended, that devotees from all parts of Galilee rub themselves reverentially against them, and believe the act a remedy for all diseases.

Tradition relates, that in this Grotto Mary lived, and over it, according to the same authority, once stood the Holy House, which , when in danger of Mahometan spoliation, was carried through the air by angels, in 1291, to Dalmatia, thence in 1294 to Recanati in Italy, and finally, in 1295, was deposited at Loretto, where it is now so well known, as the Santa Casa.[1] The Altar is raised under the half-natural, half-artifical , arch of the rock, against which the Holy House was supposed to lean. Behind this arch are two dark recesses, presumed to be primitive apartments. Why the Virgin should have lived underground, is not accounted for by the tradition.

[1] Quaresm. ii. 834.

From the Journal

26th February, 1839

Morning delightful, wind changed to the eastward. Bathed in the Red Sea; much refreshed; would have given anything for a draught of fresh water, ours being now undrinkable. Our road all day along the shore, but towards evening we turned up into the hills, where we bivouacked for the night.

27th February, 1839

Near our encampment is a small island with a ruined fortress, of which we could learn nothing. Our water was exhausted, and this morning we arrived about 12 noon, our camels and Arab attendants apparently making a great impression on the inmates of the pigmy fortress, who offered to accommodate us within the walls, but we preferred to pitch our tents outside. After we had rested and dressed, we proceeded to the fort, on the invitation of the governor, who was seated on a divan of rude stone, surrounded by his military attendants, without uniforms, and Bedouins in their sheepskins, with red and yellow handkerchiefs round their heads. We smoked and drank coffee, and arranged to have an Arab despatched to the chief of the tribe of the Alloueens, without whose permission we could go no further. (See Plate 105).

Chapel of the Annunciation Nazareth. April 21st

Church of the Annunciation

THE Church is a lofty nave, with three elevations. The highest is occupied by the Choir of the monks; the lower by the people; and communicating with the Choir and the High Altar is a handsome staircase. A door from the Choir opens into the Convent. The Convent is rich in pictures and ornaments, in which the Church largely shares; the columns and whole interior of the building being also hung with damasked striped silk, which gives it a glowing appearance. Burckhardt speaks of this Church as excelled in Syria only by that of the Holy Sepulchre. "Finding the door of the Church open," says the author of the Biblical Researches, "we went in: it was the hour of vespers, and the chaunting of the monks, sustained by the mellow tones of the organ, which came upon us unexpectedly, was solemn and affecting. The interior is small and plain, with massive arches; the hanging of the walls produced a rich effect: the whole impression transported me back to Italy. A barrier was laid across the floor, not far from the entrance, as a warning not to advance farther." A precaution, perhaps, adopted through fear of the plague, which prevailed at the time.

It is, of course, not the province of these brief descriptions to discuss the conjectures of rival monks on the subject of those localities. From the strong competition of the Greek and Latin conventuals, it frequently arises that two spots are pointed out for the same event, and the disputants refuse to be reconciled. Thus the Greeks have *their* established scene of the Anunciation, but not on this spot. They allege that the Angel, not finding the Virgin in her home, had followed her to the fountain, whither she had gone for water, and there declared his divine mission.

"And in the sixth month the angel Gabriel was sent from God unto a city of Galilee, named Nazareth, to a virgin espoused to a man whose name was Joseph, of the house of David; and the virgin's name was Mary. And the angel came in unto her, and said, Hail, thou art highly favoured; the Lord is with thee: blessed art thou among women."[1]

The most popularly honoured of all the relics of which Nazareth boasts, is the stone named "the Table of our Lord." This is a large flat slab of the common limestone of the country, fixed in the ground, at which our Lord is presumed to have dined before and after his resurrection. According to Hasselquist, it was formerly covered with sheet-iron, the nail-marks of which are yet to be seen. A Chapel has been built over it, and on the wall are copies of a Papal certificate, asserting its claims to reverence, and offering an indulgence of seven years "to all who shall visit this Holy place, reciting there, at least, one Pater and one Ave." "There is not", says Dr. Clarke, "an object in Nazareth so much the resort of pilgrims, Greek, Romish, Arab, and even Turk, as this stone. The Greek and Latin pilgrims resorting to it from devotion, and the Arab and Turk to see the wonders which it is presumed to work on the devotees."[2]

[1] Luke, i. 26,27. [2] Travels in the Holy Land.

Cana, General View

THE View is full of traditionary holiness. In the small Greek Church, at the foot of the hill, is shown by the priest, as an invaluable relic (on the authority of tradition), "one of the water-pots" in which the water was changed into wine. For preservation, it is built into the wall. The Church itself is pronounced to have been raised on the spot where the marriage-feast was celebrated. The ruins of an adjacent house are regarded, on the same authority, to be those of the dwelling of our Lord: the disciple Nathanael was a native of Cana.[1]

The nature of the Miracle may allow of some elucidation here, narrow as are the limits to which it must be confined. It seems to be implied in the narrative, that our Lord had *previously* intended to give some evidence of his divine power on the occasion of the marriage; and even that he had *declared* his intention. For his mother, on the first emergency of the feast, the failure of wine, evidently suggests it to him, as the object of his interposition; and by what other means than miracle could he have supplied it at the moment? Yet she could never have seen him work a miracle before. His answer confirms the idea of a *previous* declaration; for it is equivalent to the words, "In giving my evidence of divine power, I must not be interfered with by human suggestion. The time on which I have determined for it has not *yet* come." It is not unnatural to conceive, that HE then suffered some period to elapse; perhaps, until it was known among all the guests that the wine had been wholly consumed, and thus the deficiency distinctly felt and openly acknowledged.

The extreme succinctness of the Gospel narratives in general renders them mere outlines, which, in all humility, we are entitled to fill up with the natural features of the transaction. His mother then alludes no further to the deficiency of the wine, or rather, abandons the suggestion altogether; yet is still so fully convinced of his intention to give *some* proof of his divine power, that she bids the servants, "*Whatsoever* he saith unto you, do it."

Of course, the supreme Lord of Miracle might have wrought a wonder of a wholly different order, more stupendous in its effects, and, from its grandeur, more likely to spread his name through all ranks of his nation. But the change of the water into wine bears the peculiar characteristic by which his uniform of the divine and human natures was distinguished. It was a work of kindness as well as of power. It relieved the master of the feast from an immediate and perplexing want, and it met that want with a sudden munificence,[2] which marked the act as divine. Kindness to his mother, too, may have mingled in his choice of the miracle. He had vindicated the majesty of that great instrument of Heaven, by declaring that its use was not to be dependent on any personal and human influence; and having thus done, he soothes and honours her in the presence of the guests and attendants, by adopting her wish before them all.

Some reasons for the selection of a Marriage-feast as the scene of the primary miracle are sufficiently obvious; though it may be presumption, in the highest intellect of man, to assume that it knows *all* the reasons of any one miracle. The presence of our Lord at a festivity, and that one of the most crowded and joyous of all the social festivities of Palestine, instantly marked his Religion as wholly distinct from the frowning formalities and ascetic superstitions of the Jewish sects. His giving the assemblage an unexpected, and even a bounteous, increase of the proverbial means of enjoyment, was only an additional pledge of his sympathy with the customary habits and harmless indulgences of man. But his choice of a Marriage-feast as the commencement of his Mission may have had a reference of a higher rank. The connexion of our Lord with Church is represented, in both the Old and New Testament, under the figure of a Marriage. HE is the Bridegroom, His redeemed the Bride. The character of the Married State, — the sincere confidence, — the perfect identity of object, — the intimate, pure, and permanent union, are applied by Scripture to the sacred relation even in our world. How much more strongly to that exalted and immortal condition in which "we shall see as we are seen," and in which "the spirits of just men made perfect" go on "from glory to glory, as in the presence of the Lord!"

[1] John ii.   [2] The "measure" in the original was either the Hebrew (7½ gallons), or more probably the Attic Metretes (9 gallons). The vessels to contain water for the continual ablutions of the Jews must have been large. Dr. E. Clarke found them from 18 to 27 gallons, which would be about the "*two or three* measures a-piece."

Plate 32: Cana, General View

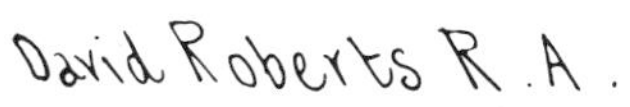

David Roberts R.A.

Above: The Artist's Signature.

The text on the opposite page describes the
following double-spread Plate.

Fountain at Cana April 21st 1839.

David Roberts R.A

Fountain of Cana

THE whole country of Galilee possesses a solemn interest from its connexion with the earlier periods of our Lord's human existence. The scene of his first miracle, and made conspicuous by his frequent return, and frequent displays of power and benevolence, the soil becomes eminently sacred, and the mind approaches its contemplation with the reverent solicitude and grateful homage due to the birth-place of Christianity.

The Fountain in the Sketch is traditionally the same from which the water-pots in the miracles were filled. The water is remarkably copious and pure; and as there is no other fountain within a considerable distance, the inhabitants of the village regard its sacred claim as beyond all question.

The large sculptured stone near the fountain is a Roman Sarcophagus, now used as a watering-trough for cattle, a purpose for which similar relics are frequently employed in Palestine. At this Fountain the Christian pilgrims rest and taste the water, as a sanctifying ceremonial previous to their entering Cana. The women of the village are constantly seen here, in groups, bearing jars of the same material and same dimensions with those described in Holy Scripture.[1]

But the claims of the existing Cana have been strongly disputed by late and learned authority. It is contended, that the site of the village in which the miracle was performed, is Kana-el-Jelil (Cana of Galilee), a ruin on the northern side of the Plain El-Buttauf; N.½E. from Nazareth, and about three hours distance. The chief reasons are its unaltered name, and its having been regarded as the true site by authorities altogether earlier than those of its competitor, and traceable up the sixth century.[2]

[1] Roberts's Journal.   [2] Biblical Researches, iii, 208.

From the Journal

2nd March, 1839

This morning the sheikh of the Alloueens arrived, when a grand palaver took place. After much beating about the bush, we came to terms, and he guaranteed our safe passage to Hebron, by the way of Wady Mousa or Petra, staying at the latter place as long as we chose. We were to pay him £45, or 4500 piastres. We invited the governor and sheikh, and their friends, to dinner, with which they expressed themselves delighted, and after giving presents to our friends the Beni-Sayd Arabs, who had accompanied us here, we made preparations for proceeding on our journey. (See Plate 109).

3rd March, 1839

Bidding farewell to the governor of the fortress, we mounted our camels and dromedaries, twenty-three in number. Our course lay up what is supposed by some to have been the ancient bed of the Jordan. The plains were covered with a heavy mist, the mountains were only seen fitfully, and the desert looked more dreary than usual. About 3 o'clock our sheikh pointed out a spot where the camels might find food, and we pitched our tents for the night; the sheikh and his son dined with us, and we afterwards took a stroll through our camp.

St Jean d Acre April 25th 1839.

St. Jean D'Acre, from the Sea

THIS view gives the sea-face of Acre, exhibiting a striking succession of domes, minarets, and that general style of ornamental building, which is so attractive to the eye at a distance, but so frequently disappoints it on a nearer view. Still the Oriental architecture has a charm of its own. Whether from association, or from its intrinsic beauty, it always gives the impression of Caliphates and Sultanries; of manners when all that was romantic in the East was combined with all that was superb; and of ages when the Asiatic Sovereign habitually lived in a state of magnificent seclusion, and mysterious voluptuousness.

Nothing has given rise to more learned, or more unproductive, dispute than the origin of the different styles. The most authentic theory seems that which would trace them all to the first dwellings of the respective nations. The Greek and Roman palace and temple were but improvements on the original habitations of climates, where the sun was genial, and the air refreshing; they are broad and lofty, spacious and open to the breeze. — The elegance of the Saracen dome is palpably modelled on the lightness of the Arab tent. — The Egyptian temple, massive, solemn, and dim, seems only a catacomb transferred to the surface; as the catacomb itself was probably only an enlargement of the first dwellings in a country of sand, and where the chief luxury of life was to escape the sun. — The Indian architecture strongly resembles the stalactite roof of the cavern, the immense solidity, and mystic grandeur of the Elephantas and Eloras — temples and palaces of Nature, worthy to stamp the taste and guide the genius of a race of Hierarchs and Sultans.

From the Journal

(Continued)

The Arabs were wrapped in their abbas, and were stretched by the watch-fires, the camels sleeping around them. The moon was shining with a splendour only seen in Eastern countries, and the mountains seemed more grave and mysterious than through the day, so that it required a very slight stretch of the imagination to transfer them to my own dear land; but this illusion was quickly dispelled by the recumbent figures of the sleeping Arabs.

4th March, 1839

At daybreak we were in motion. By 10 o'clock we dismounted by a pool of stagnant water, of which the camels drank greedily, while we enjoyed our frugal repast, consisting of Arab bread, Dutch cheese, and the remains of a kid. About 4 o'clock we arrived at the tents of the sheikh, where we were received with great kindness, and kissed on each cheek by every Arab present. A kid was presented to us by the sheikh, which we relished amazingly.

St. Jean D'Acre, from the Land

ACRE,[1] commanding the chief commerce of the corn industry of Palestine, has always been in a position of the first importance to the governors of Syria. Standing on the northern point of the Bay, of which Carmel forms the southern; heavy and massive on the sea-side; from the land it forms a striking object, with its fortifications rising above the plain, and the Mediterranean, always bright and beautiful, for its background.[2]

The Artist visited Acre previously to the memorable attack by the British fleet, and the havoc occasioned by the explosion of the great Magazine among its buildings. But it still bore formidable marks of the long siege, which closed in its capture by the Egyptian troops under Ibrahim Pasha, in 1832.

The advantages of position are generally paid for at a high price. Acre has been the prey of war from an early age. In the general inroad of the Saracens it was stormed (A.D. 636). The invasion of the Crusaders furnished another period of blood in its history (A.D. 1104). But within less than a century, the tide of Christian success had sunk, and the famous Saladin became master of a new Crusade. Once more, in the decay of the Christian conquests, it was stormed by the Saracens. But the Caliphate itself went down, and the City was given into the stronger grasp of the Turk (A.D. 1517). After a long period of oblivion, in the decay of the Sultanry, Acre was revived by the Arab Daher, a tyrant, but a bold soldier. On his death the government was seized by a barbarian, whose name, Djessar (the butcher), was amply earned by the merciless severity of his sword.

But is was now destined to form a conspicuous feature in a war which ultimately involved the civilised world. In 1799, the French army, under the great military genius of their country, advanced to the walls. The fortifications were feeble, and the garrison was composed of Turks and Arabs in a state of insubordination. But the arrival of two British ships of war, under the gallant Sir Sydney Smith, restored their courage; and Napoleon, after repeated assaults, and fifty-one days of open trenches, was driven from Acre, and from Syria.

In 1832, the revolt of Egypt exposed it to a new enemy; and it was besieged by the troops of Mehemet Ali. Abdallah, the Governor, declared, that "if an European force attacked him, he would blow himself up; but if a Turkish, he would wait, till the walls fell down upon his garrison." Closely besieged for five months and twenty-one days; 35,000 shells were thrown into it, and almost all the public buildings were shattered; yet it finally yielded only to famine.[3]

It was still to be the subject of a more distinguishable catastrophe. Syria had been conquered in two decisive fields by the Pasha; the battle of Nezib threatened to shake the Turkish throne. Negotiation with either of the contending powers had evidently become but a waste of time, and the war already menaced the peace of Europe, when England, at last, took upon herself the duty of achieving the general security. She sent a fleet to Syria. In a campaign of three months, it swept the coast of all opposition; and on the 3rd of November, 1840, appeared before Acre, the stronghold of the Pasha's conquests. In a bombardment of three hours, it crushed the fortifications, drove the garrison from the City, and concluded the War! This exploit, unexampled in the history of combat, was richly rewarded by its fruits — the peace of Syria, the independence of Turkey, and the tranquillity of the world.

[1] Anciently called also Acco, and Ptolemais. [2] Roberts's Journal.
[3] G. Robinson's Travels, 199.

Plate 35: St. Jean D'Acre, from the Land

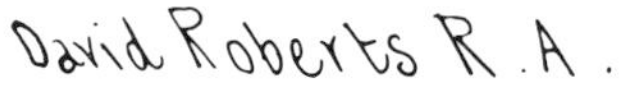

David Roberts R.A.

Above: The Artist's Signature.

The text on the opposite page describes the following double-spread Plate.

Rosia Bona near L. Sinai   David Roberts

Cape Blanco

THIS promontory forms are one of the most striking natural objects on the coast of Syria. At the foot of Cape Blanco — also called by the natives Ras-el-Abiad (the white promontory), from its bleached front — the road ascends, and winds along the face of the cliff to a startling elevation. It appears to have been the work of remote times; for it is deeply worn, and worn by the wheels of carts, a vehicle seldom used on the Coast at the present day. Huge masses of the cliff have fallen away on the seaside, and the road has become more difficult in consequence. A low parapet of loose stones is all that now stands between the traveller and a precipice several hundred feet deep, with the sea rolling in at its base. From its full exposure to the West, the effect of a winter storm, with the Mediterranean pouring its whole fury on the rocky barrier, is overwhelming, — the surges sometimes dashing up the promontory to the height of the road. The passage over the Mountain is about a mile in length. To add to its picturesque effect, the cliff is tenanted by "myriads" of wild pigeons, which, on the discharge of fire-arms, rush out and cloud the air.

All the wonders of Syria are attributed to Alexander the Great, as all the churches of Palestine claim the Empress Helena for their founder. But the tradition which gives to the great Conqueror and Civiliser a work of such difficulty, usefulness, and grandeur, is not unsuitable to the genius of the most daring, yet most cultivated, master of mankind.

The artist had the advantage — which, perhaps, none but an Artist could fully appreciate — of seeing Cape Blanco under the influence of a coming storm. "The sky was dark and louring; heavy clouds swept over our heads, and the rolling surge beat with a thundering noise on the rocks. It was certainly the most sublime scene I had yet beheld on the coast of Syria."[1]

Descending the northern side of the promontory, the traveller enters upon the celebrated Phœnician Plain, which extends from three hours south of Tyre to the Nahr-el-Auly, an hour north of Sidon; the whole being a distance of about eleven hours. Its breadth is unequal, generally half an hour, except round Tyre and Sidon, where the hills recede. The soil is now nearly waste, but obviously capable of tillage.[2] The actual domain of Tyre never exceeded a circumference of twenty miles.

This was a singularly small territory to maintain the mightiest traffic of the ancient world. The trade of Tyre extended eastward through Persia, or even, perhaps, through India; and westward through the Ocean; at a period when, to all other nations, the mouth of the Red Sea was the "Straits of Death, " and the Pillars of Hercules were the boundaries of the earth. In the Ocean, northward it reached the British Isles, and southward ranged the coast of Africa.[3] For ages before Greece or Italy had attained regular government, and while both were the chosen seats of popular fable and poetic monsters, the bold mariners of Phœnicia were familiar with their seas, and had formed settlements in their ports; Carthage, Cadiz, and Marseilles, were their colonies; and the tin and wolf-skins of Britain met the gold and silks of the remote East in the marts of Tyre.

The wealth of her merchants, the magnificence of her buildings, and the strength of her battlements, were the wonder of all nations. Even when, at length, she fell before an enemy commissioned by an avenging Providence, she rapidly rose again, resumed her fame, and recommenced the Commercial Empire of the world. It is remarkable, that though Commerce has often raised feeble states to sudden power, there is no other instance in history of that unrivalled and universal influence, except our own. — Tyre and England, at the distance of thousands of years, alike, and alone, exhibiting the natural results of vigorous enterprise, guided by wisdom, cheered by national encouragement, and left free in its direction, its impulses, and its rewards.

[1] Roberts's Journal.　[2] Bibl. Res. iii. 410.　[3] Vincent, Commerce, &c. of the Ancients, ii. 624, &c.

Port of Tyre April 27th 1839   David Roberts R.A.

Port of Tyre

THE site of Tyre, now named Sur, was once apparently a mere ledge of rocks, distant half a mile from the shore. The gradual accumulation of sand enlarged it, and the Causeway was widened by the same means into an Isthmus. Thus two bays were formed, the Northern and the Southern; the former being the principal roadstead.

The Northern port, or basin, was formerly enclosed by a wall running from the north end of the Island, in a curve towards the mainland. This wall, of which but fragments remain, displays even in ruin great massiveness. Its foundations often exhibit marble and granite pillars laid side by side , not unlike vast pieces of ordnance. But enclosure has long since been useless; for the port has been nearly choked with sand, and it now gives a place of refuge to scarecely more than the few fishing vessels of the neighbouring peasantry.

The memorable prophecy of Ezekiel against the elder Tyre, regarded in merely its human aspect, would supply almost a study of the commerce of antiquity; closing with the sentence of ruin: "These were thy merchants in all sorts of things, in blue clothes, and in broidered work, and in chests of rich apparel, bound with cords, and made of cedar, among thy merchandise." The previous detail embraces nearly all the wants and luxuries of man.

Then follows the condemnation: "All the inhabitants of the isles shall be astonished at thee, and their kings shall be sore afraid, they shall be troubled in their countenance. The merchants among the people shall hiss at thee; thou shalt be a terror, and never shalt be any more."[1]

[1] Ezek. xxvii. 2-36.

From the Journal

5th March, 1839

Started early, as usual. About 12 o'clock we struck into a chain of mountains on our right, forming part of the range of Mount Hor. At 3 o'clock we pitched our tents at the entrance to Wady Mousa; and, anxious to get a glimpse of Petra, I ascended the mountain and found another hill intervened, but the view of the valley forming the ancient bed of the Jordan was magnificent.

6th March, 1839

Petra. To-day we encamped in the centre of the remains of this extraordinary city, which is situated in the midst of mountains, surrounded by the desert, but abounding in every vegetable production. Our sheikh had endeavoured to persuade us to leave our camels and baggage behind us, and go along with him into Petra, that we might the more easily get away if the Fellaheens came upon us. This we refused to do, and getting all the caravan in motion, we began to ascend the mountain by a path along the verge of a deep ravine, filled with oleander and laurel. (See Plate 99).

Tyre, from The Isthmus

THIS view represents Tyre as it now exists, with the Causeway connecting it with the mainland. The length of the Island is a mile. On the right lies the principal harbour. The tower on the same side marks the two fountains of the Island, and the Ras-el-Ain.[1] The town spreads loosely along the eastern shore. On the south, the ruins of the Cathedral are seen; and the square Saracenic tower on the left is built on the extremity of a wall once extending across the Causeway, and, perhaps, forming a species of fortification. Between the houses and the western shore remains a broad strip of land used for tillage.[2] The interval between the southern wall and the end of the Island in that quarter is a rocky space, used to "dry nets upon." The western coast is wholly a ledge of rugged rocks, in some parts fifteen or twenty feet high, on which the Mediterranean dashes with a perpetual surge. This shore is strewed with columns of red and grey granite, the last evidence of the ancient grandeur of Tyre.

The early history of Tyre ascends to the first ages of the commercial intercourse of nations. The Indian trade seems to have been in every age the fountain of wealth, or rather the great stimulant and reward of the commercial activity of man. This trade flowed to the West through the two channels of Tyre and Egypt, giving to the one its opulence and its arts, and to the other its opulence and its knowledge. Between them lay Palestine, withheld from the pursuits of both, but obviously withheld for the express purpose of being preserved from the corruptions of either, and of retaining religion for mankind. By a striking contrast, Egypt was the great producer, yet with a strong distaste for naval adventure: while Phœnicia produced comparatively little, yet was the chief merchant: the one the manufacturer, the other the carrier, of the world.[3]

Whether the original Tyre was on the mainland or the island has been a question. But that the City which first obtained distinction was on the mainland is acknowledged. It is mentioned as a "strong city" so early as the Division by Joshua. It retained the same character in the time of David, and was "the strong city, Tyre." The well-known compact between Solomon and Hiram its king gives further evidence of its power. Hiram disposes of the forests at Lebanon, at his will, for the building of the Temple. "So Hiram gave Solomon cedar-trees and fir-trees, according to all his desire: and Solomon gave Hiram twenty thousand measures of wheat for food to his household, and twenty measures of pure oil."[4]

The superior quality of the Island, with the alarm excited by the growth of the Assyrian power, probably impelled the population to take refuge in the new Tyre. If such were the reason, it was amply justified by the event; for on Shalmaneser's invasion (B.C. 720), while the Palætyrus (Old Tyre) was taken at once the City of the Island resisted for five years, and finally repelled him. The more warlike ability, and perhaps more disciplined force, of Nebuchadnezzar, though it destroyed Old Tyre,[5] wasted thirteen years in the blockade of the New. Even the great military genius of the ancient world, Alexander, besieged it for seven months, and ultimately conquered, only by throwing the stones of Old Tyre into the sea, and thus forming the Causeway, by which he was enabled to assault the walls. The City was at length absorbed into the general tide of Roman conquest. But it then obtained, even if unconsciously, the highest distinction in its history. It was visited, or at least, approached by our Lord. "And He arose, and went into the borders of Tyre and Sidon, and entered into a house. And a certain woman, whose daughter had an unclean spirit, heard of him, and came and fell at his feet."[6] It was also the seat of an early Christian Church visited by St. Paul on his way to Jerusalem.[7] In the Crusades it fell into the hands of the Christians (June 27, 1124), and was held by them until the memorable year 1291 — the era of the expulsion of the Franks from Palestine; when Melek-el-Ashref, Sultan of Egypt and Damascus, so terrified the people by his severities at Acre, that on his approach to Tyre, the Franks fled on board their ships, and left the gates open. From that time it sank into a decay, which has defied all restoration.

[1] Roberts's Journal. [2] Bib. Res. Res. iii. 499, &c. [3] Stevenson, Hist. of Commerce. [4] I Kings, v. 11. [5] It is evidently to this destruction that the strong denunciations of the prophets are to be chiefly referred. Ezekiel, xxvi. 21, 27, &c. [6] Mark, vii. 24. [7] Acts, xxi. 2-4.

Plate 38: Tyre, from the Isthmus

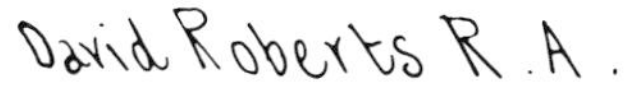

David Roberts R.A.

Above: The Artist's Signature.

The text on the opposite page describes the following double-spread Plate.

Tyre ancient Tyre from the Isthmus about 24th 1839

General View of Tyre

THIS scene comprehends the sites of two of the most memorable Cities of antiquity — the Tyre of the mainland, and the Tyre of the Island, with the Causeway connecting them. The former Tyre was early ruined, and if any remnants of it exist, they are buried in the sand which continually accumulates over the plain: or, are to be found in the materials for the Causeway by which Alexander the Great approached the second Tyre; and in which the sand has been swept away by the wind and the surge.[1]

This once renowned City is now but a diminutive town, carrying on a struggling commerce in the tobacco of the neighbouring hills, with some wood and charcoal from the more distant mountains. The streets are narrow and winding, and the houses mean, seldom exceeding a single story, with flat roofs. But the palm-trees, which are always beautiful, and full of Oriental character, mixed with the buildings, give a grace and freshness to the distant aspect of Tyre.[2]

The chief trade is carried on by the Christian population, who amount to a considerable portion of the inhabitants, and whose industry is said to arise from their being free from the Conscription, if it may not equally arise from the spirit and habits of their religion. At the time of the Sketch, some vessels were lying in the Bay; few, but sufficient to carry on the traffic of this once Queen of the Commercial World.[3]

Its ancient architecture was proverbially of the stateliest kind; some columns of Egyptian granite, ten feet in diameter, remain fixed in the walls. And on examining the foundations of those walls (which are evidently of a later date), pieces of marble, granite, and earthenware, are discovered; though fixed in a cement so strong, that where the action of the sea has honeycombed the stone, it still has left the cement unimpaired. But the only gate of Tyre is Saracenic, and the only fortifications are the work of the middle ages.[4]

The Cathedral of Tyre stood in the south-eastern corner of the present town. It was in the Greek style, and must have been a remarkable fabric; its length being at least 250 feet, and its breadth 150. The eastern end is yet partially standing, and some portions of its western extremity exist; but the area is filled up with hovels. Adjoining one of those, lies an immense double column of Syenite granite, consisting of two parallel, connected shafts of exquisite shape and beauty, which once belonged to the Cathedral. Djezzar Pasha proposed to

have carried these pillars to Acre, for one of his Mosques; but their weight defied the skill, or the industry, of his Syrian engineers.[5] An earthquake in 1837 did considerable damage in the Island; when a lofty arch, and a portion of the finer architecture of the ruin, were thrown down.

The history of the Cathedral is obscure. But it is known, that so early as the fourth century, there was in Tyre a Cathedral, built by its Bishop, Paulinus; for which the consecration sermon was written by Eusebius, and which he pronounced to be "the most splendid of all the temples of Phœnica."[6] From that Period, it singularly lapsed into oblivion. Even during the Crusades, an era when all the recollections of Eastern antiquity were revived with extraordinary ardour, when Tyre itself was erected into an Archbishopric under the Patriarchate of Jerusalem; and when William of Tyre, the well-known Chronicler of the Crusades, was consecrated Archbishop (A.D. 1174) and wrote his History here ; still, no record of the Cathedral is to be found. An unsettled tradition reports, that the bones of the Emperor Frederic the First, who was drowned in the Calycadnus, or the Cydnus, on his march to Palestine (A.D. 1190), were buried in Tyre, his heart having been deposited in the Cathedral of Antioch.[7]

The population of Tyre is reckoned at 400 taxable Mahometans, and 300 taxable Christians, thus giving a population of nearly 3000 souls. The Christians are chiefly Greek Catholics, who have a resident Bishop. There are but few Jewish inhabitants. The water of the town is supplied by two fountains rising in the Island, close to the sea; they are, however, supposed to have some secret communication with the springs of Ras-el-Ain, three copious reservoirs, at an hour's distance in the plain.

[1] Roberts's Journal.   [2] Bibl. Res. iii 398.   [3]. G. Robinson's Travels.   [4] Bibl. Res. iii. 399.   [5] Volney, Voyage, ii. 196.   [6] Hist. Eccl. x. 4.   [7] Will. Tyre, xxi. 9, and others, quoted in Biblical Researches, iii. 399.

Ruins called the El Hammâm near Tyre.   April 25th 1839

David Roberts R A !

Ruins of an Ionic Temple

PASSING northward from Acre, on descending the first headland, the traveller reaches the small village of Nachora. The road, in its general massiveness, gives striking vestiges of the work of antiquity: even the bridge over the inconsiderable stream which crosses it is formed of immense blocks, which scorn decay.

On ascending a promontory at some distance from the village, the eye is struck with a bold ruin, the remnant of an Ionic temple, which must have once formed a magnificent object from both the hills and the sea, having a front of at least 200 feet, with a depth of 400. One standing shaft alone retains its capital. But fragments of Ionic columns, in the best taste, remain, flung about in every direction, and confusedly mingled with Doric: earthquakes are the great enemy of architecture in this country. The Artist observes, as one of the most singular instances of Asiatic oblivion, or Antiquarian neglect, that neither this noble ruin, nor the stately City which obviously surrounded it, has found a name. Fragments of sculpture and building extend widely within view of the Temple; and he conjectures, that they may have once been the City built by Alexander, whose site had been erroneously conceived to lie a mile farther to the north. The country in the rear rises in a succession of hills, which, though now desolate, give evidence of former cultivation. Beyond the Temple, the road again ascends until it meets the precipices of Cape Blanco.[1]

The mixture of the Doric and Ionic architecture may be accounted for by the acknowledged affinity of the two orders; the latter being palpably but the former refined into elegance: the triglyph exchanged for the dentele; the strong and single architrave for the delicate lines and ornamental sculpture of the triple; the robust and plain shaft for the shapely and fluted: and the massy capital for the graceful volute — the Doric the emblem of masculine strength; the Ionic the emblem of feminine beauty.

[1] Roberts's Journal.

From the Journal

(Continued)

We crossed a ridge of the mountain, and were about to descend into the valley of Petra when we were surrounded by a party of the Fellaheen Arabs, who intimated by violent gesticulations that we would not be permitted to proceed further. Their sheikh informed us that the sheikh of the Alloueens had no right to come, or bring any travellers there; so, after a long altercation, we agreed to pay them 300 piastres, and erected our tents in the centre of the city.
(See Plate 87).

Our first stroll was to the Khasne, and I cannot say whether I was most surprised at the building or its extraordinary position. It stands, as it were, in an immense niche in the rocks, and the fine colour of the stone, and perfect preservation of the minute details, give it the appearance of having been recently finished.
(See Plates 86, 88).

7th March, 1839

I am more and more astonished and bewildered with this extraordinary city, which must be five or six miles each way in extent; and every ravine has been inhabited, even to the tops of the mountains.

Sarepta

HERE the scenery changes from the general aspect of the south of Palestine: the hills assume a bolder character, and the chain of Lebanon, capped with snow, rises majestically in the background.

In front of the village on the hill, and close to the sea, is a small Mosque, traditionally covering the site of the house in which the prophet Elijah took refuge, and restored the widow's son to life by prayer.[1] The name of the village is now Surafend.

Sarepta had the high distinction of being named in both the Old Testament and the New. In the history of the great prophet it is recorded, — "And the word of the Lord came unto him and said, Arise get thee to Zarephath (Sarepta), which belongeth to Zidon, and dwell there."[2]

And our Lord, in rebuking the stubborness of his nation, repeats the record, — "I tell you of a truth, many widows were in Israel in the days of Elias, when the heaven was shut up three years and six months, when a great famine was throughout all the land; but unto none of them was Elias sent save unto Sarepta, a city of Sidon, unto a woman that was a widow."[3]

Sarepta was erected into a Bishopric by the Crusaders, who raised a Chapel over the reputed spot where Elijah restored the widow's child.[4] In the twelfth century it seems to have been a fortified city, with a port, and some stately buildings. The true Sarepta evidently stood on the shore. The village of Surafend, its present substitute, was probably formed by refugees from the decayed City, and has grown subsequently to the Crusades.

[1] Roberts's Journal.   [2] I Kings, xvii. 9, 10.   [3] Luke, iv. 25.   [4] Le Quien, Oriens Christianus, iii. 1338.

From the Journal

(Continued)

The valley has been filled with temples, public buildings, triumphal arches, and bridges, all of which have been laid prostrate, with the exception of one arch, and one temple, and of this temple the portico has fallen. The style of the architecture varies from all I have ever seen, and in many of its parts is a curious combination of the Egyptian with the Roman and Greek orders. The stream still flows through it as heretofore; the shrubs and wild-flowers flourish luxuriantly; every crevice of the rock is filled with them, and the air is perfumed with the most delicious fragrance. (See Plates 91, 94).

Sidon

SIDON, a name familiar to all the readers of ancient history, and renewed in our recollections by the brilliant Syrian campaign of 1841, is one of the oldest cities in the world; and has been distinguished for its commerce, its opulence, and its vicissitudes, from almost the earliest period of its existence. It is named in the Pentateuch,[1] and by Homer.[2] In the division of Palestine it was alloted to Asher,[3] but was never possessed. In the general invasion of Phœnicia by Shalmaneser (B.C. 720), it was conquered; and sank into a tributary to the successive empires of Assyria and Persia. Tyre, its younger rival, resisted and repulsed the invader; perhaps not more from its insular position, than its superior wealth, population, and the public spirit resulting from both. Joining the general revolt of Phœnicia against Artaxerxes Ochus (B.C. 350), it was captured and destroyed by the conqueror. But its situation made it powerful once more; it was rapidly rebuilt, and on the invasion of the Persian Empire by Alexander the Great, probably warned by example, it received him with open gates, and thus escaped the ruin which befell its haughtier and more powerful neighbour, Tyre. After the death of that most illustrious of Pagan conquerors, Sidon became alternately the prey of the Kings of Egypt and Syria, until they, too, sank into the all-absorbing dominion of Rome. Yet the City remained distinguished, at once for Oriental indulgence and Western activity.

But another and still more memorable period of its existence was to come. Our Lord himself trod the regions of Tyre and Sidon.[4] Christianity took root there so early as the first preaching of the Apostles; and St. Paul, on his way to Rome, found converts, and apparently a church.[5] A Bishopric certainly existed in the territory of Sidon at an early period, though the first of its Bishops on record was Theodorus, who was present at the Council of Nice (A.D. 325).

The Age of the Crusades was destined to exhibit a general change in maritime Syria. The Crusaders commenced their operations against Jerusalem from the north, and the general march from Antioch (A.D. 1099) followed nearly the line of the sea-shore. In the first instance the Cities were passed by, and the march was directed full upon the grand object of the invasion. But the position of Sidon rendered its possession essential, and it sustained two attacks from Baldwin, the new monarch of Jerusalem (A.D. 1107 and 1108). In the first it bought off, and in the second it repulsed, the Crusaders. But it was attacked a third time (A.D. 1111), and captured, after a six weeks' siege.

Sidon enjoyed comparative security under its Christian governors, until towards the close of the century. But the banner of the Kingdom of Jerusalem had long been shattered, and after the decisive battle of Hattim, the City opened its gates to Saladin (A.D. 1187). It now underwent the usual unhappy casualties of the seat of war. It was reconquered by the Christians only to be again lost to the Moslem, and possessed by the Moslem only to be again assaulted by the Knights who still wandered over the sacred soil. Yet, by a singular exception to the emporiums of the East, a remnant of population clung to its ruins, until it resumed the shape of a City again. At length, in the seventeenth century, it rose into sudden distinction, under the famous Emir of the Druses, Fakhr-ed-Din. The Emir adorned it with stately public buildings, his policy attracted merchants from Europe, and his power protected the industry and intelligence of the people. After his ruin, its commerce was chiefly with France. It exported cotton and silk, and was the chief mart of the rich silk manufacturers of Damascus.[6] But Djezzar Pasha drove out the French, and the trade declining once more, was carried on by the natives alone. Beyrout has since become the port of Damascus, and unless some new change of masters shall change its fortunes, Sidon is likely to perish by natural decay.

[1] Gen. x. 19.   [2] Iliad, vi. 289. Odyss. xv. 415; xvii. 424.   [3] Josh. xix. 28. Judges, i.31.   [4] Matt. xv. 21. Mark, vii. 24.   [5] Acts, xxvii. 3.   [6] Volney, Voyage en Syrie, ii. 192.

David Roberts R.A.

Sidon, from the North

THE site of the City was admirably chosen at once for commerce, strength, and beauty. Standing on a bold projection of the land, which sufficiently separated it from the level country of the interior, and which was probably fortified, it was safe from casual insult, while it enjoyed the fertility of plains even now remarkable for their richness. The approach to Sidon is through plantations of mulberry-trees, cultivated for the food of the silkworm, and through groves and gardens of the vine, the pomegranate, the orange, and the fig-tree; those are in such abundance and excellence as to have nearly superseded the olive, that favourite production of Syria.

The lover of nature in the East is continually liable to impediments arising from the absurdity of the people. The Artist and his party were placed under a guard, in a species of quarantine; but his admiration of the scene induced him to encounter all difficulties, and transfer the landscape to his portfolio. Sidon struck him as superior to the generality of the coast towns; the houses solid and spacious, and the people well dressed. But the antiquities were few, and apparently limited to some granite columns lying in the road, and vestiges of tessellated pavements.[1]

The small building in the foreground is called the Tomb of Zebulon, and is held in great veneration alike by Moslems and Christians.

[1] Roberts's Journal.

From the Journal

8th March, 1839

To-day we wound our way up a steep ravine, a broken staircase extending about a mile. We reached a building, rarely visited, called Dier, or Convent, which is hewn out of the face of the rock. It is 100 feet in height, and 1000 feet above the level of the city. Facing this, on the summit of a high rock, are the ruins of what has been a magnificent temple; the bases of the portico and colonnade on each side still remain, and the adytum, hewn out of the rock, has a beautifully-ornamental recess, in which the idol has been placed. In a vault underneath is a capital of white marble. The view here is magnificent, embracing the valley of El Ghor, Mount Hor (the tomb of Aaron crowning the summit), and the whole defile, leading through rocks which make you giddy to look over; while the ancient city, in all its extent, is seen stretching along the valley. I have often thrown my pencil away in despair of ever being able to convey any idea of this extraordinary place.

(See Plates 85, 93).

Citadel of Sidon — April 28th 1839

David Roberts R.A.

The Citadel of Sidon

ON the south of Sidon, and on a height commanding the City, stands the large square tower now designated as the Citadel, though formerly perhaps no more than a blockhouse, or advanced post of the general fortifications. It, however, boasts a romantic antiquity, being supposed to belong to the age of the Crusades, if not to have been actually built by Louis IX. (A.D. 1258).[1]

On a coast where good harbours are so rare, and where the winds from both the sea and the mountains blow with such violence, the harbour of Sidon early attracted a memorable commerce; and its command, even in later periods, was obviously a matter of importance. It thus exercised the rude engineering of the Crusaders, who built another Castle on a rock in the sea, connected with the shore on the north by a causeway of nine arches. But, as the harbour also exposed the City to hazard from the Turkish fleets, the still ruder science of the celebrated Fakhr-ed-Din found no other expedient for its protection, than partly filling up the inner harbour with the fragments of ancient pillars, so that boats alone can enter it. Large vessels lie outside the entrance, on the north of a ledge of rocks, where they find sufficient protection from W.S.W. winds, but lie open to those from the north.

The Artist strikingly observes: "From a little farm-house, with a garden of olives and mulberries, we had our first view of Sidon. It is one of the finest that I have yet seen in this country. This once noble City, jutting out upon its promontory into the clear, blue sea, and connected with its ancient Citadel by a bridge and causeway; with the snow-clad peaks of Lebanon in the distance, reflected in the Mediterranean in all the glories of a Syrian sunset, formed a superb spectacle."[2]

[1] Nau. p. 585. Pococke, ii. 87. Turner's Tour, 87, quoted by Robinson, Biblical Researches, iii. 418.   [2] Roberts's Journal.

From the Journal

9th March, 1839

Explored the grand entrance to Petra, which may be about a mile in length, winding between the high rocks by which the valley is enclosed, in many parts overhanging so as almost to meet each other. Others shoot up perpendicularly, and range from 300 to 600 feet in height. This was the grand entrance into Petra, and is still used by the Arabs. In spite of the torrents which rush through it, a large caravan consisting of forty camels, passed yesterday on their way to Maan, on the line of the Mecca and Damascus road. The stream in this defile has originally been covered over, but the force of the torrent has torn up the pavement, and the luxuriant foilage of the trees and shrubs almost chokes up the passage. About the middle there are the remains of a temple or gateway. Beyond this the road, following the course of the stream, opens to the mountains, which at one time must have been cultivated to the very summits. The meadows are covered with wild-flowers, the groves filled with singing-birds. Partridges and wild-pigeons are plentiful, and on the high rocks are seen large white eagles. (See Plate 95).

The necropolis lies between the main entrance and the meadows; some of the tombs hewn out of the rock, though mutilated, are still magnificent. Several have porticoes and colonnades, and the columns of one I observed were Doric of the purest kind. They seem now to be used as pens for cattle. (See Plate 101).

General View of Sidon, looking towards Lebanon

THE view of Sidon and the hills from this point is of a very commanding character, and may give some conception of the "Queen City," in the days of her original opulence and beauty. But the buildings to which Sidon owes its chief present distinction, the Serail, the Khan, and other stately structures, were the work of an extraordinary individual, so late as the seventeenth century.

The defeat of the Druses by Amurath III. (A.D. 1588) had changed a nation of free, but rival tribes, into a dependent government. Fakhr-ed-din, a Druse, was the chief appointed by the Sultan. He commenced his career by a display of activity and courage. The Arabs, taking advantage of the war, had covered the country between the mountains and the shore, with blood and plunder. The new Emir suddenly gathered an army, attacked the invaders, and after a succession of bold encounters, drove them back into the Desert.

His victory had brought him to the sea-shore; and his views enlarged with his fortunes; the soldier became a statesman. Venice was then carrying on the richest commerce of the world. Fakhr-ed-din drove out the Aga of Beyrout; made himself master of the city, and commenced a commerce with the Venetians. Within the next twenty years he had extended his authority over the principal cities of Northern Syria. The Pashas of Damascus and Tripoli vainly complained, fought, and intrigued against him. He beat them both in the field, and bribed higher than either at Constantinople. But at length the jealousy of the Porte was fully roused; a Turkish force was marched into Syria, and the Emir of the Druses felt that he must look beyond the barren resources of his principality, or perish in a conflict with a power which still made Christendom tremble.

Fakhr-ed-din now formed the bold resolution of enlisting his European allies in his cause; and from Beyrout he put to sea for Italy. The court of the Medici was then in its splendour; he sailed to Florence, and was received with the pompous hospitality of the Italians, augmented at once by the gallantry of his achievements, and the mystery of his origin. It had long been a national dream, that a remnant of the Crusaders had formed a sovereignty among the mountains, and the daring valour and old independence of the Druses were regarded as proofs of their descent from that noble band. The Emir also either found or feigned a chivalric connexion with the House of Lorraine, and the priesthood and poets of

Italy were soon enthusiastic in the cause of a prince who had come to restore romance and religion among the forests and valleys of Lebanon.

Fakhr-ed-din returned, after an absence of nine years. But Florence had been to him what Capua was to the Carthaginian. The hardy mountaineer returned the Italian voluptuary. He built gilded palaces and marble baths, planted European gardens, and even adorned his pavilions with pictures, the abomination of the Koran. He rashly abandoned his stronghold in the hills, and led a life of luxury among the shades and breezes of the shore.

But his evil day was at hand; his indignant subjects deserted him; his sovereign Amurath IV., resolved on his extinction; and the Pasha of Damascus marching a powerful army against the Emir's troops, after two defeats, gained a third bloody battle, in which Fakhr-ed-din saw his gallant son Ali fall, and himself undone. Still his spirit was unbroken; he took refuge in one of his mountain fortresses; and though now deprived of all allies, and advanced in age, he made a daring defence, and after a year of heroism, saw the enemy retire in exhaustion from the walls. But intrigue accomplished what could not be done by arms. He was seized by a band of conspirators, and betrayed to the Sultan. The captive was received at Constantinople with honour, but his fate was already sealed in the Divan; he was thrown into a dungeon and after a brief period of confinement , strangled, at the age of seventy (A.D. 1633).[1]

[1] Sandys's Travels.   D'Arvieux,i.

Plate 45: General View of Sidon, looking towards Lebanon

David Roberts R.A.

Above: The Artist's Signature.

The text on the opposite page describes the following double-spread Plate.

SIDON. Looking towards LEBANON

PLATE 45: GENERAL VIEW OF SIDON, LOOKING TOWARDS LEBANON

Baalbec, General View

THE plain between the Libanus and Antilibanus is divided into the Bekaa, and the territory of Baalbec.[1] But little is known of the ancient history of this once beautiful City. Probably owing its wealth, if not its origin, to the traffic which was carried on between Tyre and Palmyra; it was, like them, an early seat of idolatry and corruption.[2] But its Temple, the source of its existing fame, was due to Rome. The importance of the City as a military position had attracted the eye of the Imperial Government, and in the reign of Augustus it was made a fortress; 149 years after, Antoninus Pius built the present Temple, on the site of a former one. In the reign of Constantine, the fabric shared the general fate of the heathen shrines, and was first abandoned, and then consecrated as a Christian Church. The Sacacen invasion at length threw it into the hands of Moslem. In the fluctuations of their fortune, it was again turned into a fortress. The frequent earthquakes of Syria added their share of devastation; and the chief matter of surprise is, that, exposed to so many agents of ruin, any portion of this magnificent fabric should survive, to excite the curiosity, or delight the taste of Europe, at the end of seventeen centuries.[3]

There have been frequent descriptions of the Temple, but the limits to which we are necessarily confined and the changes which are constantly occurring in the buildings, from earthquakes, and the barbarism of the Arabs, induce us to prefer the brief, yet expressive and graphic, notice by the Artist himself.

"Leaving Zahley, and continuing our course along the base of Libanus, we struck into the plain, and bearing N.E., for about two hours, we came in sight of Baalbec.

"Next day though the rain continued to fall without intermission, and though I was seized with fever; such was my delight and wonder at the stateliness of the Temple, that I could not resist visiting and examining every portion of it, until I became totally exhausted, and was confined to my bed for some time.

"I feel that, it must be difficult to convey, even with the pencil, any idea of the magnificence of this ruin, the beauty of its form, the exquisite richness of its ornament, or the vast magnitude of its dimensions. The whole is contained within an irregular oblong enclosure, which has once been obviously used as a place of defence; a comparatively small portion of it being occupied by the Temple. The Portico, which, with two of the sides, has been thrown down, originally contained eight pillars in front and fourteen each side, each pillar being six feet three inches in diameter, and thus reaching, base and capital included, a height of seventy feet. The whole was evidently constructed without mortar, but the joints of the pillars have been fixed by cramps of bronze.

"The grand doorway is of immense size, formed of vast stones, and sculptured with the richest decoration. From the marks of fastenings, the entrance was probably closed with a curtain or veil as in the Jewish Temple, and in some of the Spanish churches at this day. The enclosure is divided into three great Courts, in the innermost of which the principal building stands."[4]

An arched avenue, or portal, 150 paces long, formed its approach. The breadth of the Temple itself is 32 yards; the whole length 64, of which, however, 18 are taken up by the Ante-Temple.[5]

[1] Burckhardt, Travels, 35. Bekaa, in Hebrew, signifies a mulberry-tree; which abounds in this place. This, with the common Syrian prefix, Baal, might have made the name of the City. But Pococke regards it as a corruption of Baalbeit (or Beth), the House of Baal. [2] Macrob. [3] Baalbec, like all the principal relics of Asiatic antiquity, had remained almost unknown, until the commencement of the last century. The existence of our mercantile factories on the Syrian coast then directed a considerable degree of intelligence and interest to the cities of the interior; and Baalbec and Palmyra began to be visited by European travellers. Maundrell, Pococke, Volney, Burckhardt, Irby and Mangles, Richardson, Lamartine, and other accomplished investigators, have given striking details of the architecture of Baalbec. But the folio of Dawkins and Wood, containing designs and descriptions of the most elaborate order, remains still the standard volume. [4] Roberts's Journal. [5] Maundrell's Travels.

PLATE 47: BAALBEC, REMAINS OF THE WESTERN PORTICO

Baalbec,
Remains of the Western Portico

THIS View, from its being simply a lateral elevation of the external wall of the Adytum, with the remains of the Portico, partly prostrate and partly standing, perhaps conveys a more true representation than some of the others, where the perspective becomes more abrupt; at the same time it is necessary to mention that the columns seem *stunted,* and effect produced by their being built up to the height of about six feet in a wall, when the whole structure had been turned into a place of defence. "The enormous size of the marble blocks of which the columns are composed is distinctly shown here, even from the efforts which have been made for their overthrow; most of them being of two blocks, and none more than three. Between the remaining shafts and the wall is seen a portion of the Soffit, which connected the colonnade with the external wall. The intricate pattern and rich sculpture of this portion cannot be looked on without the highest admiration at the fancy and skill of Roman workmanship. There is something also that exhibits remarkable contrivance, in the fine polish of the joints of those pillars, while their exterior is left in the rough; the inner faces of the blocks being wrought so fine, that they could require no cement; the edge of a pen-knife can scarcely be forced between them. No cement has been used, but they have been fixed together by square metal cramps, of great size; an ancient means of preservation, which, though probably effectual against time, and even against earthquakes, has, unfortunately, tempted the barbarian masters of the country to destroy them, for the value of the metal. This mode of fixing the chief portions of the edifice seems to have been extensively employed. The sockets are still visible, in which were placed the bars for the support of the Pediment and Frieze. Had these been left in their places, the earthquakes would have probably spared a large proportion of its beauty; they might have shaken the building, but they might have failed to destroy."[1]

The material of which the Temple is constructed is a compact limestone resembling marble. In its original state, it must have been most imposing; around it was a row of beautiful Corinthian columns, forty-five feet high, nineteen feet in circumference, and eight or nine feet apart, and at the same distance from the wall covered by a carved ceiling of remarkable delicacy. Of the columns, there were originally fourteen on a side, sixteen in front, and eight in the rear, counting the corner ones of both numbers. Of those, nine still remain on the north side,

with the ceiling, four on the south, and six on the west. Some of the columns have slipped from their pedestals, and recline unbroken against the wall of the Temple; the remainder have fallen over into the area below.

A late traveller thus touchingly conveys his impression of this noble and solemn scene:—"The sun was fast sinking behind Lebanon, and the shadows of the mountain were gradually encroaching on the silent and desert plain, when a sort of consciousness of danger bade me return into the enclosure. At that moment a beautiful moon was just appearing over the hills to the eastward. As I entered the Grand Court, a general silence prevailed throughout; even the shepherd's pipe, which, but a few moments before had caught my ear in the plain, had now ceased to be heard. I directed my steps to the more perfect Temple, standing in the area below, but the masses of prostrate columns and fractured marbles seem to interdict an approach." At length, after repeated falls, and disturbing a whole host of wild pigeons, he reached the interior. "One half of the building, which is roofless, lay in gloomy shadow, while the moonlight rested softly on the upper story of the remainder, and gave a fanciful embellishment to its elaborate sculptures. Viewed by day, these beautiful structures, though replete with interest and delight, carry with them a mingled feeling of humiliation at the transitory greatness of all human conceptions, and regret that such proud relics of genius should be in the hands of a people incapable of appreciating their merits; and consequently heedless of their complete destruction. While by the uncertain light which reigns at this hour, the greater part of the deficiencies are supplied by fancy, and the mind is irresistibly carried back to the period of their perfect state."[2]

[1] Roberts's Journal   [2] Robinson's Travels, ii. 104.

Upper Temple of Baalbec   May 5th 1839

Looking towards Mount Lebanon

David Roberts R A

Baalbec,
looking towards Lebanon

THIS is the most entire portion of the buildings, but is placed in a much lower horizontal plane than the Great Temple; though, on the south side, a subasement has been raised considerably from the ground. The view exhibits a portion of the Eastern Portico, and also gives some conception of the strength of the columns; in the instance of one which, though fallen against the wall, and breaking it in by its weight, has yet remained solid in its joints, in consequence of their being fastened by iron pins. Some of those pins were evidently a foot long, and a foot in diameter.

"When we compare," says Wood, "the ruins of Baalbec with those of many ancient cities which we visited in Italy, Greece, Egypt, and in other parts of Asia, we cannot help thinking these the remains of the boldest plan we ever saw attempted in architecture. Is it not strange then, that the age and undertaker of works, in which stability and duration have been so remarkably consulted, should be a matter of such obscurity?"[1]

The inhabitants of the country, Mussulmans, Jews, Christians, all confidently believe that Solomon built both Palmyra and Baalbec. But, that the City had both its name and worship from Heliopolis (the City of the Sun) in Egypt, we have classical authority. "In the City called Helipolis, the Assyrians (Syrians) worship the Sun with great pomp, under the name of Heliopolitan Jove, and the statue of the god was brought from Egypt."[2] The Temple in its early state, was renowned for divination, the express province of Apollo.

From the Journal

10th March, 1839

Heavy rain to-day, notwithstanding which I have made several sketches of this extraodinary place.

11th March, 1839

Aroused at early morn by a cry of robbers, and found that a brace of pistols and a bag of percussion-caps had been carried off. At 8 the camels were loaded, and I repeatedly turned back to look on the deserted city, so sad a memorial of divine judgement. In its strength it must have scorned all human means of destruction, for, in comparison, all walls built by man were insignificant. Although in the desert, its climate is unsurpassed in salubrity, and the population must have consisted of hundreds of thousands. Yet its history is almost unknown. We ascended the mountains to the south-west, all of which are excavated, and present handsome façades similar to those in the city. Near the summit are various square monuments. Keeping Mount Hor to the right, we descended by a steep and rugged path to the main valley. I regretted much that I was unable to ascend to Aaron's Tomb in consequence of my shoes being completely worn out. For miles after leaving the city, terraces are seen on the hills, supporting the soil, showing that the whole must have been under cultivation. (See Plate 98).

[1] Wood and Dawkins, p.b. Macrob. Saturnalia, lib. 1.   [2] Wood and Dawkins, p.9.

HOLY LAND,

Syria, Idumea, Arabia, Egypt & Nubia.

FROM DRAWINGS MADE ON THE SPOT BY

David Roberts, R.A.

WITH HISTORICAL DESCRIPTIONS, BY

THE REV? GEORGE CROLY, L.L.D.

LITHOGRAPHED BY

LOUIS HAGHE.

VOL 2.

146

David Roberts. R.A

Drawn from Nature & on Stone. Mar 9th 1839.

LONDON, PUBLISHED TO THE SUBSCRIBERS, BY F. G. MOON, 20. THREADNEEDLE STREET.
PUBLISHER IN ORDINARY TO HER MAJESTY.
MDCCCXLII.

PLATE 49: BAALBEC, FROM THE FOUNTAIN (TITLE PA

Baalbec, from the Fountain

(Title-page)

THE grandeur of the ruins of Baalbec can best be appreciated by the large drawings in this Work of the eastern portico of the temple; of the doorway, so unrivalled in enrichment; and others of our illustations of the remains of this extraordinary city; but from no point are the ruins of Baalbec seen in such picturesque combination as from the Fountain, where temples, bridges, water, and varied foliage, make up, with the ruined columns in the foreground, a scene of most singular beauty.

From the Journal

12th March, 1839

This morning we left at half-past 6, and proceeded towards Hebron. During the day we came upon an Arab encampment, with large flocks of sheep and goats. We bought a goat for about 2s. The Arabs seemed very friendly, and several of the women came out of their tents to see us. We pitched our tents early, in a place where there was abundance of food for the camels.

13th March, 1839

Started this morning at 7. Our course still lay through the Wady El Ghor, or Wady Araba, and we came to what was called a well, surrounded by long dark rushes, but which being a stagnant pool, our camels passed untasted. Towards noon we struck into the hills on our left, and filled our skins with some rain water, that lay in a basin in the rocks.

PLATE 50. BALBEC. THE DOORWAY

Baalbec, the Doorway

ON a subject of this order, no description can be so valuable as that of the individual who has surveyed at once with the intelligent curiosity of a traveller, and the accurate eye of an Artist.

"This is, perhaps, the most elaborate work, as well as the most exquisite in its detail, of anything of its kind in the world. The pencil can convey but a faint idea of its beauty. One scroll alone, of acanthus leaves, with groups of children and panthers intertwined, might form a work of itself. Even independently of the beauty of the sculpture, and its excellent preservation, we are lost in wonder at the size of the stones, and at the nature of the machinery by which such masses were raised. Earthquakes have shaken this extraordinary remnant; but from the magnitude of the blocks which form the lintel, the central one, being wedge-shaped, has slipped only so far as to break away a portion of the blocks on either side, and thus remain suspended.

"But its effect is injured by a wall which crosses the eastern Portico, and within a few feet of the doorway, so that the spectator is forced to look at it almost directly upwards. An eagle, with expanded wings, hovers in the centre of the lintel, bearing festoons of fruit and flowers. The fair proportions of this extraordinary work are injured below still more than above, by being buried ten or twelve feet in the ground, so that it necessarily looks stunted." Yet the whole performance, shattered, shortened, and hidden as it is, excited the highest admiration that can be given to a work of genius and beauty.[1]

The Artist proposes the question, whether the Eagle may not be rather the Egyptian emblem of sanctity than of the Roman empire, from the similitude of its position to that of the "Sacred Vulture," invariably placed on the lintels of the Egyptian temples. In this idea he nearly coincides with M. Volney, who remarks that the tuft upon its head proves that it is not the Roman Eagle. The same bird, too, is found on the Temple of Palmyra, and is, therefore, and Oriental Eagle, consecrated to the Sun, which was the divinity of both temples.

On the northern side of the portal is sculptured a winged form, hovering over head, and extending its wings two-thirds of the breadth of the gate; and on each side of the central Eagle is also sculptured a youth, or Genius, on the wing. The Eagle carries in its pounces a caduceus, and in its beak the strings coming from the end of the two festoons, whose other ends are supported by the two youths, or Genii.[2]

The breadth of this incomparable entrance is twenty-two feet; the height can be ascertained only when its bases shall be cleared from the accumulation of ruins and earth. The measure of the Temple within is forty yards long by twenty broad. Round the interior are two rows of pilasters. Between the pilasters are niches, which seem to have been designed for the reception of statues. There are eight pilasters in a row, and seven niches, exclusive of those of the Adytum.

About eight yards from the upper end of the Temple, stood, until recently, two fine channelled pillars, which seem to have formed a partition, and to have supported a canopy over the head of the great Idol, whose place was probably in a large niche at the end. On those portions of the partition which remain are carvings in relievo of Neptune, tritons, fishes, sea-gods, Arion and his Dolphin, and other marine figures. The covering of the whole fabric is broken down. "But this I must say" (it is Maundrell, one of the most exact of travellers, who speaks), "that it strikes the mind with an air of grandeur beyond anything that I ever saw before, and is an eminent proof of the magnificence of the ancient architecture. About fifty yards distance from the Temple is a row of Corinthian pillars, very great and lofty, with a most stately architrave and lintel at top. This speaks itself to have been part of some very august pile."

[1] Roberts's Journal. [2] Pococke conceives them to be Zephyra, or emblems of the Atmosphere, as the Eagle was of the Sun.

Circular Temple at Baalbec May 7th 1839

Baalbec, The Circular Temple

ABOUT a hundred and fifty yards S.E. of the Great Temple stands a detached Temple, which must have been one of the most beautiful of those fine buildings in its early day. The entablature and cornice are supported by six columns on projecting bases, like the radii of a circle, forming a grand stylobate, with two columns on each side of the door. A broad flight of steps led to the entrance. The stylobate curves inwards between every two columns, thus forming a graceful corridor. It seems to have been crowned with a cupola, and to have been about twenty-three feet high from the ground. The study of ornament in all these fabrics is remarkable; wherever a wreath, a bust, or a statue, could be introduced, it has been placed there. In every interval between the columns, niches have been formed, evidently for statues, for the pedestals remain. The contrast of this Temple, in its diminutive size and delicate beauty, with the colossal piles in its neighbourhood, must have been peculiar and striking.[1]

The interior consisted of two stories, the upper surrounded with Corinthian pillars, the lower with Ionic; and in the time of Maundrell, it appears to have been used as a Church. An exact architectural description of the fabric is given in the folio of Wood and Dawkins, Plates XLII. &c.[2] Dismantled as it is, the eye is instantly captivated by its style. But, a few years will probably level it to the ground. The wild inhabitants have but little value for ruins, beyond their iron and limestone. Earthquakes are continually shaking the soil, and the only hope of saving the last honours of Syria is by rescuing and reviving them in England.

[1] G. Robinson's Travels, ii. 100.   [2] Wood and Dawkins — Baalbec, p. 27, Plates xlii. &c.

From the Journal

14th March, 1839

After breakfasting at the foot of the mountains which separate Wady El Ghor from Judea, we commenced the ascent, which is very steep, the roadway being partly hewn in steps out of the rock. On the summit stood the remains of a building of square stones, which may either be Saracenic or Roman. After crossing the hill we descended into a valley covered with rich vegetation, and thickly studded with wildflowers. Again we ascended a hill, and descended into a similar valley, where we found numerous camels grazing belonging to a tribe of Arabs, from whom we purchased a dish of delicious milk, which, after the bitter waters we had been drinking, we relished highly. Overhanging a deep ravine, through which flows a stream, are the ruins of an ancient tower or fort, that seems to have been thrown down by an earthquake. I could not discover to what style or period of art the ruins belonged.

16th March, 1839

Approaching Hebron, the hills are covered with vines and olive trees. On turning round the side of a hill, Hebron first bursts upon you. The situation is beautiful, and the houses, gleaming brightly in the noonday sun, reminded me of England. The children, who came out to meet us, were healthy and pretty, their blooming countenances very unlike the squalid children of Egypt. (See Plate 57).

Baalbec,
Portion of the Eastern Portico

THE Great Temple, with all its connected buildings, stands at the western extremity of the City, and just within the modern walls. A wall of moderate height, and flanked by square towers at intervals, encompasses the remaining portion of the city. The interior is covered with the ruins of private and public buildings.

The chief entrance to the Sacred Enclosure, in its original state, was a grand Portico of the Corinthian order, looking to the East, and approached by a broad and stately flight of stone steps. This entrance is now walled across, and flanked at the extremities by two square towers, evidently a later work, being built up with fragments of cornices and columns. Two Courts lead the way to the Great Temple itself. The first is a Hexagon of 144 feet diameter. From this there was an ascent into a vast Quadrangle of 347 feet in length, by 317 feet in breadth. Both Courts were evidently surrounded with buildings, probably for the dwellings of the priests; but those of the Hexagon are in such a state of dilapidation, as to defy any distinct conjecture. Those of the Quadrangle being in a ruined condition, give evidence of a succession of arcades and covered recesses of various less sizes; probably, Exedræ, or places of lecture for the priesthood and students, similar to those in the public groves of Greece; some of them squares of 43 feet, and some semicircular, of 30 in diameter. The whole with its noble columns, cornices, and elaborate sculpture, forming a scene, in its day of early beauty, to which the architectural world has no parallel.

The roofs of those chambers, which were all open to the Court, have fallen in, and have long since been in dust; but the exterior walls, from which they sprang, remain, and is in sufficient preservation to give an idea of the immense labour bestowed on their decoration. A row of niches for statues extends the whole length of these walls, which are ornamented with rich mouldings, and divided by pilasters. There are similar niches in the buttresses between. Wild herbs have now sprung up on the summit, and added their green and picturesque luxuriance to the general ruin. A foundation wall is discoverable in the middle of the Quadrangle, but whether of a temple, it is hopeless to ascertain.

Still advancing to the westward, the stranger enters upon a grand Esplanade, a parallelogram of 230 feet by 118. This court had arches similar to the former along its western and northern sides. On the southern side stood a row of magnificent Corinthian columns, surmounted by a highly sculptured architrave, making the whole height sixty or seventy feet above the epistylia. Of this colonnade six only are now erect; the remainder lie around them. The whole Esplanade being artificially raised above the level of the surrounding country, they form a very conspicuous object among the ruins.

The magnitude of the materials strikes the eye with scarcely inferior effect to the general decoration of those splendid reliques of ancient genius. "I cannot help," says one of our latest and most intelligent travellers, "making a few observations on one mass of ruins, the imposing grandeur of which peculiarly struck us. I allude to that remnant of a Colonnade, of which there are six columns standing. The beauty and elegance of those pillars are surprising. Their diameter is seven feet, and we estimated their altitude at between fifty and sixty, exclusive of the epistylia, which is twenty feet deep, and composed of immense blocks of stone, in two layers of ten feet each in depth; the whole most elaborately carved in various devices. The space originally included by those pillars was 10 paces long by 50 broad."[1] The magnitude of the stones generally used in these buildings is extraordinary. In the west wall there are three stones which together measure 182 feet, with proportional depth. The largest which the Artist had ever previously seen were those in the Egyptian Temple of Dendera, 29 feet.[2] Some of the stones in the walls of Jerusalem were also of great size. But, "these are, perhaps, the most ponderous masses that human skill ever moved into a wall; and here they are raised between twenty and thirty feet from the foundation."[3] The largest stone of the three is 62 feet 9 inches long, the two others are about 60 feet each.[4]

[1] Irby and Mangles' Travels. [2] Roberts's Journal. [3] Richardson's Travels.
[4] Pococke.

LIST OF LITHOGRAPHS IN THE SERIES OF DAVID ROBERTS "THE HOLY LAND"

terra sancta arts

אמנות ארץ ישראל

Note: The sequence of the Plates slightly differs from the First Edition, due to technical limitations.

Ioppa Shaalbin Ramah Bizath Gian Iericho Gilgal
Iamnia Modin Gibeon Shilo Vallis Achor Debir Macherus
Rakkon Hazshemesh Iabneel Iehud Beneberek Ithlah Chephehaam Reken Adumin Geliloth
Mejarkon Gibethon Kiriath-iearim Mona Mishmash Zeboim
Gallim Anathoth Manahath Vallis Ketiz Lapis Bohan Lashta Ashdoth-Pisgah
Shicron Baalah Ramah Gibeah saulis Nob Hozor Betharabah Neballat

EPHRAIM

Gath Bethshemesh Emaus Ierusalem Mons Olouzi Enshemesh
Goth Rimmon Elon Fons Nephtoah Bahurim Kidron flu.
Ekron Templum belzebub Emaus Vallis Hinnom Fons Enrogel Meddin
Timnah Gebah Zebzah Nebshan Socatah
Dan Hepher zarah Bethlehem Zebzah
Metheg-Amah Eltokeh Sepulcrum Sampsonis Diiam Teko Libnah Zoar
Adullam Mispeh coa Tekoæ Spelunca Lot
Ashdod Azekah Desertum Zoar
Sorek torens Beth-marcaboth Spelunca Dauidis Shillim Spelunca Saulis Engedi
Beth-labaoth Ziglag Hareth Tappuah Lahmam Desertum Engedi
El-tolad Bazalah Azem Iim Hezkath Kithlish
Askalon Balah Sansana Keilah Nezib Migdalgad Iesimon
Azem Ain Bethpalet Hezekah Eglon Ziph
Sharuhen Gedor Zenam Bozkath Lahmam Desertum ziph
Hazorsusah Danugh Kabon Hachilah
Simeon Iarmuth Hebron Desertum
Hazor-shual Aenda Sepulcrum Abner Zior Maon Sela Hammaheoth
Shebah Hazargaddah Shamir Humtah
Gerar Esek Kiriath Sepher Debier Dumah Zanoah
Maladah Rechoboth Anab Socoh
Beersheba Goshon Carmel Iezreael
Sitnah Bethul Arah Gilon Iockdeam
Gaza Tochen Hormah Ashtemoth Iuttah
DESERTVM Beer-la-haroi Baalath Kedesh Ithnan
Majuma Ramah meridionalis Eshean Hazor
Bered Hazor Hezron Ianun Adadah
KADESH Kerioth Holon Beth-huppua Dumonah
Bealoth Ziph Aphekah
Rinocoloura Telem Amam Arad Kinah
fluuius Ægipti Hadattah Shema
Azmon Iattir Desertum Iud Eder Iagur
Desertum Shur Karkaa Zin Kabzeel
Adar
MERI Hezron DI Desertum Zin ES

Iohn Goddard Sculps:

Zeboim

Sodom

Gomorah

Admah

Viro amplissimo.
Dno Guilielmo Paston, Equiti aurato
disjunctissimarum regionum Aulorij
Omnia perlustra quæ profert charta
 Condona errantice recta tuere precor
Nam Tibi Iudæa est, tibi tam sunt ostia
Quam tua mendicis hospita nota domus.

PARS

TERRÆ

MOAB

SCALA MILLIARIV.

PHILISTIA

IVDA

5 10 15 20

3. JUDEA & THE JORDAN RIVER

Then ye shall answer them,
That the waters of Jordan were
cut off before the Ark of the
Covenant of the Lord; when it
passed over Jordan the water of
Jordan were cut off: and these
stones shall be for a memorial
unto the children of Israel for
ever.

Joshua 4,7

ואמרתם להם אשר נכרתו מימי הירדן
מפני ארון ברית־יהוה בעברו בירדן
נכרתו מי הירדן והיו האבנים האלה
לזכרון לבני ישראל עד־עולם.

יהושע ד׳, 7

Contents

Note: The sequence of the Plates slightly differs from the First Edition, due to technical limitations.

3

JUDEA & THE JORDAN RIVER

DAVID ROBERTS R.A.
THE HOLY LAND

24 Coloured Facsimile Lithographs
24 Coloured Photos of the Sites
Introduction and Historical descriptions
of the Sites by Rev. G. Crolly, L.L.D.
David Roberts's private Journal
Text and Lithographs by Courtesy of the
Victoria & Albert Museum's Library, London

Introduction

WE now enter on that portion of our Volume which traces the early steps of Christianity; and we approach it with a reverence due to the most solemn transaction of the world.

Religion is the key of History; and the more closely we investigate the course of Providence, the more distinctly shall we comprehend the course of man. The three great Revelations, the Patriarchal, the Jewish, and the Christian, will be found to have been adapted to the three great periods of Society, and to have been adapted with a foresight and a completeness, which argue their origin Divine. In each instance, the Religion long preceded the period, a proof that it was not the work of human necessities; and the Period was always the subject of both Prophecy and Miracle, a proof that it was also the operation of the will of Heaven.

The first stage of human society after the Disperion of the descendants of Noah was Clanship; an existence by small tribes, widely separated, and roving over the wastes of the world. That this form of society was by a Divine ordiance is evident, from the prophetic name of the Patriarch, PELEG (Dispersion), in whose time this extraordinary change was to be effected; and from the miracle expressly wrought to counteract the establishment of an Empire at Babel; that miracle, too, having the object of even increasing the dispersion, by breaking up the universal language. The Religion had been given five hundred years before, by the Covenant with Noah, itself only a renewal of the Religion given at the gates of Paradise; its simple tenets being, the Existence of a God, the Sin of Man, and the hope of a Redeemer; its simple ritual being Sacrifice, and its only priest the father of the family. A Religion whose simplicity, while it contained all the essential truths of Revelation, was obviously suited to the narrow means and rude capacities of wanderers through the wilderness of the globe.

But another Period was to come, when a new and vast stimulant was to be given to the progress of mankind, by a new system of Society. The scattered clans were to be gathered into condensed masses. Government was to begin; and the passions, powers and enjoyments of mankind, were to be moulded, excited, and elevated by the force, the fear, and the splendour of the Sceptre. In this period, the civilized world was to be placed under four successive great Sovereignties: and the singularity of this system was, that, unlike the perpetual competitorships of later kingdoms, each was to be, for its time, wholly without a rival, the supreme governor and guardian of civilized mankind. That this period was equally the work of the Divine will is proved, as in the former instance, by both miracle and prophecy; the miraculous vision of Nebuchadnezzar revealing the existence of the four successive and only Empires; and the prophecies of Daniel giving the detail of their origin, their objects, and their dissolution. To meet this period, a Religion had also been prepared, nearly five hundred years before — the Mosaic Covenant. For, although the Religion of the Jews was local in its ordinances, it was universal in its principles: and although expressly devised to keep the Jew separate from the profanations of the Heathen, yet in the "proselytes of the gate" it at once provided for the reception of the Gentile, and dispensed with those ordinances which were dependent on locality. But the code of Judea, besides the purest Religion, exhibited to the surrounding nations an example of the purest government. In all conditions of mankind, the two chief elements of public happiness are the Supremacy of Law, and the Security of Property. In the Jewish constitution, the Heathen saw those two elements placed in the highest point of view; a Law superior to all human change, and binding king and people; and a succession of property equally beyond the caprice of man. May it not have been with the direct purpose of impressing this example on mankind, that the Jewish kingdom was constantly connected with the four successive Empires: the lesson running parallel with them all, Judah surviving the three Eastern; and perishing only when the "Period of Empire" was to fall with Rome.

But a third Period was to come, of a totally different character from either of the past, and employing a totally different species of action. In this Period, which is our own, mankind was to be governed by separate and contemporaneous Sovereignties; thus consisting a rivalry of states, that rivalry compelling nations to cultivate their peculiar means of power, and that of cultivation, obviously tending to bring into the fullest activity all the variety and vigour of individual character. This change too was the subject of miracle and prophecy. In the vision of the King of Babylon, the division of the Western Empire into ten Sovereignties was distinctly shown a thousand years before its fulfilment; the prophecies of our Lord, and the Apocalypse, splendidly and unaswerably filling up that astonishing development of Providence. It is clear, that whatever may be the other high purposes of Christianity, one was to provide a new Religion for this new period. Its whole texture was evidently intended for a more advanced time than the era of Governments acting solely by the pressure of irresponsible power. Its constant appeals to the common-sense of man, its demands on the exercise of personal judgment, its declarations of the general accountability, and its promises of future glory to all orders of men alike, in proportion to the performance of their duty here; contain at once all the essentials of human freedom, and all the loftier excitements which can awake the human mind to the most vivid exertions of its talents and virtues. This Religion too was given about five hundred years before the time for which it was especially designed, that of the European Kingdoms.

In the few lines to which we are limited in these pages, allusion only can be made to its palpable effect, in creating a series of questions of the highest importance to mankind, yet which had never occurred before — the education of the people, the improvement of their condition, the general elevation of their habits, and the relief of their necessities under the various circumstances of human suffering. We even find all those objects contemplated from the earliest announcement of Christianity. The first declaration of our Lord was, that He came to heal the spiritual and physical maladies of the multitude, commencing by that most direct and comprehensive of all mercies —the preaching of the Gospel to the poor.[1] His whole career was an exemplification of this announcement; from day to day, He alike healed disease and preached the Gospel; often among the multitude. Even in the awful hour of the Crucifixion, as if to prove the inexhaustible spirit of a mission which reached from the highest glory of Heaven to the lowest depths of human nature; He bore with Him a repentant criminal to Paradise.

It is admitted, that Christianity has not hitherto accomplished all its purposes; that a large portion of the world still lies under despotism, and a larger still under barbarian ignorance. Yet we are to remember, that Christianity appeals only to the heart and understanding; that it makes no use of physical power; that it disdains all attempts to allure the passions or dazzle the senses; and that against it is arrayed the whole active and interested corruption of man. Still, it is beyond all denial, that in proportion as Christianity has been acknowledged, the whole condition of society has advanced; that Law has obtained higher influence; property has been rendered more secure; Science has stretched a more vigorous flight; the general mind become more intelligent; subordination been less slavish and authority at once more lenient and more limited. The Gospel, even now, draws the circle of light and darkness; Christendom is the intellectual portion of the world. But still higher results may be awaiting mankind. The future can be only a matter of hope. But there are illustrious intimations in the Scriptures that the progress of good shall not continue thus tardy beyond a certain time. Of the three great forms of human Society — Clanship, Empire, and Kingdoms, the last is probably drawing to its close. Prophecy announces one form to come; but it is still wrapt in clouds. The Atonement must for ever shine as the leading glory of the Christian triumph; but who shall say, that splendours beyond all existing conceptions may not yet follow in its train, scatter the darkness and guilt of the Fall, and more than reinstate the original grandeur of the race of man?

[1] Luke, iv. 18.

The Lithographs

Bethlehem

IN every age of Christianity Bethlehem has held a solemn place in the recollections of mankind. The history of which it witnessed the commencement can have no equal in its grandeur or in its purpose, for it extends to all the generations of the earth, and it proclaims mercy to all. The magnitude of the Gospel is so vast, that all human greatness disappears in its presence; its heights are sublime above all the imaginations of created beings; its depths are profound beyond all their penetration.

To have shared in the progress of this mighty minister of good, to have been visited by its visible presence, to have borne the vestiges of its early wonders, gives a title to the noblest honours which can be demanded by memory, or paid by gratitude. The very caverns and forests which echoed the Divine voice; the hills and waters which witnessed its power over Nature; the very dust of the Divine feet — all are consecrated. We feel that God has been there, and we involuntarily deem that His presence has not altogether departed.

"Behold the days come, saith the Lord, that I will raise unto David a righteous Branch, and a King shall reign and prosper, and shall execute judgement and justice in the earth. In His days Judah shall be saved, and Israel shall dwell safely: and this is His name whereby He shall be called, "THE LORD OUR RIGHTEOUSNESS."[1]

The place of the Nativity was distincly marked in prophecy. "But thou, Beth-lehem Ephratah, though thou be little among the thousands of Judah, yet out of thee shall He come forth unto me, that is to be ruler in Israel; whose goings forth have been of old, from everlasting."[2]

Humanly speaking, nothing could be more improbable than that Bethlehem should be the birth-place of the Son of Mary: for the country of Joseph was in the northern province of Palestine, and it was also expressly prophesied that this northern province should be the chief scene of his existence, and even the very first which was to acknowledge his glory.

"The land of Zebulun and the land of Naphtali, by the way of the sea, beyond Jordan, in Galilee of the nations; the people that walked in darkness have seen a great light; they that dwell in the land of the shadow of death, upon them hath the light shined."[3]

Yet the prophecy which assigned the place of Nativity was so distinct, as to fix the unanimous expectation of all the Jewish authorities on Bethlehem. When the Magi came to Jerusalem, perhaps conjecturing that the King to be born in his own royal city, the "chief priests and scribes of the people," being gathered together by order of Herod to determine the birth-place, "said unto him, In Bethlehem of Judæa, for thus it is written by the prophet."[4] And in Bethlehem he was sought, and found.

The village lies about two hours distance from Jerusalem, on the east and north-east slope of a long ridge; a deep valley, Wady Taamirah, being on the south side, which passes to the Dead Sea. The surrounding country, though hilly, is fertile and well cultivated.

In the distance are seen the hills of Moab, and below them is a glimpse of the Dead Sea.[5]

In the interval between the Greek Convent and the mountain border of the Dead Sea rises a hill, named the Hill of the Franks, from a legend of the Crusades. The ruins on its slope are Roman, and conjectured to be those of a palace and fortress of Herod the Great.[6]

[1] Jerem, xxiii. 5,6. [2] Micah, v.2. [3] Isaiah, ix. 1,2. [4] Matt. ii.4,5.
[5] Roberts's Journal. [6] Biblical Researches, ii. 173.

Plate 53: Bethlehem

David Roberts R.A.

Above: The Artist's Signature.

The text on the opposite page describes the following double-spread Plate.

Chancel of the Church of St. Helena

THIS once magnificent building was formed on the model of the Roman Basilica, and resembles the Church of St. Paul at Rome. The Nave is divided into aisles by forty pillars of yellow marble, of the Corinthian order. Above those pillars extends a series of scriptural subjects in Mosaic, of an elaborate kind, but now much dilapidated. A temporary screen divides the Nave from the Chancel and Transepts. An antique and gorgeous screen separates the people from the Altar. This view was taken when the priests and pilgrims were waiting for the "Holy Fire" to be brought from Jerusalem.

The Latin and Armenian Chapels are in the two transepts. A door under the platform on which the people stand opens upon a flight of steps leading to the Grotto of the Nativity. The principal entrance of this noble pile was once wide and lofty, but low, that, to enter, the head must be stooped nearly to the knees; a sufficient evidence of the alarms under which the worship has from time to time been carried on, and of the general perils and vexations which beset the Christians in former periods of the power of Islamism.

The original magnificence of this building may be estimated from the costliness of its columns, each shaft being a single piece two feet and a half in diameter, and the columns eighteen feet in height, including the capital. The distance of the intercolumniations is seven feet; that of the rows, thirty. But the roof which they were to support was either partially destroyed, or never completed, for the only roof now is a wooden one; a humiliation which the monks, with their usual ingenuity, palliate by affirming that it is of the cedar of Lebanon. They apologise for the want of size in their lamps, by saying that the larger are brought only on great occasions from Jerusalem where they are deposited, from fear of their being stolen by the Greeks.[1] The Turkish domination will now probably become more humanised; but it has hitherto been exercised over these institutions with the usual corruption and severity of Islamism; the old privileges of the Convent were regularly sold to the highest bidder, and the Greeks, being the most opulent, have made themselves masters of the largest share.

The whole site of the Greek convent is regarded with peculiar reverence by the pilgrims, and relics are exhibited, which meet with a constant sale. As this village was the probable scene of the "Massacre of the Innocents" by Herod, some of the relics are referred to that event. A withered hand is shown as belonging to one of the infants; and an Altar stands over a pit, into which tradition says that their bodies were thrown. A rude picture hung above the Altar gives a startling delineation of the various agonies of the children, and the terror and despair of their parents. Other memorials point out the traditional scenes of the history of the Nativity. Joseph has an Altar in one of the excavations, and a second Altar designates the spot where he sat, meditating, during the birth of our Lord.

But, passing by those legends: the whole scene is full of high recollections to the Christian. — Here was the place of unquestioned miracle, the display of indescribable mercy; the beginning of a period which shall finish only in Glory and Eternity.

[1] Roberts's Journal. G. Robinson, i. 151.

Shrine of the Nativity.

April 6th 1839

Shrine of the Nativity

THIS chamber, partly an excavation in the limestone, lies directly under the Church built by the mother of Constantine. It is thirty-seven feet long by eleven wide, and though now naked, when compared with the general decoration of the Greek shrines, is floored and walled with marble, and seems to have been once covered with Mosaic, of which some rich specimens still remain.

On the right are three lamps, suspended over the Manger in which our Lord was laid; opposite to this, the altar, covered with a canopy, is said by the Monks to mark the place where the Magi knelt to make their offerings. At the other end of the Grotto, in the semicircular recess, a glory represents the Star which guided the Magi. Round it is the inscription —

"HIC DE VIRGINE MARIA JESUS CHRISTUS NATUS EST."

The manger now in the Grotto is only a substitute; the *original,* according to the Italians, having been removed to Rome by Sixtus V. It is now in the Church of Santa Maria Maggiore, in a small Chapel remarkable for the costliness of its ornaments. Numerous lamps, the gifts of Christian princes, throw light over the darkness of the chamber. Above the spot where the Magi knelt, is a picture exhibiting them in the act of worshipping; one of the wise men is an Ethiopian.

From the Journal

17th March, 1839

To-day I made two coloured sketches of the town, but could not get admission to the mosque containing the tombs of Abraham, Isaac, and Jacob. The town contains 1300 families, four of which are Jewish, and one is Christian. From the latter we received the most marked attention, and we spent the night under their hospitable roof.

18th March, 1839

To-day we left Hebron at 2 for Gaza, and halted for the night at a small village called Terkumich.

19th March, 1839

Left at daybreak, passing through a richly-cultivated country. About sixteen miles from Hebron are the remains of a castle, and Roman ruins, consisting of a number of marble columns. There is a village, which takes its name from the Roman ruins, and is called Bed El Gebrin, the house of Gabriel. It is surrounded by olive orchards, the trees apparently of great age. In the evening we reached a pretty little village called Burier, containing about one hundred families. To-day we have travelled ten hours, and are within two and a half hours of Gaza. (See Plate 83).

Hebron

HEBRON is one of the most memorable sites of Palestine, as the abiding place of Abraham, Isaac, and Jacob. It possessed one of the most ancient cities in the world, built "seven years before Zoar in Egypt;"[1] whose original name was Kirjath-Arba (City of Arba), so called from Arba, the father of Anak and the Anakim; it also bore the name of Mamre.[2] From this neighbourhood Jacob and his sons went to Egypt, to dwell with Joseph. After the conquest of Palestine by Joshua, it was made one of the six "cities of refuge", and assigned to the priesthood as a residence. It became the royal city of David, where he reigned seven years and a half over Judah, and in Hebron he was anointed King over all Israel. It was in this royal city that Absalom raised the standard of rebellion. This was also one of the cities fortified by Rehoboam, and rebuilt by the people after the Captivity.[3] Hebron suffered the common reverses of Judah in its latter days. It fell into the power of the Idumæans; but was recovered from them by Judas Maccabeus. In the revolt against Rome, it was captured and burnt by Cerealis, the lieutenant of Vespasian. In later days, its sanctity as the place of patriarchal burial superseded all other recollections; and in the eighth century it was called the Castle of Abraham. This was also the name preferred by the Crusaders. The Mohammedans called it El-Khulil (The Friend), Abraham being distinguished among them as the "friend of God," from the well-known expressions of Scripture.

On the invasion of Palestine by the Crusaders, Hebron followed the fate of Jerusalem, and was given (A.D. 1100) by Godfrey of Bouillon as a fief to Gerhard of Avennes. It was not to obtain another distinction, and (A.D. 1167) was raised to the rank of a Latin Episcopal See, of which Rainold was Bishop. The title of Bishop of Hebron was retained through a succession of prelates, but the Bishopric had soon fallen (A.D. 1187) under the dominion of Saladin; the Church was made a Mosque, and its possession given into the hands of a Mahometan population, who guard it with the most jealous vigilance, and are considered to be among the most violent bigots even of Mahometanism.

It had still one disastrous chapter in its history. In 1834 the whole surrounding country rose in arms against Ibrahim Pasha. A battle was fought near "Solomon's pools," and the revolters were driven back upon Hebron; they were followed, and the place was stormed, and given up to plunder. This inflicted a blow on the town, from which its trade has not yet recovered; that trade however consisting of little more than of fruits, and of rude specimens of glass manufacture; glass lamps, and rings of the same material worn on the arms. The population is about ten thousand, among whom are about fifty Jewish families. The Artist thus describes its aspect: — "On turning the side of a hill, the little town of Hebron burst upon us. Its situation is beautiful: and the houses glittering in the noon-day sun had a look of English cleanliness, after the wretched hovels of Egypt. The children who came out to meet us, were among the most beautiful I had ever seen. The countenance was truly Jewish, but with a healthy rosy colour which I have seldom seen out of England."[4]

The conscription, a great source of suffering in all despotic governments, assumes in the East the shape of a national calamity. In the midst of all this beauty and brightness, "as we went," continues the Artist, "to show our passports at the house of the Deputy-Governor, we found many women weeping on the steps, and the Deputy engaged in the examination of a number of the unfortunate inhabitants who had been seized by the conscription. They were brought out in succession from a filthy-looking dungeon, and after inspection were handcuffed, and sent off."

The surrounding country abounds with legendary sites. The "Village of the Virgin" is supposed to have been one of the resting-places of the Holy Family in their flight into Egypt. A fine oak represents the Tree of Abraham; but it seems not improbable that the "Haram," or Mosque, whose massive enclosure seems of Jewish building, covers the Cave of Macphelah. Into this enclosure, however, no Christian is permitted to enter.

[1] Num. xiii. 22. Gen. xiii. 18. [2] Gen. xxiii. 19. [3] Chron. xi. 10. Nehem. xi. 25.
[4] Roberts's Journal.

Plate 56: Hebron

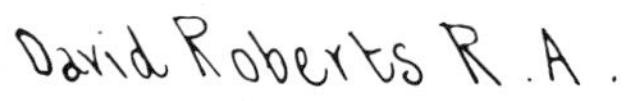

David Roberts R.A.

Above: The Artist's Signature.

The text on the opposite page describes the
following double-spread Plate.

David Roberts R.A.

1839

Bethany

BETHANY was the well-known scene of one of the mightiest miracles of our Lord — that Restoration of Lazarus to life, by which he especially proclaimed his power over the grave, in the immediate presence of Jerusalem. The results of this miracle were his kingly reception by the people, and that increased hostility of the Roman and Jewish government, which produced the unspeakable sacrifice of the Crucifixion.

Bethany owes all its present reverence, and even its present name, to this miracle; it being now called El-'Aziriyeh, from El-'Azir (Arab. Lazarus).[1] It is now a poor village, containing about twenty families, living in huts which exhibit evidence of having been formed out of the ruins of ancient buildings. Legends are of course busy. The monks profess to show the actual sites of the houses of Martha and Mary, and Simon the Leper. But the chief object of display is the Sepulchre of Lazarus, seen in the engraving as the small building on the left, with the circular dome.[2]

The Sepulchre is a deep vault excavated in the limestone rock, in the middle of the village, with a descent to it by twenty-six steps. This spot has been a place of remarkable veneration in very early ages; the "Crypt of Lazarus" being mentioned in A.D. 333, and also by Jerome about seventy years later, as the site of a Church; successive monasteries also having been built over it.[3]

1 Biblical Researches, ii. 102.   2 Roberts's Journal   3 Itin. Hieros. 596.
Onomasticon, Art. Bethania, quoted by Robinson.

From the Journal

20th March, 1839

The approach to Gaza is through extensive forests. The city stands on a height two miles from the sea, from which it is sheltered by hills of sand. Its ancient grandeur is entirely gone: the inhabitants are wretchedly poor, and there are not even the ruins of any building of importance standing. The houses and the mosques seem built from the remains of former buildings. Every house has fragments of marble sculpture and columns; and in passing through a mean suburb I noticed that one of the houses had its roof propped up by a number of beautifully-sculptured capitals piled one on another. (See Plate 73).

21st, 22nd, 23rd, and 24th March, 1839

Were kept till the 23rd, waiting for camels, and after all were obliged to start with five instead of nine. These carried our baggage, and we walked on in our Turkish dress, stopping at a small village called Burbah, near to which is Askelon, close on the sea, and once surrounded by high ramparts. The harbour has been swept away, and the city is quite deserted. Ibrahim Pasha has caused a considerable portion to be excavated for stones to build a modern city. Among other things we saw a temple with its grey granite columns, each in one piece—with bases, capitals, and entablatures in pure white marble—Corinthian of the purest kind, also a large female statue in marble. An early Christian church has been laid open, with recesses for altars, a cross encircled with a laurel-wreath, and other features common in modern Greek churches. (See Plate 69).

Semara, March 16th 1839.

David Roberts. R.A.

Ruins of Semua

THE mountain ridge which commences not far from Carmel, and runs W.S.W. to the solitude of Beersheba, formed the natural boundary, on this side, of the higher tract, or "mountains of Judah;" while the lower region, farther south, extending quite round to Beersheba, constituted the uttermost border "toward the coast of Edom, southward."

The country between Wady Mousa and Hebron has evidently been once the seat of a large population; every hill seems to have had its town, as probably every valley had its tillage and pasture. But the towns are chiefly ruins, and the valleys are abandoned to the precarious cultivation of a peasantry with whom everything is precarious.[1]

Semua (now variously pronounced, and which stands probably on the site of the Eshtemoa of Scripture[2]) is reduced to a village, in the midst of pasture lands, filled with flocks and herds at certain seasons. At the time of the Artist's visit, the cattle had been driven away to other pastures; and the inhabitants had migrated along with them. There might be an additional reason for the general solitude. The Conscription had been in force, and the young men, by whom the Egyptian service was hated, on those occasions generally fled to the mountains.[3]

The ground is strewed with large stones, the remains of vast ancient buildings, the only portion of which left standing is a tower, a relique, probably, of Roman fortification.[4]

[1] Biblical Researches, ii. 626. [2] Josh. xv. 50; xxi. 14. [3] Roberts's Journal.
[4] Kinnear.

From the Journal

25th March, 1839

Leaving our encampment by daybreak, we passed a beautiful little town called Ibrech, and arrived at Jaffa, which is surrounded by orange groves, and stands on a hill sloping to the sea. (See Plate 74).

26th March, 1839

Parted from my fellow-traveller Mr. Kinnear, who took his departure for Beyrout. We smoked a pipe at parting with the consul, who was most attentive to us. I examined the town carefully, but found very few antiquities.

27th March, 1839

Left Jaffa at 10 a.m. for Jerusalem. Mr. Pell, our guide Ishmael, and three servants, with eight horses to carry our tents and baggage. Our way lay through the gardens which surround Jaffa, and across the plain of Sharon, through a richly-cultivated country. The ground is carpeted with flowers—the plain is studded with small villages and groups of palm-trees, and, independent of its interesting associations, the country is the loveliest I ever beheld. The mountains of Judea bound the view, and beyond is the Holy City. About 3 we arrived at Rameh, and were kindly received at the Latin Convent by the superior, who accompanied me through the town and showed me its antiquities. There is nothing very remarkable except the great mosque, originally the church of the Knights of St. John of Jerusalem, which, in the interior is divided into a nave, having aisles on each side, with clustered columns. (See Plate 70).

Jericho

THE ancient Jericho has wholly disappeared, with the exception of some foundations of the external walls. The modern, which bears the Arab name of Eriha, is a miserable village, with a Saracenic tower, entitled the Castle, in its centre. The houses are ruins, formed of ruins, and generally surrounded with a thorny hedge, within which the cattle are brought at night, thus increasing the squalidness of the scene. The population amount to about two hundred souls. Yet it stands in a plain capable of the highest fertility, once the famous soil of the palm, the vine, the balsam-tree, and almost every other rich product of the earth.

The climate of Jericho is excessively hot, and especially unhealthy for strangers. In traversing the short distance between Jerusalem and Jericho, the traveller passes from a pure and temperate atmosphere into the sultry heat of an Egyptian climate. Nor is this surprising, when it is considered that the caldron of the Dead Sea and the Valley of the Jordan lie several hundred feet below the level of the ocean, and nearly three thousand feet lower than Jerusalem.[1]

To the left of the Castle are the ruins of a Christian Church, on the walls of which may still be seen some very good Greek paintings. The dark tents of a party of Bedouins occupy the foreground; the cattle are enclosed in the centre of the circle during the night for protection. The more extensive encampment of the pilgrims lay behind the sand-hills, at some distance from the Castle.

The Artist's description of this scene and its accompaniments brings the whole clearly and gracefully before the eye.

"Our encampment was soon buried in sleep as the night came on, though occasionally I caught sounds of the song and the dance, either from the tents of the pilgrims or our Arab guard. The night was one of the most beautiful which I had seen even in the country, and the moon was reflected in all its brightness on the silent waters of the Dead Sea...

"I lay down, with my tent-door open, watching the lights glittering from tent to tent, and wondering at the combination of creeds gathered together, to visit scenes so dear to the memory of the Christian. Many were from the most distant parts of the Russian Empire, and near me sat a black group of Abyssinians in their blue turnbans...

"Before two in the morning, the whole host were roused; and at three, a gun gave the signal that the Governor was on horseback, and had moved forward. We followed, and overtook him. Lights were carried before the Governor. The moon was casually obscured by heavy clouds; but its light now and then burst upon the long cavalcade, seen as far as the eye could reach. We moved on in silence, and the heavy tread of the dense mass was the only sound that broke the stillness of the Desert. Day at last began to dawn, and the scene became only more interesting."[2]

[1] Biblical Researches, ii. 282.   [2] Roberts's Journal.

Plate 59: Jericho

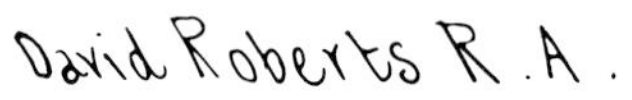

David Roberts R.A.

Above: The Artist's Signature.

The text on the opposite page describes the
following double-spread Plate.

PLATE 59. JERICHO

Encampment of the Pilgrims at Jericho

AT Easter the neighbourhood of Jericho is frequented by Pilgrims, who come to purify themselves in the River Jordan. But the land retains its ancient character for lawlessness, and the devotees are escorted by a strong military force under the direction of the Governor of Jerusalem.

The principal object in the Engraving is the tent of the Governor, Achmet Aga, who invited the Artist to accompany him to the Jordan (April, 1839). The scene at this juncture was strikingly Oriental. The numerous tents, the Pilgrims of all costumes and various countries, occupied in their preparations for the night; the officers of the escort galloping in all directions, some amusing themselves with throwing the djerrid, and others with firing at marks, at full speed; groups of men, women, and children, some at rest, some in sport, and some in prayer, and the whole illuminated by a sunset of remarkable vividness, which not merely enlightened the plain, but covered the distant mountains with golden and purple fire; formed a *coup d'œil* of singular and characteristic animation.[1]

[1] Roberts's Journal.

From the Journal

(Continued)

We dined in the ancient refectory of the convent, and spent the evening with the monks, whom we found very agreeable fellows.

28th March, 1839

Night found us encamped outside the city of Sion. All is perfectly silent save the baying of a dog and the hooting of an owl perched on the battlements, a fitting emblem of its desolation.

29th March, 1839 (Good Friday)

"It is better to be born lucky than rich" - is an old proverb, and it applies to me. This morning the quarantine has been removed, and the whole population pour out of the gates to enjoy the open country. Troops were marching, drums beating, and colours flying, and these were followed by mobs of men, women, and children. This morning I made the circuit of the city walls, proceeding northward by the gate of Damascus and the Valley of Jehosphaphat to the hill of Sion, where the tomb of David is placed, a Mahometan mosque, which no Christian is allowed to enter. Great numbers of pilgrims were in the city waiting for the Easter Festival, and we had difficulty in finding accommodation till we fortunately met with Elias, the head of the Christian family who had received us so kindly in Hebron. He found us apartments in the house of his brother-in-law, a Greek Christian. After settling ourselves in our quarters we visited several interesting places, among others the Mosque of Omar, built near the pool of Bethesda, and the Holy Sepulchre, which is approached through a series of narrow streets, the last of which opens into a court.(See Plates 8, 11).

Descent to the Valley of the Jordan

THE View is taken from the highway leading from Jerusalem through Jericho, and forming a part of the road, or system of roads, by which Jerusalem was connected with the countries on the Euphrates, and thence with Persia and India. The pass is singularly difficult, and still inherits its evil name as a place of robbers. In this scene of the Parable of the Good Samaritan, no stranger ventures without an escort. But its variety and boldness strongly attract the eye. "The view," says the Artist, "when we emerged from the rocky hills, was one not to be forgotten. The Valley of the Jordan lay stretched beneath our feet, in all the beauty of an Eastern evening. The Dead Sea, the silvery line of the rapid Jordan just visible, the gay colours of the pilgrim encampment glittering in the last rays of the setting sun, were fitter for the poet than the painter. The pencil must fail to realise it. On the whole line of road were Arab and Bedouin lancers."[1]

Lamartine describes the journey, beginning from Bethany, as singularly toilsome and melancholy. Neither houses nor cultivation, mountains without a shrub, immense rocks split by time, and pinnacles tinged with colours like those of an extinguished volcano. "From the summit of these hills, as far as the eye can reach, we see only black chains, conical or broken peaks, a boundless labyrinth of passes rent through the mountains, and those ravines lying in perfect and perpetual stillness, without a stream, without a wild animal, without even a flower; the reliques of a convulsed land, with waves of stone." He had still another ridge to cross, and on passing it the escort fired their muskets in token of joy.[2]

A large portion of the Valley of the Jordan has been from the earliest time almost a desert.[3] But in the northern part of the Ghor, the great number of rivulets which descend from the mountains on both sides produce in many places a luxuriant growth of wild herbage.[4] So, too, in the southern part, where similar rivulets exist, as around Jericho, there is even an exuberant fertility; but those rivulets seldom reach the Jordan, and have no effect on the middle of the Ghor. The mountains on each side are rugged and desolate; the western cliffs overhanding the Valley at an elevation of 1000 or 1200 feet, while the eastern mountains fall back in ranges of from 2000 to 2500.

But the Valley of the Jordan, wild as it is, comes honoured and hallowed to the heart by events of the noblest historical and religious memory. As the great barrier to Palestine, here was the miraculous passage of the Israelites, and the wondrous baptism of Israel. On this scene, too, was that second similar purification of the people consummated in the presence of "HIM whom the heaven and the heaven of heavens cannot contain," when HE came to be baptized in the waters of the River, when the Holy Spirit visibly descended upon Him, and the voice of the Eternal Majesty proclaimed to the multitude, and to mankind, THIS IS MY BELOVED SON, IN WHOM I AM WELL PLEASED.[5]

[1] Roberts's Journal.   [2] Travels in the East.   [3] Josephus, B.J. vii. 10.
[4] Jerom. Com. in Zech. xi. 9.   [5] Matt. iii. 17.

The Lake of Tiberias, looking towards Hermon

THE ancient City of Tiberias, built by Herod Antipas, and named in honour of his patron, the Emperor Tiberius, has long since perished. With the mixture of violence and policy which characterised the Oriental governments, Herod compelled a population from the surrounding provinces to fill his City; adorned it with structure, of which the very fragments are stately; gave it peculiar privileges; and building a palace which was one of the wonders of the land, declared Tiberias the capital of Galilee.[1] The ruins in the Sketch are those of the modern City prostrated by the earthquake.

The view commands various sites, memorable from their connexion with Scripture. On the West coast lies El-Medgel, the site of Magdala, the City of Mary Magdalene; Capernaum, Chorazin, and Bethsaida, once lay on the same coast; and in the vicinity, more to the South, was the City of Tarichæa. On the East coast was the scene of the great miracle, the feeding of the four thousand; and in the horizon is the majestic Hermon, 10,000 feet above the Mediteranean.

The Rabbins held that the former City stood on the site of Rakkath, while Jerome records a tradition that it was once Chinnereth;[2] but, leaving those laborious triflings to their natural obscurity, it is evident that the original Tiberias occupied a site farther to the north. There the ground is still strewed with fragments of noble architecture, — baths, temples, and perhaps theatres; giving full proof of a Capital raised with the lavish grandeur of a Herodian City. In the great, final war, which extinguished Judah as a nation, and commenced the longest calamity of the most illustrious and unhappy race of mankind, Tiberias escaped the general destruction. Submitting to the authority of Vespasian, without waiting to be subdued by his arms, the City retained its population, and, probably, its privileges. In the national havoc, it even acquired the additional wealth and honours of a City of Refuge. It had a coinage of its own, exhibiting the effigies of several of the Emperors, down to Antoninus Pius. It appears to have peculiarly attracted Imperial notice, for Hadrian, though pressed with the cares of the Roman world, commenced the rebuilding of a temple, or palace, which had been burnt in an insurrection.[2]

But the history of this beautiful City has a still higher claim on human recollection, as the last retreat of Jewish literature. On the fall of Jerusalem, and the final expulsion of the Jews from the central province, the chief surviving portion of the state, the rank, the wealth, and the learning, were suffered to take shelter within the walls of Tiberias. In the second century, a Sanhedrin was formed there, and the broken people made their last attempt to form a semblance of established government.[4]

The two great Hebraists, Buxtorf and Lightfoot, have given the history of the School of Tiberias, more interesting than the details of massacre, or the description of ruins. The protection of the City drew the principal scholars from the cells and mountains where they had concealed themselves from the habitual severities of Rome. Under the presidency of Rabbi Judah Hakkodesh the School flourished, and acquired the acknowledged title of the Capital of Jewish learning. The first natural enterprise of such a School was the collection of the ancient interpretations and traditions of the Law; and those were embodied by Rabbi Judah in the Mishna (about A.D. 220). In the third century, Rabbi Jochanan compiled the Gemara, a supplement to the Mishna (about A.D. 270), now known as the Jerusalem Talmud. In the sixth century, the Babylonian Jews also compiled a Gemara, named the Talmud of Babylon, now more esteemed by the Jews. But the School of Tiberias is said also to have produced the Masora, or Canon for preserving the purity of the text in the Old Testament, — a labour whose value, however the subject of controversy, is admitted to be incontrovertible.

The civil history of Tiberias is the common recapitulation of Eastern sieges and slaughters. Fortified by Justinian, it fell successively into the hands of the Saracens, the Crusaders, Saladin, the Syrians,[5] and the Turks. The French invasion brought Tiberias into European notice once more (A.D. 1799). On their retreat it sank into its old obscurity, and must wait another change, of good or evil fortune, to be known.

[1] John, vi. 23; xxi. 1. Joseph. Antiq. xviii. 2, 3. Bell. Jud. ii. 9, 4.   [2] Josh. xix. 35. Hieron. Comm. in Ezech. xlviii. 21.   [3] Epiphan. ad Hæret. i. 12.   [4] Lightfoot, Ap. ii, 141. Buxtorf, Tiberias, 10, &c.   [5] Niebuhr, Reisc. iii. Volney, Voyage, c. xxv.

Plate 62: The Lake of Tiberias, looking towards Hermon

David Roberts R.A.

Above: The Artist's Signature.

The text on the opposite page describes the following double-spread Plate.

City of Tiberias on the Sea of Galilee אמת ארץ ישראל

April 22nd 1839

PLATE 62: THE LAKE OF TIBERIAS, LOOKING TOWARDS HERMON

David Roberts R.A.

Banks of the Jordan. April 2nd 1839.

The Immersion of the Pilgrims

IN this View Achmet Aga, the Governor of Jerusalem, with a part of his Arab guard, occupy the foreground. The River Jordan flows so deeply beneath its banks, that in crossing the plain from Jericho it is unseen. The stream runs about fifty feet below the level of the soil. This sinking is so remarkable, that it has long exercised the conjectures of ingenious men. The Artist thinks that it may have had some connexion with the catastrophe of the "Cities of the Plain", and the formation of the Dead Sea. It would undoubedly elucidate in some degree that most memorable event, if we should be able to follow the original channel to the Gulf of Akabah.

His narrative gives a striking impression of the actual scene: — "As we approached the brink of the River, a general rush took place, and the women broke into the shrill cry of joy so often heard in Egypt. Even the camels, though heavily loaded, could scarcely be restrained. The Governor's carpets were spread on a high bank close to the River , where we could command a view of the entire scene; the military band and colours were brought round him, and seats were assigned to our party.

"One of the achievements is, to be the first to plunge into the stream; and on this occasion, a young Greek was swept away by the rapid current, and unfortunately drowned before our eyes. Young and old, male and female, were soon in the stream, in one promiscuous mass, some of them in imminent danger of being drowned. One of their superstitions is to put on slight dresses, which are to be preserved for their burial. This extraordinary display lasted about two hours, when the whole returned, the Governor now bringing up the rear."[1]

[1] Roberts's Journal.

(Continued)

This court and the Greek church on Mount Calvary, are, I imagine, the only portions remaining of the ancient structure. The court was quite a bazaar, filled with merchants and pilgrims selling and buying crosses, rosaries, staffs, etc. The ancient structure must have been beautiful. There is an arched porch with clusters of polished verdantique columns. The capitals, frieze, and cornice, are delicately carved, and similar in style to the details of the church of St. Mark at Venice. Around are the chapels of the various sects of Christians; that of the Copts is nearest the Holy Sepulchre. The Greek chapel is by far the richest, and is one mass of gold and carving, much in the style of St. Catherine's at Mount Sinai. Immediately behind is the chapel covering the site of the crucifixion, where, under the altar, is a circular brass plate over a hole in which the cross of Christ is said to have been fixed. Numerous other chapels are clustered around. (See Plates 14, 15).

30th March, 1839

To-day the governor kindly offered us a guard and horses to take us to the Jordan. Santa Saba, and Bethlehem, and offered me the upper part of his house to make drawings from.

Town of Tiberias, looking towards Lebanon.

David Roberts. R A

Town of Tiberias, looking towards Lebanon

THE Artist conceives the columns in the foreground to mark the site of ancient baths, from the hot springs still issuing round the ruins which lie on the shore of the Lake, about half an hour's walk south of the City. The whole way from the Town is marked by traces and remains of the ancient City; several columns of grey granite, twelve or fifteen feet long, lie together about half way to the baths. An old bathing house remains, and is still used by the common people; but Ibrahim Pasha, in 1838, raised, at the distance of some rods from the site, a handsome edifice for public and private bathing, consisting of a large circular apartment, covered with a dome, and having a marble pavement around a fine circular reservoir, to which steps descend. The roof is supported by columns. Many doors lead into this apartment. At the period of the Artist's visit, this bath was crowded with pilgrims, who at this season were returning from Jerusalem. The building contains private apartments for those who can afford to pay for them, which are well and orientally furnished, and some have beautiful marble baths. Above the old bathing house is a large reservoir,[1] into which the water is first received, and allowed to cool before it flows into the bath, this is necessary, for its temperature when it issues from the spring is 144° of Fahrenheit. There are four springs nearly together; the taste of the water is salt and bitter, like hot sea water, and it gives out a strong odour of sulphur.

Those waters are considered highly efficacious in rheumatic affections and debility, and are much resorted to from all parts of Syria. They are spoken of by Pliny,[2] and by Josephus,[3] and they were called Ammaus (Warm Baths). In the Talmud, the springs are mentioned as the ancient Hammath. The view of Tiberias and the Lake from this spot, backed as it is by the snowy mountains of Lebanon, is strikingly picturesque; but it wants wood, though the vegetation is rank in grass, brambles, and low shrubs.

[1] Roberts's Journal.　　[2] Hist. Nat. v. 15.　　[3] Joseph. Antiq. xviii. 2.

From the Journal

31st March, 1839 (Palm Sunday)

To-day splendid processions, in which the Greek Christians took precedence; and led by their bishops, they walked three times round the Sepulchre, bearing branches of palm in commemoration of Christ's entry into Jerusalem. The bishops, ascending the steps to the altar, blessed the multitude.
A plenteous supply of holy water was distributed, and flowers were strewn on the steps leading to the Sepulchre. Other Christian sects followed, all animated by sincere veneration. Visited the tombs of the three kings of Judea, the carving on the sarcophagi of which is probably the only thing in existence from which we can get a correct idea of art as practised by the Jews. (See Plate 17).

1st April, 1839

Having got horses, left for Jericho, taking with me my portmanteau, tent, and servant. Crossing the Valley of Jehoshaphat, and ascending the Mount of Olives, we passed close to Bethany, the principal object in which is a building like a sheikh's tomb, called the House of Lazarus. Proceeding along the road, which has been all pavemented by the Romans, we first beheld the Dead Sea. Along the whole line, Arab horsemen and Bedouins were stationed. Groups of pilgrims were moving on to the Jordan. On our left is a brawling stream, at the bottom of a deep ravine, the sides of which are perforated with caves, the former abodes of anchorites. Farther on is a pool and stream, said to be that sweetened by Elisha. Jericho lies at the base of the hills. (See Plates 56, 61).

The Sea of Tiberias, looking towards Bashan

THIS Lake bears also the name of the Sea of Galilee, from the province; of Tiberias, from the City; and of Gennesareth, from a tract of fertile land extending along its western shore, from El-Medjel on the south, to Khan Minyeh on the north; its length, according to Josephus, being thirty stadia, and its breadth twenty. It was remarkable for the abundance and excellence of its fruits, and was famed for a fertilising fountain, held by some to be a branch of the Nile, from its producing fish resembling the Coracinus, found in the lakes round Alexandria. The fountain was also called Capharnaum, probably from the town,[1] so often mentioned in Scripture as visited by our Lord.

On the sight of this Lake, De Lamartine says, in language which, though ambitious and poetic, yet conveys the common feeling of mankind:—"I had come to worship on the very shores, on the very waves which had borne HIM; on the hills where He had sat, on the stones on which He rested His head. He had a hundred times walked on that beach which I now trod with reverential homage. His feet had trodden the dust which was now under my own. He sailed in the barks of the fishermen on the Sea of Galilee; He walked on its waves, stretching His hand to the Apostle."[2]

The Artist thus gives his personal impression of the scene:—"Passing through a beautiful country, in about five hours we came in sight of the Sea of Galilee, embosomed in surrounding hills; far on the left lay Mount Hermon, covered with snow; and on a nearer hill rests the City of Safed. Here, at a glance, lay before us the scenes of our Saviour's miracles; but the population and the boats have disappeared. Towards the west the River Jordan was seen flowing from the Lake towards the Dead Sea, and below us lay the Town of Tiberias."[3]

The author of the Biblical Researches thus describes the aspect of the Lake:—"We reached the brow of the height above Tiberias, where a view of nearly the whole Sea opened at once upon us. It was a moment of no little interest; for who can look without interest upon that Lake on whose shores our Saviour lived so long, and where He performed so many of His mighty works? Yet to me, I must confess, so long as we continued around the Lake, the attraction lay more in these associations than in the scenery itself. The Lake presents, indeed, a beautiful sheet of limpid water, in a deep, depressed basin, from which the shores rise, in general, steeply and continuously all around, except where a ravine, or sometimes a deep wady, occasionally interrupts them. The hills are rounded and tame, with little of the picturesque in their form; they are decked by no shrubs or forests, and even the verdure of the grass and herbage, which, earlier in the season, might have given them a pleasing aspect, was already gone; they were now only naked and dreary. One interesting object greeted our eyes,— a little boat with a white sail, gliding over the waters: the only one, as we afterwards found, upon the Lake. The form of its basin is not unlike an oval; but the regular and almost unbroken heights which enclose it bear no comparison to the vivid and powerful effects which the wild and stern magnificence of the mountains produces around the Caldron of the Dead Sea. The position of the Lake of Galilee, embosomed deep in the higher tracts of country, exposes it, as a matter of course, in summer to gusts of wind, and in the winter to tempests. One such storm is recorded during the course of our Lord's ministry."[4]

The dimensions of the Lake are variously stated by travellers, but the most probable calculation makes it about 14½ miles long, and from 6 to 9 miles wide. Myriads of birds resort to its shores. Its water is cool and clear, and abounds with fish, though, for want of boats, few are caught, and those are consequently sold at a high price—the price of meat. To encourage and aid the inhabitants in deep-lake fishing would be one of the greatest boons which could be conferred upon them. On looking down upon the Lake, the course of the river, of which it is only an enlargement, can be distinctly traced through its centre, by the smooth surface produced by the current of "the River of the Prophets, and the River of the Gospel"—the Jordan.

[1] Joseph. Bell. Jud. iii. 8.   [2] Travels.   [3] Roberts's Journal.
[4] Biblical Researches, iii. 252.

Plate 65: The Sea of Tiberias, looking towards Bashan

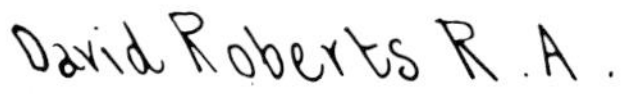

David Roberts R.A.

Above: The Artist's Signature.

The text on the opposite page describes the following double-spread Plate.

Tabarias, from the Walls — Saffet in the distance   April 22ᵈ 1839   David Roberts R.A.

Tiberias, from the Walls

THIS Sketch, in addition to the view of the City, gives, in the distance, crowning a lofty hill, the City of Safed. The land is peculiarly liable to earthquakes; Safed was fearfully visited in the middle of the last century (1759); but a still heavier vistation befell it in 1837. On the first day of the year, a succession of the most violent shocks rent the earth in many places, and almost instantly overthrew the chief part of the dwellings. The loss of life was dreadful, though perhaps too largely calculated at five thousand; four-fifths of the sufferers were Jews.[1]

Safed is venerated as one of the four holy cities of Judea; the others being Jerusalem, Hebron, and Tiberias. Its prominent position led to its being fortified at an early period. By some authorities it has been supposed to occupy the site of Bethulia, and by others, that of Kitron, a city of Zebulon. But, nothing is distinctly known of the City before the Crusades, when it afforded shelter to Baldwin III, after his defeat at El-Hûleh, in 1157. Safed is, however, chiefly celebrated for its Rabbinical school, one of the most distinguished among the Jews, and for many centuries it has been thus regarded; but the period of its scholastic foundation is not certain, it was probably long after the conquest by Bibars. Its palmy days were, however, during the sixteenth century, when the most eminent of the Rabbins lived and taught there; and at this early period (1578) it had an established printing-office, which, even as late as 1833, still gave regular employment to a considerable number of persons.[2] It has been supposed, that Safed was the "City set on a Hill," to which allusion is made in the Sermon on the Mount,[3] and that the Hill itself was the Mount of the Transfiguration.[4] But both suppositions are unsustained by evidence.

[1] Biblical Researchers, iii. 318—338.   [2] Roberts's Journal.   [3] Matt. v. 14. Maundrell, Apr. 19.   [4] Büsching Erdbeschr. th. xi. i. 488.

From the Journal

(Continued)

The present town has no pretensions to antiquity, but I found a few ruins with fragments of Corinthian capitals. Here the governor of Jerusalem passed us with a gay cavalcade, and invited us to visit him at his tent, where we were most politely received, and served with sherbet and coffee. Afterwards we pitched our tent beside his, and rode with him to the river Jordan, to see the proceedings there. (See Plates 59, 60).

2nd April, 1839

Early in the morning the whole of the pilgrims were in motion; and at 3 o'clock a gun gave signal that the governor was also moving. The long cavalcade extended as far as the eye could reach. All marched on in solemn silence, and the heavy tread of the dense mass was the only sound that broke the stillness of the desert. As we approached the Jordan a general rush took place, and the women broke out into the shrill cry of joy so often heard in Egypt. The governor's carpets were spread on a high bank close to the river, where we could command a view of the whole. I was very much struck with the breadth of the plain of Jericho, and the narrow space in which the deep and rapid stream is cooped up between the steep banks. (See Plate 62).

Jenin ancient Jezreel april 19th 1839.

David Roberts R A

Jenin

JENIN is a town situated at the mouth of a valley, opening into the great plain of Esdraelon.[1] It is the chief place of the district embracing the plain, and is the residence of the Governor of the district. Jenin had been supposed to occupy the site of the ancient Jezreel, but this opinion is strongly opposed; and the Ginæa of Josephus is asserted to be the original town. Its first occurrence in modern history is in the Crusades; but in the greater frequency of journeys to Palestine its name has become familiar, from its lying in the great route from Jerusalem to Nazareth. The town lies in the midst of plantations of fruit-trees, surrounded by fences of the prickly pear. The houses are of stone, and tolerably well built; the number of inhabitants probably two thousand.

The site of Jezreel is a matter of interest, from its connexion with the Jewish history, peculiarly in the reign of Ahab.[2] It was here that the murder of Naboth was perpetrated, which brought down a Divine malediction on Ahab, Jezebel, and their dynasty.[3] It is strongly argued, that the true position is that of Zerin, a small village standing on the brow of a deep valley, running down E.S.E. along the northern wall of the mountains of Gilboa. Zerin itself lies comparatively high, and commands a wide and noble view; to the East extending to the mountains of Ajilun, beyond the Jordan, and to the West including the whole great Plain, to the long ridge of Carmel. It is a most magnificent site for a city. The conclusion thus drawn from locality, and from the historians of the Crusades, is, that here had once been the city, and is the Plain of the ancient Jezreel.

From the Journal

(Continued)

The scene in the river was most exciting. Young and old, male and female, were in the stream in one promiscuous mass — some nude, some slightly dressed. The dresses I was told were taken home, and reserved for the funeral shrouds of the wearers. One poor young Greek was drowned, and many others narrowly escaped the same fate. The governor gave us a couple of soldiers as guides, and we set out for the Dead Sea, which we reached in about two hours. In the evening we again waited on the governor to thank him for his kind attention. He told us that Mohammed Ali, in every letter, enjoined him to pay every attention to Europeans, especially to the English, and that he was always afraid that all his exertions fell short of his Highness's wishes. Having procured guides for Santa Saba, we took leave of this friendly governor.

3rd April, 1839

We left Jericho this morning. Our route lay along the foot of the mountains, with the sea on our left; and in about three hours we arrived at a fountain of pure water. Beyond this the waters of the Dead Sea flow close to the foot of the mountains, so that we had to clamber on our way up a steep, rugged, and somewhat dangerous path, often closely overhanging the sea. The view from the summit was magnificent. (See Plate 104).

[1] The elevation of Jenin, and of the plain adjacent, is 515 Paris feet. Schubert, Reisc. iii. 162.   [2] 1 Kings, xviii. 45, &c.   [3] 2 Kings, ix. 14; x. 1, &c.

Askelon

ASKELON, known in early Jewish history as one of the chief cities of the Philistines,[1] flourished until the great fall of the Jewish cities; and from that period remained obscure until the time of the Crusades. Its position then made it important, and it became the scene of frequent and brilliant achievements. On the great adjoining plain the Moslems sustained a signal defeat by Godfrey of Bouillon (A.D. 1099); and in the Crusade under Cœur de Lion they were again routed with signal slaughter, though led by their great chieftain, Saladin.

The City lies to the westward of the road to Jaffa, within a short distance of the sea, and now exhibits only ruins. It is wholly deserted, its mole having been swept away, and thus its last hope of trade extinguished. The prophetic declarations of its solitude, as in all other instances, have been long and amply fulfilled. "For Gaza shall be forsaken, and Askelon a desolation; they shall drive out Ashdod at the noonday, and Ekron shall be rooted up. Woe unto the inhabitants of the sea-coast, the nation of the Cherethites! the word of the Lord is against you; O Canaan, the land of the Philistines, I will even destroy thee, that there shall be no inhabitant."[2]

The memorable chapter in the prophecy of Zechariah which announces the coming of our Lord—"Rejoice greatly, O daughter of Zion; shout, O daughter of Jerusalem: behold, thy King cometh unto thee!"—is headed by a general declaration against the cities of the coast, whose impurities had, doubtless, tended largely to degrade the religious obedience of Judah. "Tyrus did build herself a stronghold, and heaped up silver as the dust, and fine gold as the mire of the streets. Behold, the Lord will cast her out, the He will smite her power in the sea; and she shall be devoured with fire. Askelon shall see it, and fear; Gaza also shall see it, and be very sorrowful, and Ekron; for her expectation shall be ashamed; and the king shall perish from Gaza, and Askelon shall not be inhabited. And a bastard shall dwell in Ashdod, and I will cut off the pride of the Philistines."[3]

The plateau on which the City stood overlooks the sea. It was once a place of opulent trade, yet it never had a port, or its only port was artificial, and formed by the mole. The roadstead is open to every wind but the east: the shore seems once to have been covered with stately buildings, from the granite pillars and blocks of stone, over which the surf breaks in perpetual foam. Volney conceives the sea to have receded, but those ruins evidently contradict his theory.

In the neighbourhood of the City there exists a village called Hamami (the dove), and this, perhaps, corroborates the ancient story of the birth of Semiramis, who was said to have been born at Askelon, and nurtured in her cradle by doves. After those singular chances of her maturer life, which made her a sovereign, she assumed the name expressive of this place of her infancy,—Semiramis, in the language of Assyria, signifying a dove.

The ruins of the City are about two miles in circuit. It is a new singularity in the history of Eastern conquest, that arms should assist the researchers of taste, or the studies of the antiquarian; and it is to Ibrahim Pasha that we owe the chief indulgence which Askelon now offers to European curiosity. For the purpose of building a military station or city on this important site, he ordered the ground to be extensively cleared, and the result was the discovery of several magnificent ruins, and among the rest the ground-plan of a Temple, of which some columns remain, each of a single piece of granite, with an entablature, and capitals of marble finely executed in the Corinthian order. Another discovery was the site of a Christian Church, of which the pavement and the bases of the columns have been preserved. The capitals of the remaining columns are well executed, and upon them is represented a cross, encircled with a laurel-wreath.[4]

[1] Judges, i. 18. [2] Zephaniah, ii. 4, 5. [3] Zechariah, ix. 3—6.
[4] Roberts's Journal.

Plate 68: Askelon

David Roberts R.A.

Above: The Artist's Signature.

The text on the opposite page describes the following double-spread Plate.

Ashdod — March 24 1839. David Roberts R.A.

Ashdod

ASHDOD of the Old Testament, Azotus of the New, and Asdood of the present day, stands about ten miles from Jaffa. It is now but a wretched village, though its position in the midst of a fertile country, and commanding a portion of the route along the coast, may yet restore it to some share of its early importance.[1]

In the Jewish annals it is distinguished as one of the Five chief cities of the Philistines, and still more as the scene of one of those great miracles by which the God of the chosen people vindicated his worship, even in the midst of Jewish ruin. Ashdod was the City to which the captive Ark was brought, after the decisive defeat of the Israelite army, under the government of the feeble Eli. The victors deposited their splendid trophy in the temple of Dagon. When they opened the temple, on the next morning, the Idol was found prostrate before the Ark. It was replaced on its altar. On the next morning, it was found not merely prostrate, but with its head and hands cut off, and flung upon the threshold. Suspicious as the priests of Paganism must always have been of the imposture in which they were such adepts, they were so fully convinced that the act was Divine, that thenceforth they regarded the threshold as disastrous, or unhallowed, and neither priest nor worshipper ever after dared to tread upon the spot. But the conviction was to extend beyond the priesthood; it fell upon the people, in the shape of an agonizing disease, under whose terrors they, in a body, besought that the Ark might be sent away. It was sent successively to Gath and Ekron, followed in each instance by the disease; until it was finally restored to Israel by the voice of the nation shrinking under Divine wrath, and doing reluctant homage to Divine power.[2]

[1] Roberts's Journal. Biblical Researchers, ii. 368. Kinnear, 214.
[2] 1 Samuel, v.1, &c.

From the Journal

(Continued)

The sea was like a mirror, and reflected the mountains on its still surface without a ripple. Scarcely a word was uttered by our party to break the death like silence. We decended into Wady En Naar (the valley of fire) through which flows the brook Kedron, and after travelling about two hours reached the convent of St. Saba, situated on the brink of a ravine through which the brook flows, and which is so deep that even at mid-day the sun's rays never find their way down. All the rocks bordering this valley are perforated with cells of anchorites. The convent consists of a cluster of buildings on the face of the rock, and contains several chapels. The brotherhood is of the Greek persuasion, and numbers about thirty-five monks, who dress the same as those of Mount Sinai. (See Plate 102).

Ramla: ancient Arimathea. March 27th 1839.

David Roberts. R.A.

Ramla

ON the strength of a more than doubtful tradition, this town has been long regarded as the Arimathea of Scripture. It lies on the eastern side of a broad, low swell in the sandy plain, from which it has obviously taken its present name (Er-ramlah, *the* sand). The soil has the general fertility of this part of the coast, and the approach is through olive-groves, and gardens productive of remarkably fine fruit of various kinds. The Kharub, Sycamore, and Palm, are not unfrequent in its neighbourhood.[1]

Ramla has been rescued from the general decay of the sea-shore towns, by the annual passage of the Great Caravan between Damascus and Egypt. This has produced some struggling trade, and partially supports three thousand inhabitants, of whom one third are Greek Christians. The town contains several Mosques, some houses built of stone, and of considerable size, and the largest Latin Convent in Palestine. It lies nearly N.W. of Jerusalem, at a distance of about eighteen miles.

The Artist visited the Convent, and was well received by the Superior, a Spaniard, who, with some of the brotherhood, accompanied him on a walk round the town. "On the west were the Tower and ruined walls of a Mosque, which the Monks, as usual, pronounce to have been once a Church, but the style is decidedly Saracenic. Within its quadrangle remain some subterranean chambers, which were probably tombs, and bear evidences of Roman origin."[2]

The Empress Helena, the great authority in all the legends of Palestine, claims the credit of having built the Churches of Ramla; but the chief Mosque is stated, on less shadowy grounds, to have been the Church of the Knights of St. John.

[1] Biblical Researches, iii. 27.   [2] Roberts's Journal.

From the Journal

4th and 5th April, 1839

On looking from the heights above down on the convent, one could scarcely believe that it could possess so many comforts and conveniences within its walls. Like all Greek convents, the rooms are fitted up as divans with the richest carpets; and to us, arriving from the wild scenery of the Dead Sea, the whole scene seemed enchantment . We required no introduction. Our dinner, which we brought with us, was graced with a jug of the convent wine; and on leaving we received the benedictions of the monks without anything being expected from us. I asked and obtained leave to make a sketch of their beautiful chapel. We bade farewell at mid-day to our friendly entertainers, and, leaving a donation for poor pilgrims, set out on our way to Bethlehem, which we reached after a three hours' ride. Numerous flocks of sheep were to be seen on our way, and the immediate neighbourhood of the town abounds with fields of corn, olives, and fig-trees. The Church of the Nativity crowns the height on which the town is situated, and around it are the Latin, Greek, and Armenian convents. (See Plate 53).

Chaipas, looking towards Mount Carmel

THIS view is taken from near the mouth of the River Kishon; and in the foreground characteristically lies one of the wrecks which constantly strew this exposed shore. Mount Carmel is a ridge of about eight miles in length, rising from the memorable Plain of Esdraelon, and terminating in a bold promontory; the principal height of the chain being about 1200 feet above the level of the sea; the whole forming a striking portion of one of the finest views in this picturesque country. From the hill above Nazareth the whole prospect opens—a magnificent panorama. Beneath the eye spreads the western portion of the great plain, celebrated in ancient times for some of the most momentous transactions of Israelite history, and still teeming with fertility. On the left is seen the summit of Mount Tabor, with portions of the Lesser Hermon and Gilboa, and the opposite mountains of Samaria. The eye then rests on the long line of Carmel, with the "Convent of Elias" on its summit, and the town of Chaifas glittering at its foot. Below, on the North, extends the beautiful plain El-Buttauf, whose waters flow into the Kishon. Beyond this plain, a succession of mountain ridges stretches from East to West; and to the right is a "sea of hills," surmounted by Hermon, with its "icy crown."

The highest point of the ridge is towards the South. Thence it declines gradually northwards, and at the Convent has only the elevation of 582 Paris feet above the sea. The northern extremity bears N. 58° W. Towards the S.E., Carmel is connected with the Mountains of Samaria by a broad range of low, wooded hills, separating the great plain of the more southern coast from that of Esdraelon. The neighbouring anchorage is good, and Chaifas is, in fact, the roadstead of Acre. On the beach are the ruins of a Castle and two forts, ancient defences of the port. Towards the S.E. corner of the Bay flows a stream, now named Makattam, but more memorable by its scriptural name of Kishon. Rising in the hills which border Esdraelon, in summer, scantily supplied, it scarcely winds its feeble passage to the sea; but in winter it swells to an impetuous torrent, unfordable, and, in this bridgeless country, rendering the road hazardous to travellers. From the Convent on the ridge, the celebrated order of Carmelites probably took its name. In 1821, at the commencement of the Greek Revolution, it was destroyed by the Pasha, under suspicion of an intercourse with the insurgents. But permission or its rebuilding has since been obtained from

the Sultan, and funds alone are required for its proposed reconstruction on a new and larger scale. The prospect from the site of the Convent is of the grandest kind.[1]

But it is the memory of the great Reformer of Israel which has bequeathed its especial sanctity to Carmel. The actual site of events, however remarkable, may be forgotten in the level equality of the plain; but the mountain is itself a monument.

[1] G. Robinson's Travels, 104.

David Roberts R.A.

Above: The Artist's Signature.

The text on the opposite page describes the
following double-spread Plate.

Plate 71: Chaipas, looking towards Mount Carmel

PLATE 71: CHAIPAS, LOOKING TOWARDS MOUNT CARMEL

Christian Church of St George at Lua ancient Lydda, March 29th 1839

David Roberts R.A

Lydda

THIS village, now known as Loud'h or Ludd, and once bearing the name of Diospolis, was originally of considerable importance. Built by the Benjamites; and inhabited by them after their exile, it was transferred by Demetrius Nicator from Samaria to Judea. In the period following the death of Julius Cæsar, the City was seized, and its inhabitants sold into slavery. In the history of the New Testament it was the scene of a miracle.

"And it came to pass, as Peter passed throughout all quarters, he came down also to the saints which dwelt at Lydda. And there he found a certain man named Æneas, which had kept his bed eight years, and was sick of the palsy. And Peter said unto him, Æneas, Jesus Christ maketh thee whole: arise, and make thy bed. And he arose immediately. And all that dwelt in Lydda and Saron saw him, and turned to the Lord."[1]

Lydda was laid in ashes by the Roman troops in their march under Cestius Gallus to Jerusalem. On the conversion of the Empire it was a Bishopric of Palestina Prima, and in the Greek Ecclesiastical Notitiæ it stands as Diospolis, and in the Latin as Lydda. It was made memorable in later times by the appearance of Pelagius before a Council (A.D. 415). But its chief legendary fame is due to a tradition that the remains of St. George, who was born in Lydda, and martyred at Nicomedia in the third century, were transferred to his native place. The ruins of a Church dedicated to the Saint, and evidently once of great magnitude and beauty, lie in the eastern quarter of the village.[2] "We saw," says Robinson, "these noble ruins by the bright, yet mellow light of the full moon. The lofty remaining arch towered in imposing majesty; and the effect of the whole, though mournful, was indescribably impressive. It transported me back to the similar, though far more perfect, moonlight grandeur of the Coliseum."[3]

[1] Acts, ix. 32, &c.   [2] Roberts's Journal. G. Robinson's Travels, i. 178.
[3] Bib. Res. iii. 52, &c.

From the Journal

(Continued)

The Church of the Nativity is in form similar to the Basilica at Rome, with a double row of Corinthian columns supporting a wall, above which rises a timber roof. The wall is covered with scriptural subjects, most elaborately executed in mosaic, but much mutilated. A temporary screen divides the nave from the transepts and choir in the latter of which is the Greek church, which seems nearly as old as the rest of the building. The transepts are occupied as chapels by the Latins and Armenians, and immediately below them is the Chapel of the Nativity, which is small, and, though hung with lamps, seems poor after that at Mount Sinai. (See Plates 54, 55).

6th April, 1839

To-day, while I was sketching the interior of the chapel, a man arrived from Jerusalem with the sacred fire, which the priests say comes from heaven; and the whole of the Greek Christians turned out to receive him, carrying banners, and headed by their priests. All were soon in the greatest excitement, each struggling to obtain the first light.

Gaza

GAZA stands on the summit of a hill, half-a-mile from the sea. The hill is about two miles in circumference at the base, and appears to have been once wholly enclosed with fortifications. This position, the solidity of the ancient defences of cities, and a numerous brave population within, might promise security; yet the advantage of its possession or pillage was always too tempting; and its history has been a succession of sufferings at the hands of every invader of Palestine.[1]

Approaching by Beit-Gebrin, the country exhibits a pleasing landscape of corn-field and pasture, interspersed with clumps of trees and olives-groves, some of which are of great antiquity. The aspect of Gaza is imposing at a distance. As usual in Oriental cities, the illusion vanishes on entrance. But its connexion with the caravans renders it a place of considerable traffic, and consequently of considerable opulence.

Yet this wealth is confined to the principal traders, for the multitude live in that miserable state of discomfort, which, however it has become a second nature to the Asiatic, startles every sense, and gives pain to every feeling, of the European.

"There are no remains of its former grandeur standing," observes the Artist; "but that it must once have been filled with fine architecture is evident, from the pieces of wrought and sculptured marble everywhere built into the walls of the houses. Its seven Mosques appear to have been erected chiefly of those ruins. In passing through a wretched suburb, I remarked a number of beautifully sculptured capitals piled one above another to support the roof of a hovel! Marble and granite columns, in different degrees of preservation, are found in every quarter; and in the Cemetery, in which our tents were pitched, lay a magnificent Corinthian capital, in the purest taste."[2]

The troops in the Engraving were two regiments of Egyptian Light Dragoons and Lancers, on their march from Gaza to Sidon, armed in the European manner, and the whole in very effective equipment and condition.

A history of this City would be one of the most striking vicissitude; but our space limits it to a mere outline. Gaza was among the earliest cities of Canaan mentioned in the Old Testament.[3] It next became memorable as one of the "Five Cities" of the five Lords of the Philistines. It next was taken by the tribe of Judah; and then reverted to the Philistines, in one of those lapses of the Israelites into heathen vice, which inevitably delivered them over to be scourged by the tyranny of the heathen. To restore them, Samson was sent as the Divine champion, and Gaza was the scene of one of his astonishing exploits, and of that memorable catastrophe in the Temple of Dagon, "in which the dead whom he slew at his death, were more than they which he slew in his life."[4] Gaza was finally subdued by David, and formed the border of Solomon's kingdom.

Its history next became mingled with those of the great military nations which arose in the west of Asia. To Egypt, Gaza was the key of Palestine and Syria. It was thus seized by one of the Pharaohs, in the time of Jeremiah. Cambyses, on his invasion of Egypt, made it the depository of his treasure. On Alexander's march into Asia, its position attracted the eye of the great conqueror. It cost him a five months' siege; and his wrath at the obstinate bravery of its defenders, gave rise to one of those desperate scenes of cruelty, so frequent in ancient warfare, yet so rare in the victories of that most splendid of all masters of the sword.[5] The inhabitants were massacred, and their places filled up by strangers. It now contains about fifteen thousand people, of whom about five hundred are Christians. The inhabitants still refer to Samson's carrying away the gates, nay boldly point out the spot from which they were taken; and the small domed building on the right in the Engraving marks the spot to which he is supposed to have borne them.[6]

[1] G. Robinson's Travels.   [2] Roberts's Journal. Kinnear, 209.   [3] Genesis, x. 19.
[4] Judges, xvi.   [5] Arrian, Exp. Alex. ii. 27.   [6] Roberts's Journal.

Plate 73: Gaza

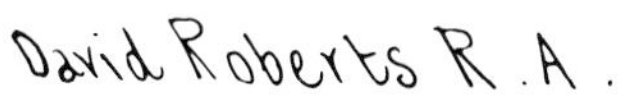

David Roberts R.A.

Above: The Artist's Signature.

The text on the opposite page describes the
following double-spread Plate.

Jaffa, looking South

JAFFA, the ancient Joppa, and now called by the Arabs Yafa, rose into early importance, as the chief harbour of Judæa. The modern town stands on a promontory rising to a height of 150 feet above the sea, and bearing to the North-west of Jerusalem, at a distance of about forty-five miles. From its commanding position, Jaffa has a striking aspect on the sea-side; and its land view is bold and extensive. On the South, it overlooks a wide and rich succession of plains spreading to Gaza; on the North, its horizon is the noble ridge of Mount Carmel; on the East, the hills of Judah exhibit every form of mountain magnificence; on the West, lies the boundless beauty of the Mediterranean. The interior, like that of all Eastern Cities, disappoints the eye. Narrow streets, loaded with mire in winter, and choked with dust in summer; a struggling population of five thousand, compressed into hovels, which seem the natural nests of disease, and where the pestilence has made many a fearful ravage; a Greek, a Latin, and an Armenian Convent, all meanly built and feebly maintained; constitute the town and the people.[1]

But the historical distinctions of Jaffa are of a high order. As Joppa it becomes known so early as the division of the Promised Land, where it was in the portion of the Tribe of Dan.[2] It was the port to which the cedars hewn in Lebanon were brought for the building of the first Temple.[3] From Joppa the Prophet Jonah embarked, when he was sent to preach to the Ninevites.[4] In Christian history, it had the distinction of the miracle wrought by St. Peter, in restoring Tabitha to life;[5] and here the great Apostle dwelt in the house of Simon the Tanner.[6] In the war which extinguished Judah, the town was garrisoned by a strong Jewish force; but it was finally stormed by the Roman troops, with a slaughter of twelve thousand of its unhappy defenders.

After a sleep of a thousand years, Joppa became again the subject of history. Its value, as the nearest port to the Holy City, attracted the enterprise of the Crusaders; and the most gallant achievement of Cœur de Lion was performed in defeating the Saracen army under its walls. But it paid dearly for the Christian triumphs, in the return of the enemy in irresistible force, and its storm, with the massacre of twenty thousand lives. The ruined walls were rebuilt by Louis IX. of France (A.D. 1250); but in the general exhaustion of the Crusades it sank into decay once more, and was lost to European recollection.

The long interval of five hundred years elapsed, when its name was revived in the Egyptian invasion of Napoleon. The brilliant but reckless ambition of that pre-eminent soldier conceived the idea of overthrowing the West by the weight of the East; and the conquest of Syria was to be the first step to the universal throne. Advancing (A.D. 1799) with a force that swept all resistance before it, he captured the Turkish posts in rapid succession, and made himself master of Jaffa after a slight combat. But there his success terminated. Our space does not allow of the further details of this most romantic enterprise. The execution of the garrison of Jaffa is a matter of painful historic record. Ill-fortune fell upon the invasion, and the proverbial skill of the leader and gallantry of the troops were baffled before the crumbling fortifications of Acre.

In after days, Napoleon, at St. Helena, was accustomed to regard the Syrian campaign as a crisis in his fortunes, — as the counteraction of a great design of conquest,— as the casualty which compelled him to remodel his plan of empire. "That campaign," said he, "cut asunder the chain which I would have twined round the East — it broke my *spell* — it forced me to turn my face to Europe."

The figures in the foreground are Polish Jews returning from their pilgrimage to Jerusalem, and waiting for embarkation.

[1] Roberts's Journal. Richardson's Travels, ii. 208. Clarke, iv. 441,&c. [2] Josh. xix. 46. [3] 2 Chron. ii. 16. [4] Jonah, i.3. [5] Acts, ix. 36, &c. [6] Acts, x. 6.

Plate 74: Jaffa, looking South

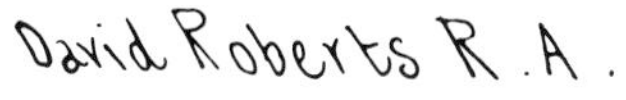

David Roberts R.A.

Above: The Artist's Signature.

The text on the opposite page describes the following double-spread Plate.

Jaffa March 25 th 1839

David Roberts R.A.

Jaffa, looking North

THE appearance of Jaffa from the sea is stately. To eyes wearied with the monotony of the shore, and the hovels which form its villages, its situation is commanding, from its being built on a cone-shaped eminence which dips boldly into the sea, and from the extreme inequality of the ground, which thus shows all its buildings in one view. Most of the streets are paved in steps; and the houses, some of which are of considerable size, stand in terraces, and thus add to the general effect. But the cypress and other trees, which so often raise their heads in the larger Oriental towns, and whose verdure adds so gracefully to the scene, are here wanting, and Jaffa is simply a succession of roofs rising above each other, bare, brown, and melancholy.

Besides its authentic history, to which reference is made in another portion of these pages, Jaffa figures in a strange mixture of Hebrew and Heathen tradition. Here Noah is said to have built the Ark!—here Andromeda to have been exposed to the Sea-monster;—and here Perseus to have bathed the wounds received in his battle with the Centaurs. But a more painful appeal is made to human memory in the Hospital, where the unfortunate French soldiery died, and which is now the Armenian Convent; and in the grave of the Turkish prisoners of El-Arish, which is still pointed out to travellers, at a mile south of the town.[1]

[1] G. Robinson's Travels.

From the Journal

7th April, 1839

Rode to the pools of Solomon, which supply Jerusalem with water. They seem to me to be of Saracenic work.

8th April, 1839

Mr. Pell and Ismael Effendi took leave of us this morning, going to Cairo by way of Hebron, while we returned to Jerusalem. In the afternoon I walked through the Valley of Jehoshaphat, and examined the tombs of Absalom and Zachariah, which are exact counterparts of those at Petra, and also cut out of the rock. (See Plates 10, 25).

10th April, 1839

After having made four drawings of the Holy Sepulchre, I waited on the new consul, Mr. Young, who arrived here to-day. (See Plates 1, 4).

12th April, 1839

On my return home after sketching, found that the consul had called for me. To-day I have wandered over the hills, but have not been able to get a good view of the city.

15th April, 1839

Left Jerusalem for Nablous at 9 A.M. Passed at mid day the town of Beer. At night our tents were surrounded by jackals.

The Dead Sea,
looking towards Moab

THE Dead Sea lies in a deep Caldron, surrounded by cliffs of limestone rock, utterly naked, the whole giving the strongest look of sterility. The surrounding region too is a naked desert; it has an Egyptian climate, and from its exposure for seven or eight months of the year to the full power of the sun, it is obviously condemned to hopeless aridity.[1] The height of the surrounding cliffs so generally screens the Lake from the wind that it but seldom loses it smoothness of surface. Yet, though the utter solitude of its shores, especially in connexion with the history of the buried Cities, impresses the spectator with the idea that he is looking upon a mighty Sepulchre, the immediate aspect of the waters is bright and even sparkling; they lie like a vast mirror, reflecting with almost undiminished lustre every colour and radiance of the bright sky above. Flocks of birds too, with their flight, and even with their songs, enliven the scene: yet under every aspect, it impresses the mind with a sense of the mysterious and monumental.

The View is taken from one of the hills of Engedi, immediately above the Convent of St. Saba, and looking down on the "Valley of Fire," through which the Kidron winds.[2]

From the Journal

16th April, 1839

Started by daybreak, and arrived at Nablous, the ancient Shechem, about 3 o'clock. The situation of the town is beautiful. It is placed between the mountains Ebal and Gerizim, and is well sheltered from the south and north winds. The town is large and populous, and the inhabitants seem more comfortable than any I have yet seen in Palestine. (See Plate 79).

17th April, 1839

I visited the synagogue of the ancient Samaritans, and was shown there two very ancient MSS. of the Pentateuch. Went to the Well of Jacob, where the interview took place between our Saviour and the woman of Samaria. It is now a heap of rubbish; and the shafts of some granite columns, half buried, but in an upright position, are all that remains of the structure erected there by the Empress Helena. Not far from the entrance to the valley is a small enclosure surrounding the tombs of Joseph and his two sons. (See Plate 78).

[1] Biblical Researches, 1. 219.   [2] Roberts's Journal.

LIST OF LITHOGRAPHS IN THE SERIES OF DAVID ROBERTS "THE HOLY LAND"

Note: The sequence of the Plates slightly differs from the First Edition, due to technical limitations.

DETAIL FROM THE MAP OF THE HOLY LAND, BY H. JAILLOT, PARIS, 1696.

4. SAMARIA & IDUMEA
PETRA

The Volumes/Parts in the Series of
David Roberts Lithographs

THE HOLY LAND

Text and Lithographs by Courtesy of the
Victoria & Albert Museum's Library,
London

And the bones of Joseph which
the children of Israel brought
up out of Egypt, buried they in
Shechem, in a parcel ground
which Jacob bought of the sons
of Hamor the father of
Shechem for a hundred pieces
of silver: and it became the
inheritance of the children of
Joseph.

Joshua 24, 32

ואת־עצמות יוסף אשר העלו
בני־ישראל ממצרים קברו בשכם
בחלקת השדה אשר קנה יעקב
מאת בני־חמור אבי־שכם במאה קשיטה
ויהיו לבני־יוסף לנחלה.

32 ,יהושע כ״ד

Contents   Page

Note: The sequence of the Plates slightly differs from the
First Edition, due to technical limitations.

4

SAMARIA & IDUMEA
PETRA

DAVID ROBERTS R.A.
THE HOLY LAND

25 Coloured Facsimile Lithographs
25 Coloured Photos of the Sites
Introduction and Historical descriptions
of the Sites by Rev. G. Crolly, L.L.D.
David Roberts's private Journal
Text and Lithographs by Courtesy of the
Victoria & Albert Museum's Library, London

Introduction

THE illustration of prophecy gives a new and powerful interest to all ancient countries connected with the Scriptures. And, with the exception of the Holy Land, there is, perhaps, no portion of the East which supplies a more striking proof of the truth of prophecy than Idumea. If there ever was a region where the skill of man exerted all its powers to confer a character of indestructibility on the labours of man it was that spot on which stands Petra. The City has not fallen, like Tyre and Babylon, into dust, and left its dwellers houseless. Its proudest portion remains in its original strength and size, almost in all its original grace and beauty, but the population have perished. The noble edifices which once stood in the midst of a flood of wealth, and were the creation of superabundant wealth, are there still, but the tide has ebbed away from their feet for ever. Human arts, so long and so richly lavished on those magnificent piles, have fled the soil; and through roads, once conveying the commerce alike of India and Italy to the storehouses of this superb city, no foot now passes but that of the Arab savage, or of the traveller hastening along, and regarding every man whom he meets as a robber and a homicide.

The fall of Edom had been pronounced by the Jewish prophets, while it was scarcely more than acquiring the shape of a state. As the restless enemy of Israel, it was the subject of Divine denunciation throughout the whole course of prophecy. Its punishments were successively proclaimed by Jeremiah, Ezekiel, Joel, Amos, Obadiah, and Malachi. By Isaiah it seems to have been taken as the emblem of the whole heathen world, and to have thus been loaded with accumulated malediction. The cruelty and corruption, the reckless vanity and furious arrogance of the national temperament, were divinely sentenced, and the general ruin was marked as irretrievable.

"Also Edom shall be a desolation: every one that goeth by it shall be astonished, and shall hiss at all the plagues thereof. As in the overthrow of Sodom and Gomorrah and the neighbour cities thereof, saith the lord, no man shall abide there, neither shall a son of man dwell in it."[1] "Thus saith the Lord God, I will stretch out mine hand upon Edom, and will cut off man and beast from it; and I will make it desolate from Teman."[2]

"The pride of thine heart hath deceived thee; thou that dwellest in the *clefts of the rocks*, whose habitation is high. Shall I not destroy the wise men out of Edom, and understanding out of the Mount of Esau? The house of Jacob shall possess their possessions, but there shall not be any remaining of the house of Esau."[3]

Malachi, in closing the prophetic volume, fixes a remarkable and final interdict on the recovery of the nation: "I laid the mountain of Esau and his heritage waste for the dragons of the wilderness. Whereas Edom saith, We are impoverished; but we will return and build the desolate places; thus saith the Lord of Hosts, They shall build, but I will throw down; and they shall call them, The border of wickedness."[4]

This weight of Divine wrath seems to have been especially heaped on Idumea (Edom) in consequence of its peculiar hostility to the chosen people. The territory had been in the possession of Esau, and his immediate descendants, who had driven out the Horites.[5] In the march of the people under Moses, when they demanded leave to pass along the chief road of the country, leading directly to Palestine, the Edomites fiercely refused, and the Israelites, who then were not commissioned to make war upon this prejudiced and inhospitable race, turned aside, and retracing their steps, were forced to make the circuit of the frontier.

The growing kingdom of Saul avenged those injuries, and probably many others by a war; and the more vigorous administration of David conquered the whole country. But in the troubled times which followed, the Edomites, enriched by commerce, and probably stimulated by the feebleness of the Jews, threw off the yoke, and fought them with varying fortune. At length the Syrian invasions of Israel prompted them to make more direct attacks, in which they carried off plunder and captives; until the hour of Jewish overthrow was ripe, and Edom was found joining the troops of Babylon.[6] In the Captivity, they even made an effort to master Palestine, and took possession of the country as far as Hebron; but were subsequently driven out by the valour of the Maccabees. The tide of conquest now recoiled, and Idumea itself was long governed by Jewish authorities.

The history of heathenism is the history of perpetual war. A new enemy from the Desert, the Nabathæi, or sons of Nebaioth, the son of Ishmael, suddenly invaded the southern border; and, changing their wandering habits for traffic and industry, became powerful. Within little more than a century (about 150 years before our era) they were in possession of the chief part of Edom. The capital had formerly been Bozrah; but Sela (a rock, petra) now became its principal city, and probably from the city was given the name of the region, Petræa.

The Idumeans were heard of once more in the siege of Jerusalem, when, entering the City in large bodies, they joined the factions, and added their violences to the sins and sufferings of the falling nation. The nominal independence of the kingdom continued for about thirty years after the fall of Jerusalem. In the reign of Trajan (A.D. 105) it was conquered and annexed to the Empire.

The position of Petra between the Red Sea and the Mediteranean poured into it the commerce which has always constituted national opulence; it became a great deposit of Eastern wealth. The troops of Antigonus (B.C. 301), in a sudden attack on the city, found there large quantities of frankincense and myrrh, with five hundred talents of silver. Even the Roman conquest, by giving greater security to the country, largely augmented its commerce. One great road stretched from Ailah to Petra, and thence to Damascus. Another from Petra strecthed to the west of the Lake Asphaltites, to Jerusalem, Askelon, and the general coast of the Mediterranean. The incursions of the Desert tribes were kept at bay by Roman stations, and in some instances by Roman towns founded along the road.

Though the region was remarkably mountainous, the palm-groves, and the romantic beauty of the country, were well known to the Roman poets, with whom, however, Idumea was a general name for Palestine, "Primus Idumeas referam tibi, Mantua, palmas." Virg. G. iii.

In the fifth century, Palestina Tertia comprehended the countries east and south of the Dead Sea. On the erection of the Patriarchate of Jerusalem at the Council of Chalcedon, the three Palestines formed its territory.[7]

But a formidable change was to break down at once the religion and the prosperity of the land. A.D. 630, Mahomet invaded the country.[8] The formation of the Mahometan kingdoms of Syria, Arabia, and Egypt, destroyed the traffic of Idumea. The roads were neglected, the population perished, and the land was abandoned to the savage and the wilderness.[9] In the twelfh century, the Crusaders under Baldwin I. made expeditions through the interior; but in 1183, they were finally expelled by Saladin.[10] From this period Petra was unknown to Europeans for six centuries. At length Volney, in his Syrian narrative (about 1785), told, as an Arab rumour, that on the south of the Dead Sea there were more than thirty ruined towns. In 1806, Seetzen passed round the south end of the Dead Sea, but without reaching Edom. In 1812, Burckhardt explored the Wady Mousa (Valley of Moses). The country has been since largely explored by Laborde, Robinson, and other intelligent travellers.

[1] Jeremiah, xlix. 17   [2] Ezekiel, xxv. 13   [3] Obadiah.   [4] Malachi, i. 3, 4   [5] Genesis, xxxvi.   [6] Ezekiel, xxv. 12. Obadiah.   [7] Reland, quoted by Robinson, ii. 563.   [8] Abulf. Ann. Moham j. 171.   [9] Ritter, Gesch. 209.   [10] Gauf. Vinisauf, quoted by Robinson, ii. 568.

The Lithographs

Jacob's Well at Shechem

THIS most memorable well is universally honoured by the Jews and Samaritans as the Well of Jacob, and by the Christians as the Bîr-es-Sâmirîyeh (the Well of the Samaritan Woman). The conviction of its identity with the latter alone could have prompted the zeal of the early Christians to build a Church over it, but which is now to be scarcely distinguished in its heap of ruins. The broken shafts of some granite columns, half buried in the soil, mark where their zeal and devotion had acknowledged the truth of the tradition in favour of this well; for, two other fountains, within three or four hundred yards, might have disputed the interest, and the honour of being the historic well; but, as in the case already shown, of the Tomb of Joseph, which lies in the inclosure seen in this view, all agree as to which is the true object of reverence. The Church is supposed to have been built in the fourth century, "though not by Helena, as reported in modern times; for Eusebius and the Bordeaux Pilgrim mention, as early as A.D. 333, the well, but not the Church." It is, however, spoken of by writers of the fifth and sixth centuries. At present only the broken columns of the scattered ruins mark that such a structure existed there.[1]

Robinson enters, with his usual intelligence, into the investigation of the subject: he says,— "Before the days of Eusebius, there seems to be no historical testimony to the identity of the well with that which our Saviour visited, and the proof must therefore rest, so far as it can be made out at all, on circumstantial evidence. I am not aware of anything in the nature of the case, that goes to contradict the common tradition; but on the other hand, I see much in the circumstances, tending to confirm the supposition, that this is actually the spot where our Lord held his conversation with the Samaritan woman. Jesus was journeying from Jerusalem to Galilee, and rested at the well, while 'his disciples were gone away into the city to buy meat'[2] The well, therefore, lay apparently before the city, and at some distance from it. In passing along the eastern plain, our Lord had halted at the well, and sent his disciples to the city, situated in the narrow valley, intending, on their return, to proceed along the plain on his way to Galilee, without entering the city. All this corresponds exactly with the present character of the ground. The well, too, was Jacob's Well, of high antiquity; a known and venerated spot, which, after having lived for so many ages in tradition, would not be likely to be forgotten in the two and a half centuries, intervening between St. John and Eusebius. I think we may thus rest with confidence in the opinion that this is Jacob's Well, and here the parcel of ground that Jacob gave to his son Joseph. Here the Saviour, wearied with his journey, sat upon the well, and taught the Samaritan woman those great truths, which have broken down the separating wall between Jews and Gentiles: 'God is a Spirit; and they that worship him, must worship him in spirit and in truth.' Here, too, as the people flocked to him from the city to hear him, he pointed his disciples to the waving[3] fields which decked the noble plain around, exclaiming, 'Say not ye, There are four months, and then cometh harvest? Behold, I say unto you, Lift up your eyes, and look on the fields, for they are white already to harvest!' We returned to our tent, wearied indeed in body, but refreshed in spirit, as we read anew, and in the midst of the very scenes, the account of our Saviour's visit and sublime teaching."[4]

[1] Biblical Researches, iii. 109. Roberts's Journal [2] John, iv. 3—8. [3] The epithet "waving," if it imply the maturity of the crop, wants the Author's habitual accuracy. Our Lord's allusion was obviously to the contrast between the physical nakedness of the field at that moment, and the spiritual harvest, which *his* eye saw ripening. [4] Biblical Researches, iii. 108—10.

Plate 77: Jacob's Well at Shechem

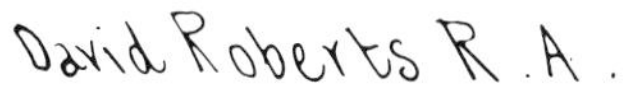

David Roberts R.A.

Above: The Artist's Signature.

The text on the opposite page describes the
following double-spread Plate.

The Tomb of Joseph at Shechem

AMONG the relics associated with Biblical history at Nablous, the Tomb of Joseph is an object of great veneration. The Artist describes it as standing nearly in the centre of a small inclosure, at the eastern entrance to the valley which lies between the Mounts Gerizim and Ebal, and not far from the ruins of the early Christian Church now covering the Well of Jacob. The Tomb is plain, and plastered over, with a small recess at the foot, in which he observed that some small lamps were placed, probably by pious Jews, by whom also the walls were covered with writing in the Hebrew character. The people hold this spot in deep reverence. At the head and foot of the Tomb are two rude altars, which the guides pointed out as the Tombs of Ephraim and Manasseh, the sons of Joseph.[1]

Joseph died in the faith, that the Land of Canaan was to be the inheritance of his people. And, on his death-bed, he directed the children of Israel "to carry up his bones" from Egypt; "and they embalmed him, and he was put in a coffin in Egypt."[2] "And the bones of Joseph, which the children of Israel brought up out of Egypt, buried they in Shechem, in a parcel of ground which Jacob bought of the sons of Hamor, the father of Shechem, for an hundred pieces of silver; and it became the inheritance of the children of Joseph."[3]

The reverence with which the resting-place of the great protector of his people has been so long regarded, leaves but little doubt of its actual identity. It is now, and has been for ages, pointed out as the spot of his sepulture; and in this belief in the tradition, Jews and Samaritans, Christians and Mahommedans, agree.[4]

From the Journal
(Continued)

Leaving Nablous in the afternoon, in two hours and a half we came within sight of the ancient Samaria, now called Sebaste. The town has a noble and imposing appearance, and is surrounded by a fertile and richly-wooded country. The remains of a Christian convent overlook a beautiful valley, which might almost pass for a scene in England, and contrasts strongly with the bleak and desolate appearance of Jerusalem. We pitched our tents at the foot of the hill, and ascended and examined the convent, together with the vast field of columns, still surrounding two sides of the hill, on which stood the ancient palace of Herod. The convent has pointed arches, the ornamental details are similar to the early Norman. It has a nave and aisles with circular apse, and in the centre a sheikh's tomb. (See Plate 82).

[1] Roberts's Journal.   [2] Gen. 1.26   [3] Joshua, xxiv. 32.
[4] Heb. xi. 22. Acts vii. 16.

Entrance to Nablous   April 17th 1839

Entrance to Nablous

THE Shechem of the Old Testament, and Sychar of the New, once the capital of Samaria, was a city of very high antiquity, and eminent renown. Few in the Holy Land are so beautifully situated. Nablous, its present name, is derived from the Romans, who established themselves here, rebuilt the city, and gave to it the title of Neapolis (New City). It is approached through long avenues of ancient olive trees.[1] It lies in a narrow valley, between Mount Ebal on the north, and Mount Gerizim on the south, or right hand of the View. The actual width of the valley in which Nablous[2] is situated is only about five hundred yards, between the bases of the mountains. The City is long and narrow; the houses are high, and generally well built, with domes upon the roofs, as at Jerusalem. It is situated at the summit of the valley, so that the waters nearly on its crest flow off in different directions; on the eastern side into the plain, and to the Jordan; on the western, the waters of some of its fountains flow down the valley towards the Mediterranean. The mountains rise boldly on either side, with a general character of sterility, which is more marked in Mount Ebal. But this only increases the effect of the beauty and fertility of the valley, as Nablous appears embosomed in gardens and groves of fig, mulberry, and other fruit trees. Robinson says, that as he and his companion approached it, "a scene of luxuriant and almost unparalleled verdure burst upon our view. The whole valley was filled with gardens of vegetables, and orchards of all kinds of fruits, watered by several fountains, which burst forth in various parts, and flow westwards in refreshing streams. It came upon us suddenly, like a scene of enchantment. We saw nothing to compare with it in all Palestine."[3]

[1] Roberts's Journal.   [2] According to Abulfeda, the more correct name is Nabuls.
[3] Biblical Researches, iii. 96.

From the Journal

18th April, 1839

I carefully examined the hill formerly occupied by the capital of the ten tribes, which is thickly strewn with shafts of columns. There are the remains of two large circular towers, which, in all probability, defended the entrance, and from which a double row of columns extends round what must have been the citadel. These are of limestone from the surrounding hills. In the middle of the city (if a few wretched hovels deserve such a name), rising over vast arches of hewn stone, are the ruins of a Christian church, the architecture of which must have been very perfect. We struck our tents, and at night halted at a considerable village called Abate, which is situated on a hill adjoining a large lake. There are few men, and these all aged or infirm, the young being drafted off to the army. The groups of women with their waterjars at the fountains are very picturesque. The dress consists of a loose white robe, and a red sash; a red handkerchief is bound round the head; a scarf of the same colour, covering the under part of the face, falls down over the back, and a string of large silver coins hangs dangling from the dark hair.

Nablous, ancient Shechem

THIS View of one of the oldest and most interesting cities in Palestine is taken from the western entrance of the valley in which it stands. The bright and copious stream which is seen passing under the bridge irrigates the valley, and produces the remarkable fertility of a spot, in which the olive, fig, mulberry, palm, pomegranate, orange, and citron flourish, and which shelters numberless nightingales; above it rises Mount Gerizim, the sacred hill of the Samaritans, the whole forming a scene of striking beauty. Nablous contains some fine fragments of its former grandeur. Near the centre of the City are several porphyry columns of large dimensions; [1] but neither those, nor the beauty of its site, are, in general, the chief objects of attraction to the traveller: the history of Nablous, as associated with the Old and New Testaments, constitutes its more natural and powerful interest. Here Abraham came "unto the place of Shechem, unto the oaks of Moreh."[2] Here was the scene of the revenge taken by Simeon and Levi. Here was the "parcel of ground" bought by Jacob, and given as an inheritance to Joseph. Here the twelve sons of Jacob were buried; and though only the Well of Jacob (the Well of the woman of Samaria) and the Tomb of Joseph are pointed out, tradition relates that Eleazer, the son of Aaron, and Joshua, the chief of his people, were also buried here. Here Joshua carried into effect the command of Moses,[3] when six of the tribes stood over against Gerizim, to bless the people who obeyed the law, and six against Mount Ebal, to curse the disobedient, when Joshua read aloud the whole of the law. The situation was singularly suited to the event, for a voice from either side might, on a calm day, be distinctly heard by the people assembled. Here, in the midst of the valley, was placed the Ark of the Covenant, surrounded by the priests and elders, and the officers, with Joshua, bearing the banners of their tribes, — a national spectacle of sacred magnificence. Here, from Mount Gerizim, Jotham's fine parable against Abimelech was uttered.[4] Here all Israel came to make Rehoboam king. Here the tribes rebelled, and the City became for a time the royal residence of Jeroboam.

After the fall of the Ten Tribes, Shechem was chiefly known as the principal city of the people who took the name of Samaritans, but who were Babylonians and others, gathered by Shalmaneser in the first instance, and afterwards by Ezarhaddon, to colonize the land. The depopulation of the country had exposed it to the ravages

of wild beasts; and the new colonists, being molested with lions, and regarding this calamity as the result of a curse, applied to the Assyrian monarch, for one of the Jewish priests "to teach them the manner of the God of the land." A priest was sent accordingly, but they mingled their original idolatry with the true worship; and, though they received the Pentateuch, were rejected from all communion with the Jews. The refusal of the Jews to allow the Samaritans to assist them in rebuilding the Temple at Jerusalem increased the national hatred. The Samaritans, in defiance, then raised a Temple on Mount Gerizim, and Shechem became the religious metropolis of Samaria. The hatred of the two nations rose at length to such a height, in their contests for the superior sanctity of their respective temples, as to lead to the destruction of that on Gerizim (129 B.C.). Yet the worship continued, for coins of Neapolis are extant, on which Mount Gerizim, with its temple (probably rebuilt), are represented as the symbol of the City.

The Samaritans are now reduced to a few hundred persons, who continue in the creed of their fathers; and on the days of the Passover, and other feasts of their religion, ascend Gerizim and worship God upon "the mountain," where, on the site of their ancient Temple, they make their sacrifices "as of old." They pretend to possess at Nablous one of the most ancient copies of the Pentateuch.[5] As a sect, the Samaritans are now greatly reduced; and a few small communities exist only here, and in Cairo, Gaza, and Damascus.

[1] Roberts's Journal.   [2] Gen. xii. 6.   [3] Deut. xxvii. xxviii. Josh. viii. 30—35.
[4] The height of Gerizim is about 2500 French feet above the sea, or nearly that of the Mount of Olives. Nablous is 1751 French feet above the sea. Gerizim and Ebal rise in steep, rocky precipices; and, from the valley, are about 800 feet in height. Schubert, Reise. Bibl. Res. iii. 96. Judges, ix. 7.   [5] The Samaritan priest displays this MS. to travellers, and pronounces it to be 3460 years old, the work of Abishua, the son of Phinehas. It is, however, conjectured to be modern. Bibl. Res. iii. 105.

Plate 80: Nablous, Ancient Shechem

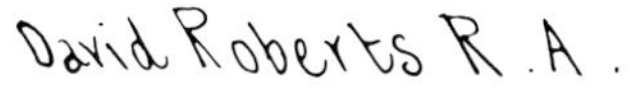

David Roberts R.A.

Above: The Artist's Signature.

The text on the opposite page describes the following double-spread Plate.

1839

Ruins of the Church of St. John, Sebaste

Ruins of the Church of Saint John, Sebaste

ON approaching from the West the ruins of the ancient City of Samaria, now the village of Sebaste, the most conspicuous object is formed by the ruins of the Church of Saint John the Baptist, which overhang the steep declivity below the village of Sebaste. This Church was built on the spot where tradition holds, that this "more than prophet," the herald of our Lord, was imprisoned, martyred, and buried.[1]

The alcove for the Altar, occupying the greater part of the eastern end, which thus assumes a rounded form, is an imposing piece of mixed architecture, the Greek style predominating; the arches of the windows are round; and the whole alcove is highly ornamented, expecially on the outside. But the upper arches on the inside of the alcove are pointed, as are also the great arches in the body of the Church. The latter rest on columns of no defined order; the capitals, though Corinthian in shape and size, being decorated with resemblances to the trunk of the palm-tree.

The walls are still entire to a considerable height, and the length of the Church is one hundred and fifty feet (besides a porch of ten feet), the width seventy-five feet; the windows are high up and narrow, with the pointed arches and zig-zag ornaments peculiar to the early Norman,[2] and blocks carved with grotesque heads and figures. It seems to have been, at one period, fitted for military defence. The general architecture precludes the supposition that it is older than the time of the Crusades, though its substructure and its eastern end might have had an earlier date.[3] Popular tradition attributes this, as it does so many other Christian Churches in Palestine, to the Empress Helena; it is much more probable that it was erected by the Knights of St. John, whose numerous crosses mark their reverence for the patron saint of their celebrated order. In the midst now stands the tomb of a Sheikh!

[1] According to Josephus, the Baptist was beheaded in the Castle of Machærus, on the east of the Dead Sea, near which, it may be presumed, that he was buried. Antiq. xviii. 5.2.   [2] Roberts's Journal.   [3] Biblical Researches iii. 141.

From the Journal

19th April, 1839

We started at daybreak, and shortly arrived at Jenin. We passed on through a beautiful country — Hermon on our right, Mount Tabor standing alone, overlooking the Plain of Esdrælon, said to be one of the richest in the world. A winding path leads up into the mountains, and we descended upon the hamlet of Nazareth, nestled, as it were, in the bosom of the hills. We were kindly received by the superior of the Latin convent, which is conspicuously situated. (See Plate 29).

20th April, 1839

Made two coloured drawings of the chapel, one of the Grotto or Chapel of the Annunciation, and two views of the town. Several objects of interest are pointed out to the pilgrim: — the workshop of Joseph, the stone on which Christ sat with his disciples, and the fountain to which the Virgin went for water. (See Plates 27, 28, 31).

Bird Jeloun. March 7th 1814.   David Roberts R.A.

Beit Jibrin,
or Eleutheropolis

IN the fourth century, Eleutheropolis is mentioned as an episcopal city of importance, and regarded as a central point in Southern Palestine. It was then the metropolis of the surrounding region. The names of five of its Bishops are found in the records of Councils from that of Nicæa (A.D. 325) to that of Jerusalem (A.D. 536). Epiphanius was called a native of the city, from having been born in the neighbourhood. In the seventh century, the name appears to have been corrupted to Eliotropolis. In A.D. 796 the region was laid waste by a civil war among the Saracens, and Eleutheropolis converted into a desert. The ancient name of Betogabra (later Heb. Beth Gabriel, or Beth Gebrin) was revived. The Crusaders in the twelfth century found the city in ruins; but from its commanding position, they raised a fortress on the site, to repel the Saracen attacks from Askelon, distant about twenty-six Roman miles. The defence was intrusted to the Knights Hospitallers.[1]

Robinson visited the ruins on his way from Jerusalem to Gaza. He found along the road in the vicinity traces of ancient walls. The village itself contains foundations more massy and extensive than any other in Palestine, except those of Jerusalem and the Haram at Hebron. They are evidently the remains of a fortress of great strength; rows of strong arches are visible along the circuit. The Artist regards the chief part of these works as of Roman origin. The surrounding country is rich with olive-plantations, some of them bearing marks of great antiquity.[2]

From the Journal

21st April, 1839

Left Nazareth at 11 A.M., and, after a pleasant ride of an hour and a half, arrived at Cana of Galilee, a village consisting of forty or fifty houses, most of them in ruins. There is a small Greek church, said to cover the place formerly occupied by the house in which the marriage took place, where an old man showed us what he called the identical jar in which the water was turned into wine. A ruined house is pointed out as the residence of our Saviour, and on entering the village we were shown a fountain from whence the water was said to have been taken. Passing on through a beautiful country, in about five hours we came in sight of the Sea of Galilee. Far to the left is Mount Hermon, and near to us is Safed, where the Jews expect the Messiah to reign forty years before entering Jerusalem. Not a boat is now to be seen on the Sea of Galilee, the scene of so many of our Lord's miracles, and where his followers plied their humble calling. To the south the Jordan flows from the lake to the Dead Sea, and close to the lake lies the ancient town of Tiberias, which, with 400 of its inhabitants, was destroyed by an earthquake some years since. A few temporary huts are here, the inmates of which are Jews, who come here to die, and are supported by contributions from their brethren in various parts of the world. The ruins of a small mosque stand near the entrance to the town, and we passed to-day the foundations of more than one ancient city with excavations in the rocks. (See Plates 63, 65).

[1] Biblical Researches, ii. 359, 404 &c.   [2] Roberts's Journal.

Sebaste, ancient Samaria

THE first aspect of this Village, the relique of the City, is singularly impressive. "It is difficult to conceive," says the Artist, "any place surpassing this in the beauty of its position, or any spot more commanding in situation than that of the ancient Capital of Samaria, standing as it does in the most fertile portion of Judea, and enriched by the taste and wealth of the most superb of all its governors, Herod. I never was more delighted, than when slowly winding round the brow of a hill it first burst upon me, bathed in the brightness of an eastern sunset. If, desolate as it is, the ruins of this city could thus strike the eye, what must its effect have been when its sides and summit were covered with the temples and palaces of Herod!"[1]

A lofty promontory, advancing boldly into the midst of a broad and beautiful plain; a fertile basin, surrounded by a circle of noble hills, marked the natural position for a Metropolis. It was founded by Omri, King of Israel, the father of Ahab, about the year 925 B.C.; the hill on which it was built being bought by him of Shemer, from whom its name of Samaria is derived.[2] From this period the Kings of Israel abandoned their former metropolis Shechem, and Samaria became their political capital. In history, the city is often confounded with the country.

The vast ruins which now exist at Sebaste are chiefly those of the Palace of Herod. The most remarkable are those of a Colonnade, which has been traced to the extent of 3000 feet! In the western part, above sixty of these columns are still erect, and many more are partly buried, and partly strewn around. These columns are sixteen feet high, and two feet in diameter at their bases. Robinson says, that he could discover no trace of their capitals; the Artist, however, found one, which was Corinthian. There is scarcely a doubt that this vast colonnade was the work of Herod, who enriched Samaria with splendid edifices; but its purpose is unknown, and those columns now stand in the midst of ploughed fields, "the skeleton, as it were, of departed glory."[3]

Samaria continued during two centuries to be the chief city of the ten tribes (until the Captivity, B.C. 720), and during the whole period it was the seat of idolatry. The great prophets, Elijah and Elisha, gave sacred distinction to its history; and the tombs of Elisha and of Obadiah the prophet are said to have formerly existed here. The original Samaria was taken and razed to the ground by John Hyrcanus. But it must have been soon rebuilt, for Pompey restored it to its former inhabitants;

and when Augustus gave the country to Herod the Great, Samaria was renewed by that superb monarch with extraordinary magnificence. Its name was then changed to Sebaste,[4] in gratitude to his Imperial patron. Herod filled it with a colony of six thousand veterans, made it a powerful fortress, and surrounded it with a strong wall, twenty stadia in circuit; reserving in its midst a "Sacred place," in which he raised a temple in honour of Augustus! famed for its architecture. Such appears to have been the Samaria of the New Testament, in which Philip preached the gospel, and where a church was formed by the Apostles.

Samaria early became an Episcopal city. Its Bishop, Marius, or Marinus, attended the Council of Nice (A.D. 325). The history of the Crusades adds little to that of Sebaste. It had a Latin Bishop in 1155. Saladin passed through it in 1184, on his retreat from Kerak. In the Middle Ages it was scarcely mentioned more than as an important place, from its situation, well watered, and abounding in gardens, olive-groves, and vineyards. It still contains a few Greek Christians: and a titular Bishop of Sebaste resides in the Greek Convent at Jerusalem.

[1] Robert's Journal.   [2] I Kings, xvi. 24.   [3] Biblical Researches, iii. 145.
[4] Now called by the Arabs Sebustieh.

Plate 83: Sebaste, Ancient Samaria

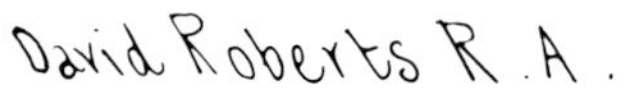

David Roberts R.A.

Above: The Artist's Signature.

The text on the opposite page describes the following double-spread Plate.

David Roberts R.A.

Site of Petra, South

THIS Engraving gives a general representation of the area which opens to the spectator on emerging from the "Chasm" by which he enters on the East. It shows the forms of the cliffs bounding the City on that site, with the various levels of the ground on which it stood. The course of the stream marks the direction of probably the chief Street, or Forum, as it was evidently covered over (though the winter floods have long since forced their way through the covering); and the nature of the ruins near the stream shows that this causeway was bordered with stately buildings. On its northern side are the remains of a Temple of large dimensions; the bases of the colonnade displaying the probable extent of its front.[1] On the southern, the site of a magnificent portico is discoverable; and at the confluence of a brook flowing from the north, with the stream, are the remnants of a circular building standing at the extremity of a broad terrace. In the bed of this brook were found the arm and shoulder of a statue, in marble, and the marble capital of a Corinthian pillar, of the purest taste, and obviously differing from the general style of Petræan sculpture.[2]

It was while the Artist and his companions were sojourning in the centre of this area (where the tents are seen), that they met the appropriate adverture of being plundered, apparently by their own escort. On the third day of their stay, they had received a warning, in the open seizure of some of their camp-furniture, which the thief, on escaping up the precipice, flourished triumphantly over his head, promising a speedy return "for something else." The chief of the escort pretended extreme indignation at the robbery, but the robber was not to be found. We give this little narrative in Mr. Kinnear's words:—

"The night was cloudy, with passing showers; and our servants told us, that the Alloeens, expecting heavy rain during the night, had removed to one of the large excavations in the neighbourhood. About midnight I was awakened by loud cries of 'El Arab! Robbers! robbers!' repeated in half-a-dozen voices, English and Arab. I started up; but on running out, no one was to be seen except our own party. The robbery was certainly boldly and cleverly executed. One or two of the tent-pins had been drawn on the outside. In this manner the thief had crept in, and deliberately selected such articles as were of most importance to these wild people: a pair of pistols, a bag of powder and balls, a shot-belt, and a box of wax-candles! To add to our discomfort, we could not help

suspecting that Hassein himself had connived at the robbery: he had long coveted the pistols."[3] His removal of the guard; his requesting that the lantern should remain lighted, thereby facilitating the movements of the thief; and his own remaining in the tent, to induce them to sleep in security, were nearly proof. The adventure shows the craftiness of these "children of nature," and how little faith is to be placed in the virtues of the Bedouin.

In closing these descriptions of Petra, it must be observed, that if its beauty and sublimity have been exaggerated, they are the exaggerations of intelligent individuals who have been upon the spot; and who have been unanimous in their admiration. It is even not improbable that some of its finest monuments remain to be discovered. The mountains cover the country; they are penetrated with chasms in all directions, and those chasms are now so choked with ruins or vegetation, that they defy the enterprise of the hurried traveller. Yet it was in one of those chasms at the western end of the valley that the unsuspected beauty of El Deir was discovered, through fragments of fallen cliffs, and an ascent of successive terraces, reached by successive flights of steps, "one of them extending over a space of a thousand feet." The chief obstacle, however, has existed in the extortion and ferocity of the Arabs; but a vigorous government would soon remove that obstacle: and, perhaps, no spot on earth would more amply repay a taste fitted to enjoy the noblest combinations of Art and Nature—that enlightened curiosity which takes an interest in the history of human genius—or those still higher feelings, which do homage to Providence, love to trace its solemn path through the times and trials of mankind, and from the desolated magnificence and blighted beauty of nations long past away, draw the high moral for the warning and the wisdom of their own.

---

[1] Biblical Researches, ii. 525, Kinnear, Cairo, &c. 150. [2] Roberts's Journal,
[3] Kinnear, Cairo, &c. 163.

El Deir

THE general view of Petra strikes every traveller with admiration. Even the least enthusiastic break out into the language of astonishment. But an artist is the most natural describer of the picturesque, and Mr. Roberts's pen brings the chief objects before the eye with a clearness and truth only second to his pencil. The following are extracts from his Journal:—

"March 6, 1839. We encamped in the centre of this extraordinary City. I did not expect to be much surprised at Petra, after seeing Thebes. But the whole is far beyond any idea which I had formed of it, in both magnitude and situation. The entire valley is strewed with ruins; the architecture a combination of the Egyptian with the Greek and Roman. Its beauty grew on the eye....

"I am more and more bewildered with the aspect of this extraordinary City. Not only the city, which must be two miles in length by nearly the same in breadth, but every ravine has been inhabited, even to the tops of the mountains. The valley has been filled up with public buildings, temples, triumphal arches, and bridges, all of which, with the exception of one triumphal arch and one temple, are prostrate. Even of this temple the portico has fallen. Those of the buildings (or rather excavations in the rock) which remain are rent by time, excepting the Khasnè, which probably owes its preservation to the narrowness of the defile, and the deep recess in which it is situated....

"To-day, accompanied by a guard of Arabs, we wound our way up a steep ravine; a broken staircase extending the whole ascent, which was nearly a mile. We at length reached the object of our journey, which was a building rarely visited, called El Deir (the Convent). It is hewn out of the face of the rock, and is of greater magnitude than the Khasnè, being upwards of 100 feet in height. The capitals of the columns and the cornices are in the rough block, the details never having been finished. In the interior, facing the entrance, is a recess, with a platform ascended by two flights of steps, in the centre of which once stood an Altar, the place where it joined the wall being distinctly visible; and over it is painted a Cross, showing that it has been used as a Christian Church.

"Opposite, and on the summit of a high rock, are the ruins of what has been a magnificent temple; the bases of the portico and colonnade on each side remain, with the Adytum, hewn out of the solid rock, and containing a beautiful ornamented recess. In a vault underneath, is a capital of one of the columns, in white marble, and in the best taste.

"El Deir stands a thousand feet above the level of the City. The view from this spot is magnificent, commanding a great extent of the valley of El Ghor; Mount Hor, with the supposed Tomb of Aaron crowning its summit; and the whole of the defile leading to the edifice, which is of the most romantic description, winding among perpendicular rocks, which turn the head giddy to look upon; while the site of the city itself is seen in all its extent below. Though the ruins of this extraordinary place are immense, they sink into insignificance when compared with these stupendous rocks. I often threw aside my pencil, in despair of being able to convey any idea of the scene."[1]

[1] Roberts's Journal.

El Khasnè, Petra

THE first object which meets the eye on the approach to Petra is a range of red sandstone cliffs, apparently impenetrable; but the brook which flows into the centre of the City passes through a narrow cleft, hidden behind a projection of the rock. Here is the opening of the extraordinary chasm, which anciently formed the only avenue to the City on this side. this is the Sik of Wady Mousa (the Valley of Moses).

The whole chasm exhibits the traces of a people lavish of ornament. A few steps beyond the entrance, a light and lofty arch crosses it, with niches sculptured in the rock beneath, probably once intended for the reception of statues. The passage varies from 12 to 40 feet; the sides are perpendicular, rising from 80 to 250 feet, and sometimes almost shutting out the sky. The fissure continues to descend, and the brook, which flows through its whole distance, fills it with vegetation; oleanders crowd it; wild figs and tamarisks start from the crevices of the rock, and it is festooned with creeping plants. The sides of the chasm exhibit continually the indefatigable taste and labour of this people of sculptors. Niches for statues, and tablets, evidently for bas-reliefs and inscriptions, are cut in the rock, and the greater part of the whole passage must have exhibited the appearance of a statue-gallery. To the stranger entering by this path, when Petra was in its day of power, the sudden contrast between the savage dreariness of the Desert, and the luxurious beauty and various magnificence of the City, with both its beauty and magnificence animated by the multitude from all regions, which then crowded its streets, its temples, and its theatres, must have been more like the work of magic than of man.

The entrance winds much, and other large fissures open from the sides, thus varying this most singular avenue. "The character of this wonderful spot, and the impression which it makes," says a writer, by no means idly addicted to emotion,[1] "is utterly indescribable. I had visited the strange sandstone caves and streets of Adersbach, and wandered with delight through the romantic dells of the Saxon Switzerland. But they exhibit few points of comparison. All here is on a grander scale. We lingered along this superb approach, forgetful of everything else, and taking no note of time. The length is a long mile; we were forty minutes in passing through it in this desultory manner."

The Sik terminates in a broader chasm, opening at right angles with it, and passing to the north-west. From this point the most perfect and beautiful relic of the City bursts upon the view—the Khasnè (the treasure), a name given to it by the Arabs, from a tradition that it contains the treasure of Pharaoh, to whom they attribute the building of all extraordinary things.

The Khasnè strikes all eyes, and the advantage of its position, which has greatly protected it from the effect of time, presents it in almost the perfection of its first day. It is universally acknowledged to be exquisitely beautiful, and to produce a more powerful impression than any surviving monument even of Greece or Rome. Its style wants classic purity, but the elegance of the general effect makes errors in detail trivial. The stone is of a rich rose colour: the symmetry of its facade is perfect; its preservation is almost complete. But the whole skill of the architect seems to have been devoted to the first impression. The interior is narrow and simple: from the vestibule the door opens into a plain, lofty room, excavated in the rock; behind this is another smaller, and small lateral chambers open from the large room and vestibule. Was this a Temple or a Tomb? The general opinion is that it was the former. Yet would a Temple be placed in the very rush and torrent of public life, or in a chasm which scarcely allowed space for the access of the worshipper, and almost prohibited the forms of sacrifice? But it stands in a valley of tombs, and is only more stately than them all. If the genius of a splendid City a thousand years past away, could be enshrined, the memory of the loveliness and grandeur of Petra could not have been transmitted by a nobler Mausoleum.

[1] Robinson, Biblical Researches, ii. 518.

David Roberts R.A.

Above: The Artist's Signature.

The text on the opposite page describes the
following double-spread Plate.

Plate 86: El-Khasne, Petra

PLATE 86: EL-KHASNE, PETRA

Encampment of the Alloeen in Wady Arabah

THE northern part of this Wady is supposed to be the Valley of Zin. The road traverses narrow sandy ravines, bounded by vast crags of calcareous rock. Solitude is sometimes grand and awful; but here it is alternately melancholy and startling. The walls of rock rise like the walls of some vast place of incarceration, but frequently torn and split into the most rugged forms by earthquakes or the elements. It is the "frowning wilderness." But this gradually improves, and the wild goat and partridge are sometimes to be seen: still the blaze of the sun is fiery; the light reflected from the rocks is blinding; breathing is painful, and thirst rapidly becomes feverish and intolerable.

A late intelligent traveller[1] has remarked, that it is impossible to look around on the ghastly and almost unearthly desolation of this scene, without feeling that the trials of the Israelites were far greater than we had ever before imagined." But admitting this, it gives only an additional proof of the fitness of the Desert for the discipline; while, by the Divine supply of food and water, the chief perils of the Desert were obviated. The purpose was to make a *new* people; and where could this purpose be more directly accomplished than in a vast and solitary region, into which civilized life could not enter, and where all the old habits of the people necessarily died away?

From the Journal

22nd April, 1839

To-day I made several sketches of the town, or rather of its remains — for every part has been more or less destroyed by earthquakes. The city wall, which is Saracenic, has been built of large square stones, now thrown down and rent from top to bottom. Towards mid-day we left for Mount Carmel, and at night rested by the only fountain in Cana. (See Plates 64, 66).

23rd April, 1839

Left at half-past 7 for St. Jean d'Acre, which we came in sight of at 3 o'clock. The situation is striking — a promontory to the north of the bay, Mount Carmel rising on the south. A large ship of war lay in the offing, and the fortifications rising above the plain, with the blue sea beyond, formed a picture that would have satisfied Turner. We pitched our tents outside the fortifications, and strolled into the town, where we saw that all the buildings had been much damaged by the late war. (See Plate 71).

[1] Kinnear, Cairo, Petra &c. 67.

HOLY LAND

Syria, Idumea, Arabia, Egypt & Nubia.

FROM DRAWINGS MADE ON THE SPOT BY

David Roberts, R.A.

WITH HISTORICAL DESCRIPTIONS BY

THE REV.D GEORGE CROLY. L.L.D.

LITHOGRAPHED BY

LOUIS HAGHE.

VOL I.

LONDON. F.G.MOON 20 THREADNEEDLE STREET.
PUBLISHER IN ORDINARY TO HER MAJESTY.
MDCCCXLII.

Temple of El Khasnè, Petra
(Title-page)

THIS view of the Temple of El Khasnè, in Petra, marks its singular locality. It is thus seen in front of the traveller on his way through the ravine which leads into the inclosed valley of Petra, and nothing can be more striking than its effect upon the spectator who has not yet emerged from the deep gorge of the Wady Mousa. The rock in which the Temple is cut seems to close the gorge and limit all further progress, like a *cul-de-sac;* but the stream which runs onward through the narrow ravine turns in its course to the right, and is joined by a small torrent from the left, at the base of the Temple El Khasnè; thence, flowing to the right, it enters the open valley which is filled by the wonders of this extraordinary place. The rocks on either side of the narrow ravine by which the city is approached are steeply escarped to a great height; in the sides the openings to numerous tombs may be seen, though many more are concealed by luxuriant shrubs, among which the rich blooming oleander is distinguished. Mr. Roberts is of opinion that these excavations, though now apparently inaccessible, were dwellings in the rocks,[1] and not tombs as Laborde supposes, and the apostrophe of Jeremiah seems to confirm this: — "O thou that dwellest in the clefts of the rock, that holdest the height of the hill," &c.

This Temple El Khasnè is not only very beautiful and one of the most striking in Petra, from its situation when seen by the traveller as he advances into the ravine, but the living rock from which it is excavated rising above it to the height of hundreds of feet, whilst the view in every other direction is limited to a few feet in width, oppressively affects the mind and prepares it for the wonderful objects and scenes disclosed in the valley beyond and throughout this, one of the most remarkable places on earth, whether considered in its physical characters or as a sublime verification of the denunciations against it made by the prophets of Holy Writ.

[1] Roberts's Journal.

From the Journal

24th April, 1839

After making two sketches of the town, I rode round the bay to Carmel. We crossed the brook of Kishon, immortalised in the song of Deborah and Barak, and in three hours reached the town of Caifa, to which we were refused admittance when it was known we had come from Acre, the plague having broken out at Jaffa. We passed on, and ascended Mount Carmel, where we were received with great kindness by the monks. They showed us the chapel, still unfinished, which, they say, covers the cave in which Elijah saw a vision of the Holy Virgin. The design is Italian, and very elegant. We saw also a statue of Elijah trampling on the priests of Baal, but they were proudest of a Virgin and Child, just received from Genoa. We ascended the belfry, from which the scene is very fine. After partaking of dinner with our Carmelite friends, we mounted our horses at sunset, and after a ride of four hours by moonlight reached our tents.

The lower Portion of El Khasnè

THIS view partially gives the profile of El Khasnè. The general architecture is Greek, but mingled with the luxurious fancy and exuberant decoration of Asia; the whole giving the impression of singular energy in the national taste, which could encounter such difficulties, yet surmount them with such success, and combine its triumph over the rudest forms of nature with such refinement of beauty.

Four Corinthian columns, thirty-five feet in height and three in diameter, supporting an entablature or pediment richly ornamented, compose the portico. On each flank stands a pilaster, and in the space between it and the last column is a colossal equestrian group in alto relievo. The entablature is ornamented with vases, connected by festoons of flowers, and in the centre of the pediment stands an eagle with expanded wings. The superstructure is more fanciful. It consists of a small circular temple, surrounded with Corinthian pillars, and flanked by two smaller temples of the same order. On the centre one stands the urn from which the building derives its Arab name, the Treasure, as the natives imagine it to contain the gold of Pharaoh, and frequently fire at it, in the hope of fracturing the depository. All the friezes and capitals are very richly sculptured.[1]

The steps to the portico are broken, and covered with grass and wild flowers. One column has been thrown down, and the *relievi* and statues are much decayed; but such is the magnitude of its general scale, and such is its grace, that those defects scarcely strike the eye. The fine colour of the stone, which is a rich rose, and the singular preservation of its most delicate carvings, give it the appearance of having been erected but yesterday.

If the Khasnè owes some of its effect to the suddenness with which it bursts upon the sight, and the contrast which its fanciful design and the freshness of its colour form with the rugged and stern aspect of the surrounding precipices; yet are we not to regard even those circumstances as evincing the singular skill of the designers? The effect is described as fascinating. "The idea of it," says Robinson, "was uppermost in my mind during the day and all the night. In the morning I returned, and beheld it with increased admiration. There is stands as it has stood for ages, in beauty and loneliness. Its rich roseate tints, as I bade it farewell, were lighted up and gilded by the beams of the morning sun, and I turned from it at length with an impression which will be effaced only by death."[2]

The Artist's farewell to the City touchingly and naturally expresses the influence of the scene:—

"The Camels were loaded, and our caravan was in motion. I repeatedly turned to look on this doomed City; so sad a memorial of Divine judgment, yet possessed of a strength which must have scorned all human instruments of destruction; placed in the bosom of impenetrable mountains, with walls so formed by nature, that to them the works of man shrank into insignificance. Though in the midst of deserts, its climate is not surpassed by any in salubrity; the soil watered by numerous streams and its mountains cultivated to the very summits; the plain below covered with the most splendid temples, and other public buildings, and the rocks themselves so filled with excavations that they resound under the foot. Yet with all this, and with a population of hundreds of thousands, all now is loneliness; its history is almost unknown, and the wandering Arab attributes its very existence to enchantment."[3]

[1] Kinnear, Cairo, &c.   [2] Biblical Researches, ii. 519.   [3] Roberts's Journal.

Plate 89: The lower portion of El-Khasnè

David Roberts R.A.

Above: The Artist's Signature.

The text on the opposite page describes the following double-spread Plate.

Approach to PETRA. An Ancient Watchtower commanding the Valley of El Ghor. Feby 5th 1839.

Ancient Watch-Tower

THIS tower is a striking object, from its position on an overhanging mass of rock, rising abruptly from the plain, on the left of the ravine by which Petra is approached through its mountain barrier. Widely overlooking the Valleys of El Ghor and Akabah, it appears to have been one of a chain of posts, or of signal towers surrounding the City; an important and customary precaution in countries so liable to invasion.

The tower is hewn out of the solid rock, and contains two chambers, but entirely plain, and without inscription or memorial of any kind.

Robinson observed similar structures in this quarter. Keeping on directly towards the middle pass, Es-Sufah, near the foot of the mountain, he came to the ruins of a small post or castle of hewn stones. It was obviously intended to guard the pass.[1] The Artist, on leaving Petra by another route, saw the foundations of other towers of the same kind, and apparently intended to keep up a chain of communication. This chain could be traced nearly to Hebron, particulary in crossing the high ridge called Nukb al Sujah.[2]

[1] Robinson, Biblical Researches, ii. 590.   [2] Roberts's Journal.

From the Journal

25th April, 1839

Heavy rain this morning compelled us to remain till midday, and at night we pitched our tents near the old Roman fountain.

26th April, 1839

This morning we descended on a small village called Nakhura, and travelled along the old Roman road, still in many parts in excellent preservation. On a height we found the remains of an extensive Greek temple, some of the capitals being Ionic, and others Doric. This building must have been at least 400 feet in length, and 200 feet in depth, and it is singular it has passed unnoticed. Proceeding along the bay, we began to ascend the Cape Blanco by a road carried along the face of the rock, the base of which the sea washes with a tremendous surge. With the heavy clouds rolling above, and the wild sea lashing below, it was the most sublime scene I ever saw, and I could not resist stopping to make a coloured study of it. By-and-bye we approached the fountains called the Wells of Solomon, the water from which drives a number of mills, besides supplying the aqueduct for the use of Tyre.

Another hour's ride along the sands brought us in front of ancient Tyre. In riding along, I could see fragments of the ancient village in places where the wind had cleared away the sand. (See Plate 36).

PLATE 91: THE ARCH CROSSING THE RAV

The Arch Crossing the Ravine

NEAR the mouth of the chasm El Sik, an Arch, at a considerable height, connects the rocks on either side. Time has destroyed whatever evidence might have existed of its actual purpose, and the question now is, whether it was formed for ornament, for defence, or for simple communication. But with that fondness for decoration which seems to have neglected no opportunity of exhibiting itself, the portion below the Arch is excavated into niches, which, it may be presumed, contained statues, possibly idols, the protecting deities of this extraordinary city. Some remains of a gateway, or barrier built of large square stones, show that the security of the entrance was intrusted to more sufficient guardians.

Petra, though deserted, is not untrodden; a rude and infrequent traffic passes through it still; and it happened, that while the Artist was employed on this sketch, a caravan from Gaza, consisting of forty camels on their way to Màan on the Damascus road, passed through the ravine.

From the Journal

(Continued)

The present town is a mere village, with a mosque rising in the centre, and the prophecy that it should become a rock for fishermen to dry their nets on is literally fulfilled. Enormous pillars of Egyptian granite, some of them 10 feet in diameter — remains of the town's ancient grandeur — are built into some parts of the wall, and a group of these lay piled on the shore with the waves breaking over them. The houses are in pretty good condition, and (for Syria) the streets clean. A few vessels are in the bay, but the city that sent out colonies to found Carthage is now little more than a naked rock in the midst of the sea. (See Plates 38, 40).

27th April, 1839

Made some sketches. Found a ruinous tower of Saracenic construction — the stones of great size, with foundations of similar structures stretching across the isthmus, jutting into the sea. Leaving Tyre at 11 A.M., we came upon the remains of what must have been a large town, with two beautiful little bays. The hill behind is perforated with caves. Further on is a picturesque village, said to occupy the site of the ancient Sarepta. In front of this is a small mosque, said to stand on the site of the house where Elijah sojourned with the widow. Further on we came in sight of Sidon. Night came on long before we could reach our destination, and to add to our discomfort, we were stopped by a guard, who demanded our bill of health.

The Theatre, Petra

THIS view exhibits another of the wonders of Petra. The Stream of Wady Mousa, here turning to the south, enters a ravine gradually narrowing. The cliffs are perforated, as usual, with numberless excavations; but the largest labour of this order, and the one which most directly meets the eye on entering the City from the eastward, is the Theatre. Its form, parts, and dimensions, are still ascertainable. The diameter of the Podium is 120 feet,[1] the number of rows of seats is 33, and of the Cunei 3; and as the benches are capable of containing about 100 persons each, the entire would thus give room for upwards of 3000. Behind the upper bench runs a narrow corridor. The Scena was built, and not excavated; the whole, therefore, has fallen. But the bases of four columns remain on its interior face. All the rest was hewn out of the living rock. Above the highest row of the seats are small chambers excavated in the cliff. The Theatre fronts the east-north-east. From the upper or southern front is obtained, perhaps, the most striking view in the whole valley. The opposite or eastern cliff, as it here skirts the track, is low; while above it, farther back, is another higher precipice, extending towards the north.[2]

The Engraving affords a view of the general height of the cliffs enclosing the Ravine which leads to the City. Its entrance and its termination were alike defended by small fortresses formed in the rock, but now ruined by earthquakes. Immediately facing the Ravine, and on the left of the spectator, is a rock, formerly crowned by a circular Monument, of which but the lower portion remains.[3] The ancients knew the power of first impression, and in all their cities seem to have studied to render the entrance most impressive. But the site of their City supplied the Petræans with singular advantages, which they employed to the utmost. In entering Petra on this side, the eye of the stranger was met by a succession of objects the most novel, bold, and striking. He first saw this Monument, probably a noble tower, suspended above his head. He next saw the Theatre, an immense work of wealth and labour, which, though now reduced to the simple excavation of the seats, we may justly suppose to have possessed the pillar and the portico, with every decoration which could embellish the most favoured resort of a splendid people. Above both Monument and Theatre, he followed both excavations of the richest and most fantastic style, ascending to the summit of the cliffs, and those cliffs themselves exhibiting the hues of painted scenery on the most colossal scale. Even now, in all its

desolation, all is beautiful. Nature has hung the rocks with prodigal and glowing vegetation; where the sculptured ornament has mouldered away, the shrub and the flower have partially supplied its loss, — have festooned the cliff, and coloured and tissued the ruin.

[1] Irby and Mangles.　[2] Biblical Researches, ii. 521.　[3] Roberts's Journal.

Plate 92: The Theatre, Petra

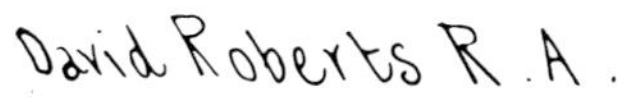

David Roberts R.A.

Above: The Artist's Signature.

The text on the opposite page describes the following double-spread Plate.

PLATE 92: THE THEATRE, PETRA

Louis Haghe, lith.

David Roberts, R.A.

Tomb of Aaron,
Summit of Mount Hor

AMONG the hills in the approach to Petra, the most striking is Mount Hor, from its boldness and height, and still more, from its connexion with Scripture. The ascent to the supposed Tomb of Aaron, which stands on its brow, occupies about an hour, and in its latter portion is extremely steep, often requiring to be climbed on the hands and knees. In many parts, where it would have been otherwise impracticable, the steepness is relieved by flights of stairs. The upper clefts of the mountain are enriched with a large growth of juniper and other shrubs; and on the summit is a grotto, in which a kind of Arab hermit dwelt for forty years, the greater part within the present century. He has lately died and seems to have had no successor.

The Tomb is alluded to prior to the Crusades; it is in a vault, and for preservation it has long been enclosed in a building similar to a Mahometan Saint's Sepulchre. An iron grating once protected it from the unhallowed touch, but it has been broken down, and all may now approach. The visitors, however, are compelled to descend into the vault with naked feet, an embarrassing necessity, in a place which may naturally be supposed to breed vipers and scorpions. It is still much resorted to by the Christian pilgrims, and is held in veneration even by the Mahometan.

We had none, but I told them that I had a firman from the Pasha Mohammed Ali, and if they stopped me they must be answerable for the consequences, as I should in the morning inform the governor of Sidon. This had the desired effect, for they immediately desired us to remount, and they sent a soldier with us, who led us to a spot close to the sea, and south of the town, where, with great difficulty, we pitched our tents in the middle of a thunderstorm. (See Plates 41, 42).

28th April, 1839

Our guard having remained all night with us, we were prevented entering the town. Wherever we walked he preceded us, beating every one out of the way, and calling out we were in quarantine, till the people actually believed we were plague subjects.

I was determined to sketch, however, and I got one or two views of an ancient fort, connected with the land by a bridge of several arches. The houses of Sidon seem large, but I could discover few antiquities, except some granite columns lying in the road, and some tesselated pavement. The people seem well dressed, and the town thriving; and on the whole I was much pleased with it, and thought Lady Hester Stanhope has shown good taste in selecting it for her residence. After breakfasting and bathing, we struck our tents, and left Sidon for Baalbec.

The Eastern end of the Valley

IN advancing towards the termination of the valley, two masses of sculpture peculiarly attract the eye. One, the more distant in the present view, resembling the Khasnè, but having eight Corinthian pillars. The edifice in front is of larger dimensions, and has four entrances, adorned by pilasters and ornaments in the florid style. A part of the work has fallen down, probably in some earthquake, but it still has four stories, with a row of fourteen pilasters extending across each of the three upper ones. Only three pilasters of the highest tier, however, remain. The excavations within form four apartments; but they are totally destitute of decoration, and they all contain simple recesses, of whose purpose nothing distinct is known. Travellers have, in general, pronounced them "*either* temples or tombs." But while this indecision lasts, there still is room for conjecture; and the writer of these pages conceives, that their primary purpose was *neither*. That places of public worship should be formed in the face of cliffs, some a thousand feet above the City, and almost inaccessible to the frequent approach of the people; without the space in front, of the depth within, which were essential to all ancient worship, whether Eastern or Western, seems improbable; and that these places of worship should be multiplied almost in every direction seem equally improbable. We are to remember also, that the actual City was *below*, in a valley of two miles every way, where we still discover vestiges of the public buildings. It is in this extensive area that we are naturally to look for the site of edifices so important, and in such constant public use, as the temples of heathenism.

The opinion now offered is, that the majority of those sculptured excavations were for the sole purpose of gratifying the eye; a noble indulgence of the national taste for ornament, a natural and fine employment of the superfluous wealth of an active and opulent people compressed within a boundary, narrow but singularly adapted for the most novel and magnificent decoration. In other sites, the wealth of cities flows into the surrounding landscape. But Petra saw round it only a circle of cliffs, from three hundred to a thousand feet high; those cliffs rugged, and forming the strongest contrast to the profuse elegance of an Oriental City, reared by the richest traffic in the world. The Citizens, unable to pass beyond their barrier, converted it into beauty; exchanged the wildness of its rocks for resemblances of the most graceful and stately architecture; and thus surrounded themselves with that picturesque, singular, and richly-embellished scenery, which, to this hour, excites the admiration of mankind.

Nor is it necessary to the conception, that this embellishment should have begun in any public design of the community. An unemployed architect, finding an easily wrought material, open to all, might have naturally adopted it to display his ability, in a position conspicuous to every eye. An opulent and childless citizen might have thus exhibited his taste, or transmitted his memory. The example set by individual caprice might have been followed by public munificence. The habits of ancient times were highly favourable to the conjecture. The want of those innumerable channels by which superfluous wealth finds its productive discharge in our day; the local pride of small commonwealths; the love of public decoration congenial to climates where nothing decays, and where the population live in the open air; and the actual existence of the finest monuments of the ancient world in their unmutilated beauty, naturally stimulated the popular spirit to respond to a call so deep as that uttered by the stupendous grandeur of the rocks of Petra.

That some of those excavations may, in after ages, have been used as temples or tombs is perfectly possible. That they may have been used as dwellings is probable, for such is the course of a declining state; pauperism readily takes refuge in a shelter which costs it nothing. But that the original and general purpose was the gratification of public taste — the expenditure of national means on the most striking and splendid national ornament, and the conversion of a rude and savage circumvallation into a circle of the most superb imagery of Europe and Asia; if but a conjecture, is one not unsuitable to the incomparable effect before the eye, to the striking locality, or the operation of a people of genius and power.

Ruins of a Triumphal Arch

IT is to be remembered that against Petra itself the Divine denunciation has been explicitly fulfilled. The whole area of the valley is a bed of ruins. The "line of confusion and the stones of emptiness" are scarcely more than the obvious expression for the havoc of the actual City. Though the fabrics, such as they were, formed from the rocks, are nearly indestructible, and will excite the wonder of many a future age, — Bozrah has become "a desolation, a waste and a curse."

The Arch-way in the Engraving, in the lower Roman style, is little more than a heap of stones. There appears to have been a central arch with two side ones, opening upon the esplanade which extended from the Theatre to the Doric edifice immediately under the rock of the Acropolis. In front a bridge, of which a portion remains, crossed the stream. On the hill are considerable ruins of temples and other public buildings, and portions of the esplanade still sweep round its base.[1]

Among the relics of the Arch lies a large stone, bearing a figure with expanded wings, which probably occupied a place on the Arch. From the pilasters and the fragments scattered round, the whole structure seems to have been loaded with ornament.[2] This profusion, and the Greco-Roman character of the sculptured fronts in various instances, render it more than probable that the City was the object of considerable decoration by its Western masters, from the second century, when it first became a Roman province. But the Roman style was unfit to mingle with the Petræan. Both were lavish of ornament; but the former was often lavish without luxuriance and costly without grandeur. The latter, alike from the magnitude of its scale and scene, was never rich without being superb nor simple without being sublime.

The fulfilment of the prophecy does not require that this extraordinary and once beautiful City should be either wholly untrodden by man, or a place of unexampled horror. The denunciation which condemns it to eternal flame[3] seems to regard it only as a general representative of heathen blasphemy. But the peculiar allusions to its fall are perfectly compatible with a certain degree of habitancy. The Fellaheen, or Arabs, who haunt its cliffs and chasms, amount to several hundreds. It is not wholly destitute of quadrupeds; the camel is everywhere in Arabia, and the wild goat browses among its recesses; the eagle soars above its coloured pinnacles; partridges and pigeons wing the lower air; the note of the blackbird, and many of the smaller songsters, is heard;

and in the season of flowers the sheltered chasms and the sides of the rocks are covered with bloom and filled with fragrance. But the inhabitants are the savage and the robber, and civilization is gone for ever.

"Hear the counsel of the Lord that He hath taken against Edom; and his purposes, that He hath purposed against the inhabitants of Teman: Surely the least of the flock shall draw them out: surely He shall make their habitation desolate with them. The earth is moved at the noise of their fall, at the cry the noise thereof was heard in the Red Sea. Behold, He shall come up as the eagle, and spread his wings over Bozrah."[4]

[1] Roberts's Journal. [2] Kinnear, 150. [3] Isaiah xxxiv. [4] Jeremiah, xlix. 20-22.

Plate 95: Ruins of a Triumphal Arch

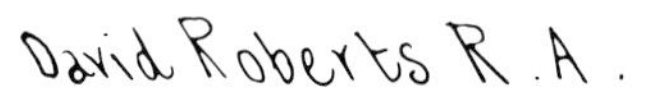

David Roberts R.A.

Above: The Artist's Signature.

The text on the opposite page describes the following double-spread Plate.

Remains of a Triumphal Arch at Petra.
March 8th 1839.

David Roberts

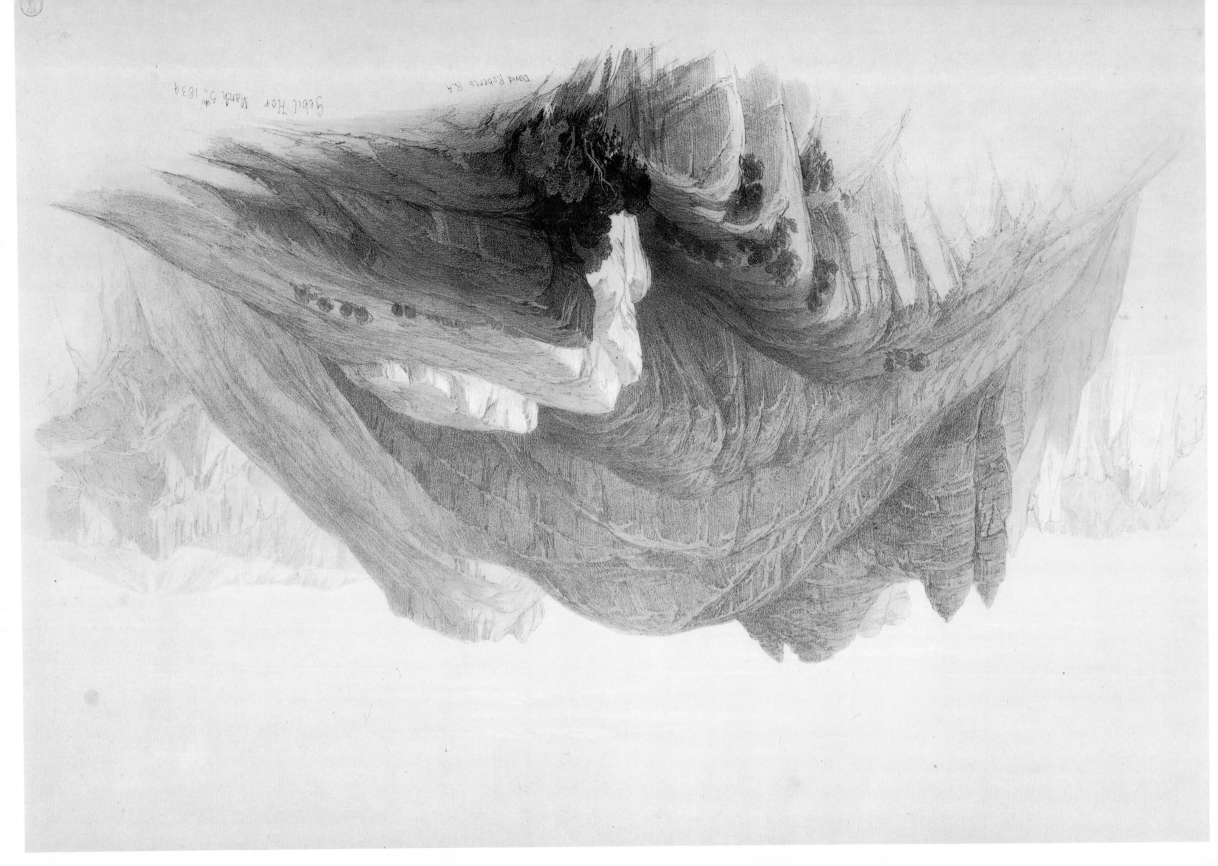

Mount Hor, from the cliffs encircling Petra

THIS view was taken from a great height. On the evening previous to his entering Petra, the Artist scaled one of the hills, which promised to give him a glimpse of the great object of his journey. But on reaching the summit, he found himself in the midst of a region of hills. His disappointment was amply repaid by the general scene. The view was magnificent, commanding El Ghor and the Wady Arabah, while above him towered the naked majesty of Mount Hor, and around and beneath lay the rocks of Mount Seir, bathed in the splendours of an Eastern sunset.[1]

But an interest more powerful than any which can arise from mere beauty or grandeur of landscape is connected with the scene. It is impossible to forget, that on this spot was transacted one of the most solemn events of Scripture; that in the ravines and plains immediately surrounding the spectator, the Camp of Israel was pitched; that on the wild declivity before the eye, trod the leader of the chosen people, ascending to be present at the death which was so significant of his own; and that on its summit, and in the sight of the assembled nation, the first high-priest of Israel surrendered his office and passed to glory.[2]

[1] Roberts's Journal. [2] Numbers xx.

From the Journal

(Continued)

We proceeded along the coast through a beautiful valley, with a stream flowing through, its banks thickly gemmed with flowers. Crossing the stream, we ascended the mountain by an ancient Roman road, sadly dilapidated, and attained the summit of a conical hill, a branch of Mount Lebanon, when night overtook us, and we pitched our tents.
(See Plate 45).

29th April, 1839

Started this morning at daybreak; ascended and descended the mountains all day, the roads being bad, and the climbing fatiguing both ourselves and the horses. The scenery was magnificent—a great part of the hills covered with natural wood, and the valley with flowers; the sides of the hills were sown with corn and barley. We were now in the country of the Druses, a sect belonging neither to Christians nor Mohammedans, though occasionally conforming to the latter. We pitched our tent at night on the summit of a mount. Owing to our being kept out of Sidon, we are in want of everything. Our light is from a bit of rag in a dish of butter; tea we have none; coffee, but no sugar. Wine and spirits have long been unknown: my only solace before turning into bed is a pipe of tobacco.

30th April, 1839

After two hours' ride we descended into the country of the Maronites, a primitive class of Christians, who have maintained their independence for 1200 years.

Conference of Arabs

THE Engraving gives a conception of the manner in which the more serious affairs of the natives are conducted. A party of the Fellaheen Arabs had come armed, to demand their share of the piastres which had been paid by the Artist and his fellow-travellers for protection; a violent altercation ensued, and 150 piastres were obtained from their former extortioner, "old Abed, who pulled the money from his bosom, and dashing it on the ground, cursed them and their fathers to the lowest depths of Jehennem," (Gehenna).[1]

To this succeeded a scene curiously contrasted in its quiet and formality. One of the Fellaheen was charged with having stolen an ass, and the three sheiks were called on to give judgment in the case. The whole party now seated themselves on the ground, and old Abed, who had just divided spoil with such angry reluctance, "opened the court" with great gravity, by reciting a part of the introductory chapter of the Koran, and what seemed some of the Bedouin laws; all which was listened to in silence and with great attention. While speaking, he held a drawn sword in his hand. When he concluded, the sword was taken up by another speaker, and another, and so on, none attempting to interrupt the holder of the sword. When the decision was given, the Fellaheen suddenly and quietly disappeared among the rocks.

[1] Kinnear, Cairo and Petra. Roberts's Journal.

From the Journal

(Continued)

We passed through a succession of villages, neatly built, with flat projecting roofs. Every foot of ground is cultivated, and the country seems literally covered with flowers. The inhabitants are well clothed and happy-looking. The children sitting round the doors reading their books reminded us of home The chief employment of the people is rearing the silkworm, and the vine and the mulberry are the principal productions. In the groves around the villages the blackbird, thrush, and cuckoo are heard; and these, with clear streams of water rushing down the face of the mountains, also recall our own country.

1st May, 1839

At daylight we were again on our way, and descended into a vast plain, between the mountains of Lebanon and Anti-Lebanon; a river winds through the plain, and from mountain to mountain every portion is cultivated or in pasture. About mid-day we came to a large mountain town called Ab Elias, with the ruins of a monastery picturesquely situated on the heights above. I stopped here to make a sketch, and two well-dressed men came and told us that one of them wanted to be made an Englishman—that is, as my servant explained to me, a Christian. About 4 o'clock we reached the principal town of the district, called Zahleh, where, stopping to make some purchases, our servants brought us word that an insurrection had broken out in Baalbec.

Excavations at the Eastern end of the Valley

THE cliff opposite to the Theatre is largely excavated, but among those works the one given in the Vignette is of superior design and preservation. The front presents an entablature and pediment, supported by four columns, and surmounted with an urn. The entrance is about twelve feet from the ground, and recedes considerably within the cliff, the rock extending fifteen feet forward on each side. The rock is on each side also hewn into an open gallery, supported by five pillars, two tiers of built arches supporting the ground between the colonnades, which thus forms a kind of terrace in front of the entrance.[1]

The architects of Petra had evidently a strong sense of beauty. Their choice of position, in all their more elaborate designs, is always admirable. The view from the platform in front of those edifices, whatever might have been their purpose, must have been most captivating. The City, in its pomp and animation below; the surrounding cliffs, in every variety of form and colour, and the whole seen through an atmosphere without a stain, and under a heaven without a cloud, must have formed a combination altogether unrivalled.

[1] Roberts's Journal.

From the Journal

(Continued)

Buckling on our swords, and looking as martial as possible, we sought the house of the sheikh and produced our firman, which was gravely perused. Coffee was served, and we learned that war had not actually broken out, but was hourly expected. The governor told us he would send three mounted soldiers as our escort. The town of Zahleh is one of the prettiest I have seen. It lies embosomed in the mountains, and has a considerable stream running through it. All the people seem employed and cheerful; long may they continue to wear the same happy faces.

2nd May, 1839

We left Zahleh, and in about two hours came in sight of Baalbec. The rain fell heavily all day, and with difficulty we found our way through the ruins into the town, where we erected our tents, and were in a miserable plight, our bedding and clothing being thoroughly drenched. The rain continued; the horses and mules were drawn in close for shelter; and in the middle of the night I was awakened by the falling of the tent. I felt very unwell, and in the morning, learning that there were some Greek priests in the town, I waited on them, and they kindly procured me a room, of which I at once took possession. (See Plate 46).

The Ravine, Petra

THIS view is taken from the Theatre, and represents the Excavations in the opposite cliffs, and the continuation of the chief eastern entrance to the City. The face of the rock is perforated in every accessible spot; and the prominent masses seem to have borne towers, and other defences of the pass. The bottom was flagged with large stones, not unlike the great Roman ways. But their level is now much broken up.

Laborde conceiving that these excavations are tombs, remarks on the singular neighbourhood of this scene of mortality to the animation of the Theatre. "What a strange habit of mind," he observes, "the people of Petra must have possessed, thus to familiarize themselves so constantly to the idea of Death; as Mithridates (!) accustomed himself to poison, in order to become insensible to its effects."[1]

Yet it is by no means clear, that any of these excavations were originally meant for tombs. For the excavations in the acknowledged Cemetery, outside the City, are not merely on a much smaller scale, but of a different form, being generally niches, cut into the shape of a coffin, and frequently in pairs, as if for members of the same family, and also frequently covered with mould and verdure; in all those points resembling the tombs surrounding Jerusalem; while within the Ravine they exhibit no imitations of the shape of the coffin, no verdure, nor any other covering than dust, nor that dust any other trace than those of the serpent and the lizard.[2]

The picturesque effect of the scene is less open to disputation. The rocks present an endless variety of colours, varying from crimson to the softest rose, and sometimes verging into orange and yellow; those are sometimes exhibited in broad stripes, changing and blending into each other like the hues of shot silk. But the general contrast of the cliffs with the sculptures singularly strikes the eye. Nature in her most savage wildness is brought into immediate connexion with art, sometimes capricious and romantic, but often graceful, and always new. All above is a succession of vast crags, battlements stayed by time and tempest, and sheets of colouring, which time and tempest may have only brightened. All below is a succession of colonnades, porticoes, and corridors; some approaching the purity of the Greek, and others mingling the styles of East and West; some minute and delicate, others broad, bold, and colossal; and all displayed with the rich effect of an Eastern climate, and in positions affording every advantage of light and shade.

In those examples of every style two are predominant, the Egyptian and the Roman-Greek; the former visible in the frequent recurrence of truncated pyramidal forms, and the slightly inclined fronts and sides of the more massive monuments; the latter in the general floridness of decoration in the remaining columns, architraves, and bas-reliefs of the ruins which cover the site of the city, and in the principal sculptures of the rocks. Those styles may be accounted for, by the intercourse of a people of opulent traders with the chief sources of ancient commerce. Its connexion with the Egyptian traffic naturally determined it to the solid and grave dignity of the architecture of Memphis and Thebes. Its connexion with with Greek Isles, and with Italy, through its subjugation by the Cæsars, would as naturally determine its adoption of the elegance of Greece, and the imperial exuberance of Rome.

The geology of the Mountains of Edom offers a wide field. Argillaceous rock forms the base, lofty masses of porphyry constitute the body, and long limestone ridges extend above all. The porphyry cliffs average 2000 feet above the Arabah. Wady Mousa is about the same height above it, and the limestone ridges may rise 3000 feet. The whole breadth of the Mountain tract between the Arabah and the Desert is under twenty geographical miles.[3]

[1] Laborde.   [2] Roberts's Journal.   [3] Biblical Researches, ii. 551.

Plate 99: The Ravine, Petra

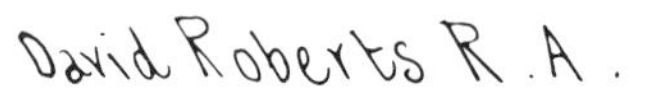

David Roberts R.A.

Above: The Artist's Signature.

The text on the opposite page describes the
following double-spread Plate.

PLATE 99: THE RAVINE, PETRA

The Acropolis (Kusr Faron)

THIS gives the central view of the City. On the right lie the ruins of the Triumphal Arch, whose site was near the brook, and fronting to the east. Its style is florid and corrupt. It seems to have formed the approach to the Palace, or pile of building in the centre, called by the Arabs Kusr Faron (Pharaoh's Castle). Its age is dubious, but it has the distinction of being the only structure of mason-work now standing in the valley. Joists of wood are, in different parts, let in among the courses of stone, intended, doubtless, to receive the fastenings for ornaments of stone or stucco. The walls are chiefly entire, but the columns of the northern front, which were composed of separate pieces, are gone. The distribution of the interior into chambers and stories shows that it was not a temple. This edifice, even in its dismantled state, has an interest, from its probably supplying some idea of the general architecture of the larger buildings of Petra. South of the Kusr stands a lone pillar, the last of a temple, of whose other pillars the fragments lie scattered around. Those objects are the only relics in the midst of a great tract of ruins. The course of the brook, when it has emerged from the Chasm, is through a strip of level land, on the north and south of which the ground rises into irregular eminences, and those again backed by a steeper ascent. It is this lower tract, half a mile square, which formed the actual circuit of the original City; the access being open on the north and south, where, however, we may presume that it was defended by walls, and the east and west being shut in by the cliffs, and capable of being approached only by the "Chasms."[1] The site was thus "an area in the bosom of a mountain, swelling into mounds, and intersected with gullies, but the whole ground of such a nature as might be conveniently built upon, and with neither ascent nor descent inconveniently steep."

The whole area was once evidently occupied with buildings. Along the immediate edge of the stream, its wintry violence has cleared away the ruins; but higher up, the whole space on both sides is covered with foundations and fragments. The stones are hewn, and the houses must have been solid and well built. They cover a space perfectly capable of accommodating thirty or forty thousand inhabitants.

To the left of the Kusr Faron is the rock which Laborde regards as the site of the Acropolis. The conjecture is probable, from the commanding position of the rock, and from the known habit of ancient nations to have a place of strength in the midst of their cities. But there is no further evidence. The crag is now inaccessible, though this does not preclude ascent in more ancient times. The Artist thinks that he discovered fragments of building on its summit.[3]

The rising ground on the left and front is covered with ruins.

All the impressions created by the general aspect of this City are characteristic and forcible. The choice of the site may have been natural to a people desirous of security in ages of violence; for such a position, defended by resolute men, must have been impregnable. The sublimity was the work of Nature; but the taste, the labour, and the ornament, were the work of man. "The most striking feature" is not so much in the existence of any one work of surpassing stateliness, as in their multitude, in the unwearied variety of such labours along the whole extent of the perpendicular rocks adjacent to the main area, and throughout the lateral valleys and chasms, the entrances of many of which are decorated with every imaginable style of architecture; many more, probably, remaining to reward the research of travellers in safer times.[4]

[1] Biblical Researches, ii. 523.   [2] Irby and Mangles.   [3] Roberts's Journal.
[4] Biblical Researches, ii. 529.

The Necropolis

IN the valley which conducts to Petra, and which lies outside the "Chasm," is the chief Cemetery. The ravine suddenly narrows to a space of about fifty yards, shut in by sandstone cliffs forty or fifty feet high. Here commences the Necropolis. The tombs begin immediately on the right: they are numerous, but the first which peculiarly strike the eye are three on the right, strongly resembling those in the Valley of Jehoshaphat. They are isolated masses of rock, fifteen or twenty feet square, cut away from the cliffs, and leaving a passage of several feet between. In one of them is a small sepulchral chamber, with a low door. Another has columns, but too much defaced to leave their order discoverable. These tombs differ from those of Absalom and Zechariah chiefly in their being flat-roofed, and in their sides being slightly inclined in the Egyptian style. They are mentioned by Burckhardt. A little farther on the left, in the face of the cliff, is a tomb with six Ionic columns. Immediately over this is another, bearing four slender pyramids, sculptured on the rock, the only instance of the kind here.

The valley then contracts more and more, and the cliffs become higher, forming a street of tombs. The rocks are of red sandstone.[1] The large tomb on the left of the Engraving is curious, from its giving some idea of the Petræan style of embellishment. The cornices and architrave, with the capitals and bases of the pilasters, were "let into" the sandstone, and were probably of some richer material, marble, if not bronze.[2] The whole must once have been a scene of stately melancholy.

[1] Biblical Researches, iii. 415.   [2] Roberts's Journal.

From the Journal

(Continued)

I was, however, so much struck with the magnificence of the temple, that I could not resist visiting and examining it, but in the afternoon I felt the fever increasing so much that I was complelled to go to bed, and for some days I suffered severely.

4th May, 1839

Have begun my studies of the temple, of the magnificence of which it is impossible to convey any idea, either by pencil or pen. The beauty of its form, the exquisite richness of its ornament, and the vast magnitude of its dimensions, are altogether unparalleled. The whole is contained within an irregular oblong enclosure, which has once been obviously used as a place of defence, a comparatively small portion of it being occupied by the temple. The portico, which, with two of the sides, has been thrown down, originally contained eight pillars in front, and fourteen on each side, each pillar being 6 feet 3 inches in diameter, and, including base and capital, 70 feet in height. (See Plates 47, 51).

LIST OF LITHOGRAPHS IN THE SERIES OF DAVID ROBERTS "THE HOLY LAND"

terra sancta arts

אמנות ארץ ישראל

Note: The sequence of the Plates slightly differs from the First Edition, due to technical limitations.

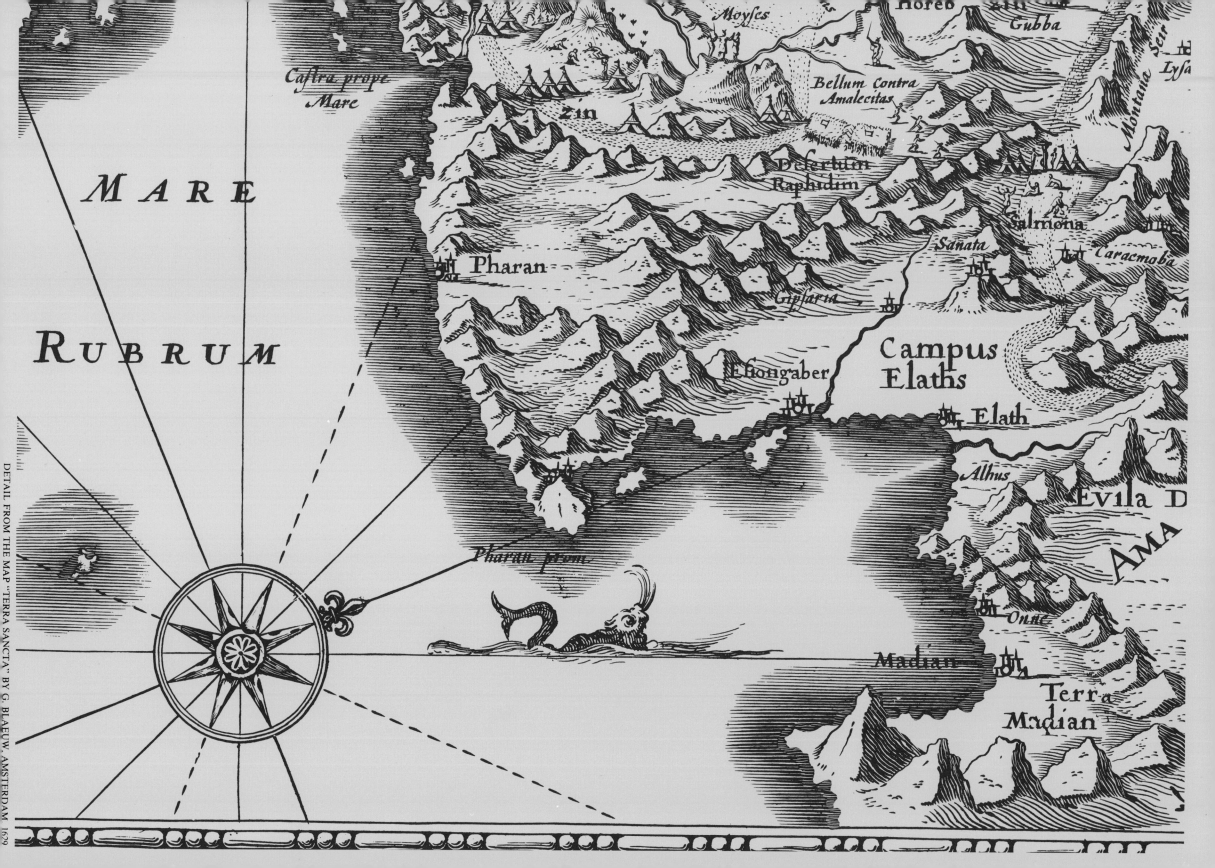

MARE

RUBRUM

Caſtra prope
Mare

Zin

Moyſes

Horeb

Gubba

Lyſa

Bellum Contra
Amalecitas

Montana Seir

Deſertum
Raphidim

Salmona

Pharan

Sanata

Caracmoba

Gipſaria

Aſiongaber

Campus
Elaths

Elath

Alhus

Evila D

Pharan pmm

AMA

Onae

Madian

Terra
Madian

5. THE DESERT
NEGEV & SINAI

The Volumes/Parts in the Series of
David Roberts Lithographs

THE HOLY LAND

Text and Lithographs by Courtesy of the
Victoria & Albert Museum's Library,
London

And he gave unto Moses, when he had made an end of communing with him upon Mount Sinai, two tables of testimony, tables of stone, written with the finger of God.

Exodus 31, 18

ויתן אל־משה ככלתו לדבר אתו בהר סיני
שני לחת העדות לחת אבן
כתבים באצבע אלהים.

שמות ל״א, 18

Contents   Page

Note: The sequence of the Plates slightly differs from the First Edition, due to technical limitations.

5

THE DESERT
NEGEV & SINAI

DAVID ROBERTS R.A.
THE HOLY LAND

22 Coloured Facsimile Lithographs
22 Coloured Photos of the Sites
Historical descriptions of the Sites
by Rev. G. Crolly, L.L.D.
David Roberts's private Journal
Introduction by Prof. M. Har-El
Map of the Route of David Roberts
Text and Lithographs by Courtesy of the
Victoria & Albert Museum's Library, London

Introduction

"THE NEGEV DESERT AND IT SURROUNDINGS": The Negev, which is the widest and the most arid region in the Land of Israel, is made up of five types of world deserts: sand dunes, hamada, badlands, rugged mountains and salt marshes. The Negev is divided into three latitudinal regions — southern, central and northern. In the south of the southern region are the barren mountains of Eilat, rising to a height of 800 meters above sea level, and extending to the high plateaus of Paran and Nahal Paran in the north. The rugged central region contains the Ramon Crater, which is 1000 meters above sea level, and runs to Nahal Zin in the north. The northern region is made up of anticlines and synclines, whose peaks reach upward to 700 meters above sea level, and comes to an end at the Beersheba-Arad Valley in the north, where most of the land mass of the Negev is situated.

The Negev has two climatic zones. One is a north-south zone that begins at the Beersheba-Arad Valley, which receives 200mm. of rainfall annually and is composed of fertile loess soil, and extends to the Gulf of Suez and the Gulf of Eilat, which receives 20mm. rainfall yearly. Along this axis the Negev changes gradually from desert to wilderness. The other climatic zone starts at the Mediterranean and runs to the watershed which is located in the mountain region of the Negev. Its average annual rainfall is 100-200mm. From the watershed eastward to the Arava, the region receives from a high of 100mm to a low of 20mm. of rainfall each season. This is considered to be absolute wilderness whose landscape is marked by deep canyons, suitable for raising camels, who graze in the shrubs of the dry watercourses of the Arava.

The natural limiting factors of life in the Negev are the arid climate, and the lack of fertile land and fresh water. To overcome these obstacles to make possible the creation of permanent settlements, man must be able to control the periodic floods which occur in the dry riverbeds of the region, dig wells and drill water holes, and build connecting roads.

Three geographic factors determined man's existence in the Negev in the past. First, the dry riverbeds were the only overland routes that contained sources of water. In ancient times there were three main arteries of transportation: the hill country route originating in the southwest from Egypt and Sinai and continuing to the northeast and the Land of Canaan; the Arava Valley route extending from the Gulf of Eilat opposite Edom in the south to the Dead Sea near Moab in the north; and the East-West route from Rafiah on the Mediterranean Sea in the west, to the Valley of Sodom in the east.

Indeed, the "Via Maris" on the coast from Egypt to El-Arish and north and "The Way of Shur" that traverses the Sinai from the lakes near the Suez Canal to Kadesh Barnea and Beersheba all point in a northeasterly direction.

Many settlements were erected along the principle highways, starting from the days of the Israelites and than the Nabateans in the Second Century B.C. and continuing to the northeast and the Land of Canaan; the Arava Valley route extending from the Gulf of Eilat opposite Edom in the south to the Dead Sea near Moab in the north; and the East-West route from Rafiah on the Mediterranean Sea in the west, to the Valley of Sodom in the east.

The longitudinal direction the the Arava caused the uncovering of ancient copper mines in Punon and Timna and enabled King Solomon to establish Etzion Gever as a port city on the Gulf of Eilat. From here passed the treasures of the ancient world, from Africa in the west and Southeast Asia in the east, including incense and perfumes, spices and precious stones, gold and other precious objects, all being brought to Jerusalem, the capital and to Gaza, the Negev port city on the Mediterranean.

The latitudinal direction of the Beersheba-Arad Valley resulted in the deposit of fertile loess soil in the northern Negev. In this region, wells were sunk and the land routes that passed from the two arms of the Red Sea northward converged. As a result, the main permanent settlements of the Negev were located there: Sharuhen in the west, Beersheba in the central region and Mashosh, Malhata and Arad in the east. Even today Beersheba is the principle city of the Negev.

SINAI OF THE EXODUS: The Sinai Peninsula is a total wilderness receiving in most areas less than 50mm rainfall yearly (except for the high mountain region where snow falls during the winter). Accordingly this is an excellent place for raising camels and flocks of goats, which are better able to withstand the blazing dry heat of the Sinai than sheep.

The Sinai is divided into three main regions; the High Mountain region in the south, the Plateau region in the central Sinai and the Northern region. The High Mountain region in the south contains the highest mountain ranges in the Sinai. The summits reach heights of from 2070 meters at Serbal to 2258 meters at Mt. Musa, 2568 meters at Mt. Um Shomer, and 2642 at Mt. Catherine. These mountains are snow covered in the winter and for that reason have many oases and natural springs, the most famous being the Firan Oasis. Many monasteries and churches were built near the oases during Justinian's reign in the 6th Century A.C. Of particular significance are those at Catherine, Firan and A-Tur on the coast of the Gulf of Suez.

This region geologically consists of basic rock formations and in the north Nubian sandstone, in which are found turquoise and copper ores and the ancient Egyptian Temple Serabit el-Khadim.

The Plateau region of central Sinai is built of limestone formations whose peaks rise to 1600 meters at el-Igma and descending as they go northward to 1000 meters at Badiyat E-Tih. The Land of Goshen where the Children of Israel lived is identified as being Wadi Tumilat west of Ismailia. From this plateau descend the tributaries of Nahal El-Arish, the largest of the Sinai watercourses that flow to the Mediterranean.

The northern region consists of high plateaus, isolated mountains and wide dunes running from southwest to northeast from Africa and Egypt to Asia and the Land of Canaan. Among the mountains there is Mt. Yellek 1090 meters high, Maghara 735 meters and Halal 890 meters. The largest oasis in northern Sinai, Ein Quedirath at Kadesh Barnea, is located in this region. The routes mentioned in the Bible in connection with the Exodus also converge in this region: "The Way of the Land of Philistines" on the Mediterranean coast, "The Way of Shur", from Goshen to Kadesh Barnea and to Beersheba, and "The Red Sea-Desert Way", crossing from the Gulf of Suez to Eilat.

At no time was the Sinai Peninsula ever ruled by local chieftains. Nevertheless, it was very important because of its copper and turquoise mines, its holy sites, like Mt. Sinai to Christians and Jews and churches and monasteries to Christians, and the Darb el-Haj, that was the way of the Moslem pilgrims who came from North Africa and Egypt to Mecca.

Today there are 50,000 Bedouin in the Sinai, who originated from the Hejaz and who are engaged in raising camels, sheep and goats, fishing in the Mediterranean and Red Sea, and serving tourists in the Sinai and at the monasteries. The Bedouins are under the jurisdiction of the Governor of El-Arish on the Mediterranean coast, which is the only city in Sinai.

Prof. M. Har-El

The Lithographs

Mar Saba

THE convent of St. Saba is about four leagues to the south-east of Jerusalem. The surrounding country is desert. The road from the City leads over a succession of yellow and bald hills, at a distance resembling mountains of sand, and the valleys are in general mere collections of the stony wrecks of those hills. Bird, beast, and man, equally shun this arid region, and the only living things seen there are an occasional tribe of Bedouins, who make as short a stay as possible. Their black encampments even contribute to the general melancholy of the scene.[1]

The immediate approach to the Convent is striking. "It was night," says one of its describers, "when after having descended into the bed of a ravine, where the Kidron passes to the Dead Sea, and arriving at the foot of the Mountains of St. Saba, we saw the convent above us, by the uncertain light of the moon. It looked a lofty and colossal structure, rising in stories or terraces, one above another, against the sides of the mountain to its summit, and there crowned with towers. We ascended flights of steps, climbed up a ladder, crept through a small door only large enough to admit one at a time, and found ourselves in an antechamber, surrounded by above a hundred Greek pilgrims.

"The next morning my first step was to the principal tower, which commands a view of the whole Convent. All round, and particularly in the mountain opposite, were ranges of grottoes, once the residence of anchorites. . . . It was a fortunate moment for the picturesque of the scene. It was Passion Week, and the concourse of pilgrims was considerable. An old white-bearded monk, leaning on his staff, was toiling up the side of the hill, leading a long procession of devotees. Below, apparently growing out of the rock, was a large palm-tree, said to be planted by the hands of the saint in the fourth century. Half-way down the slope was a cemetery."[2]

History, and probably legend, contributed its share to the effect. In a Chapel, behind an iron grating, in one of the grottoes, was a pile of skulls. The tradition of the Convent said they were those of hermits, who, to the amount of several thousands, had been slaughtered by the Osmanlis.[3]

Monasteries in every part of Europe have been generally built in picturesque situations, as was natural when the founders had their choice of ground. But in the East security necessarily became a principal object; and in the midst of a lawless population, whether under settled government, or the mere wanderers of the wilderness, the Monks were compelled to build their houses as strongholds, and their strongholds among rocks. The Monastery of St. Saba looks down upon a succession of precipices and defiles. In older times it might stand a siege, and even now would be nearly impregnable to the rude tactics of a native force. The entrance-doors are low, narrow, and formed of iron or very thick wood. The Monks even pay and keep a regular guard of Arabs at the principal entrance; and in one of the towers a sentinel is constantly posted, to announce the approach, whether of travellers, or of Bedouins.

But the Monks receive strangers with courtesy; and they not merely permitted the Artist to sketch their Chapel, but as their service was beginning before he had finished his design, they would not suffer him to lay aside his pencil.

There are generally about thirty Monks resident, of the Greek Church, who employ themselves a good deal in cultivating the gardens which they have formed in little terraces on the slope of the mountain, by conveying earth from below. The Monastery boasts of great antiquity, and is said to have been founded twelve hundred years ago.[4] Its surrounding hermitages perforate the rocks in all directions, and might have contained a large population in the days of its renown.

[1] Correspondence d'Orient.   [2] Stephens's Incidents of Travel.
[3] Carne's Letters.   [4] Roberts's Journal.

Plate 102: Mar Saba

David Roberts R.A.

Above: The Artist's Signature.

The text on the opposite page describes the following double-spread Plate.

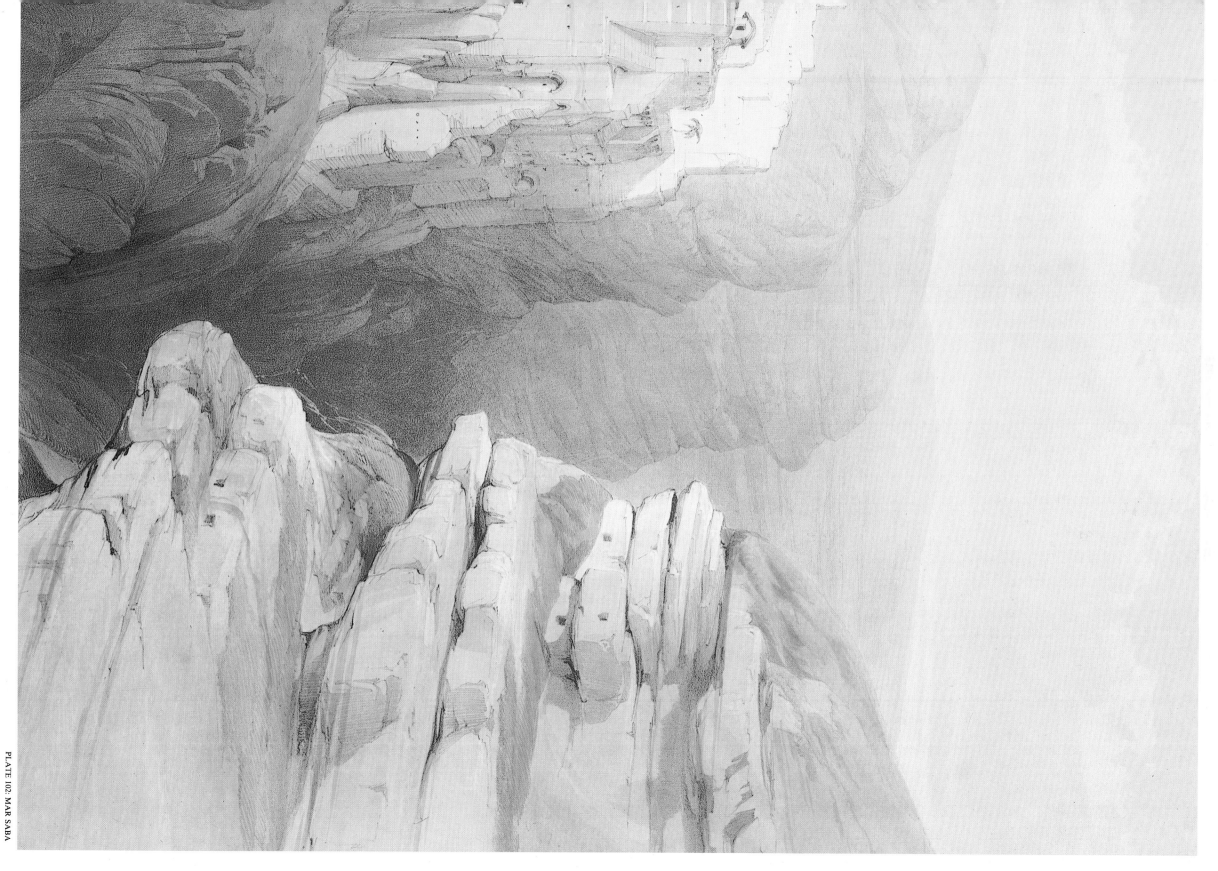

Chapel of the Convent of St Saba
April 5th 1839.

D Roberts R.A.

The Chapel of St. Saba

THE Chapel belongs to one of the chief Greek Monasteries of Palestine. It is ancient, and highly ornamented, though too much in the extravagant style of decoration frequent in the Greek churches. One of the pictures, which obviously excites the especial admiration of the pilgrims, is a representation of the Day of Judgment. The Deity is enthroned among angels and the spirits of good men. Beneath is a gigantic figure, weighing the souls as they ascend. On one side, an equally gigantic minister of punishment stands in the midst of flames. On the other, Elias is warring with Antichrist; and, in the background, the graves are giving up their dead.[1] Yet if a subject of this order goes beyond the limits of painting, it must be remembered that it has exercised the pencil of Michael Angelo.

Still, the Chapel in its general effect is beautiful; and the Russian government has signalized its care of the Greek churches in the East by adding to it some very striking ornaments. A short period before the date of this sketch, a number of pictures had been sent by the Imperial command, principally of saints, with the flesh painted, but the draperies and backgrounds in chased silver. The Convent, too, had undergone a thorough repair, as was presumed, from the same Imperial patronage.[2]

[1] Stephens's Incidents of Travel.   [2] Roberts's Journal.

From the Journal

4th May, 1839

The capitals (Corinthian) are of the most exquisite proportion, and, with the ornamentation of the frieze and cornice, are so deeply and boldly cut, that I should think they must have been carved after being erected. The whole has evidently been constructed without mortar, but the joints of the pillars have been polished and fixed by cramps of bronze. The grand doorway is of immense size, formed of vast stones, and sculptured with the richest decorations. From the marks of fastenings, the entrance was probably closed with a curtain or veil, as in the Jewish temple, and in some of the Spanish churches of this day. The enclosure is divided into three great courts, in the innermost of which the temple stands, and in the same court is a range of columns, larger in dimensions, and on a higher elevation, though of the same order of architecture. The central court is larger, and it has also been occupied by a structure, now, alas! a mass of ruins. The substructure of these buildings contains large apartments extending the full breadth and length of the enclosure, and are composed of huge stones, some of them 70 feet in length.

(See Plates 49, 50).

The Wilderness of Engedi

THE country to the west of the Dead Sea is a succession of hills and ravines, covered in the early part of the summer with rich vegetation, but soon exhibiting the fiery force of the season, and becoming scorched, until all look of vegetation withers away. A good deal of the discrepancy in the descriptions of Palestine obviously arises from the different periods of the year at which it has been visited. The traveller who sees it in spring, sees it glowing with shrubs and flowers; a few months after, the plain looks a waste of sand, the hill a pile of burnt rocks, and the mountain-chain the very emblem of sterility.[1]

The descent of the pass to the fountain Ain-Jidy ("Engedi") is among the most formidable even in this country of ravines. The path descends by zig-zags, often at the steepest angle practicable for horses, and is carried partly along ledges or shelves on the perpendicular face of the cliff, and then down the almost equally steep débris. Much of the rock is a compact, reddish limestone, smooth as glass, though with an irregular surface. "My companion," says Robinson, "had crossed the heights of Lebanon and the mountains of Persia, and I had formerly traversed the whole of the Swiss Alps, yet neither of us had ever met with a pass so difficult and dangerous. Of those which I had seen, the Gemmi resembles it most; but is not so high, and the path is better."[2]

The Artist's impressions of this remarkable spot fully coincide with those of the traveller. "There was a death-like silence around us. We descended into the Wady-en-Nar (the Fire Valley), through which the Kidron has formed for itself a channel. Ascending the opposite bank, we proceeded for some time over undulating ground, covered with rank vegetation, which, however, was beginning to be parched; and at length came in sight of the Towers of St. Saba. It is impossible to imagine a more romantic scene. The ravine cannot be less than five hundred feet in depth, perhaps more; the heights are wild."[3]

This was the country to which David fled from the persecution of Saul. The Monks, who find a place for everything, point out the Cavern in which the famous future King of Israel took shelter. But later authorities indignantly differ, some fixing the scene of the memorable encounter of David and Saul near the convent, others at the pass of Ain-Jidy. A dispute of air. The spot may well be conceived beyond all power of modern identification.[4]

After a descent of about three-quarters of an hour the fountain which gives the name to the district is reached. The Ain-Jidy bursts forth at once a fine stream from a narrow shelf of the mountain, still more than four hundred feet above the level of the Dead Sea. The course of the stream is soon lost in the profuse vegetation of trees and shrubs.

At the fountain are the remains of several buildings, apparently ancient. The fountain itself is limpid and sparkling, with a copious stream of sweet water. The thermometer stood in it at 81° Fahrenheit. The borders of the stream are covered with a thicket, flourishing luxuriantly. The botany of the spot is interesting. Among the trees, are the Seyal, producing the Gum Arabic; the thorny Nubk, or Lote Tree, bearing a small fruit like a thorn-apple, much enjoyed by the common people; the Fustak, or Pistacia, a large tree, with long and beautiful clusters of white blossoms (but which Robinson imagines to be the El-Henna, the "camphire" of our translation of the Bible (Lawsonia inermis, Linn.), for which this region was anciently celebrated); and, most singular of them all, the Osher, or Apple of Sodom. Among the shrubs is the Egg-plant Nightshade (Solanum Melongena); and the Hubeibeh, whose ashes are called El-Kuli (Alkali), apparently one of the numerous species of Salsola.[5]

In the foreground is the pass leading to the Monastery of St. Saba. The Dead Sea is in the distance.

[1] Roberts's Journal.   [2] Biblical Researches, ii. 208.   [3]Roberts's Journal.
[4] I Sam. xxiv. 1-4.   [5] Biblical Researches, ii. 210.

Island of Graia, Gulf of Akabah

THIS name has been given to the Island by Laborde; why, it is difficult to say. The Beni-Sa'id Arabs called it "Ascala el Dair," from the ruins of a Castle or Convent which existed on it, and which was occupied, according to the Arabs, before the times of the Crusades. Their tradition is, that a great City once existed in the Island, with a magnificent harbour, and that the entrance was defended by a chain, which was stretched across four or five miles! and tribute paid by all vessels entering. Now, not a solitary sail is ever seen. The waters teem with fish; but only one man was seen at Akabah pursuing fishing as an employment; he sat across a log of wood, and used two palm-branches as oars; yet he caught a great number of excellent fish, and supplied the Caravan of the Artist's party with a great treat after the fare of the Desert.[1]

Whether the site of Akabah, or of the ruined City on the Island, be that of the great port of the Edomites (the probability is in favour of the latter) — still this locality is interesting, as associated with sacred history. Elath was not retained by the Jews more than 150 years after the conquest of the Edomites, by David. In the reign of Joram they revolted,[2] but were defeated by him, and again rebelled. Under Azariah, the power of the Jews was re-established; he is said to have built and restored Elath to Judah; but it was taken by Rezin, King of Syria,[3] in the reign of Ahaz, and never again recovered by the Jews. Elath afterwards fell into the hands of the Ptolemies, then of the Romans, the Greek Emperors, the Arabians, the Sultans of Egypt, the Turks, and finally of Mehemed Ali. Its importance was destroyed by the change in the course of commerce, which, instead of finding its great outlet to the Mediterranean at Tyre, took the Western arm of the Gulf to Alexandria.

Burckhardt, on the authority of Makrizi, the Egyptian historian, says, that it was once the frontier station of the Greeks; that here formerly existed a triumphal arch of the Cæsars; and that, in the time of the Islam, a fine town, inhabited by the Beni-Omeya, containing many mosques. It was taken by the Franks during the Crusades; but Saladin recovered it, by transporting ships upon camels from Cairo. Near Akabah was a large handsome town, called Afzyoun (according to the name, Ezion-Geber), and this supports the idea that Elath and Ezion-Geber were distinct cities.

De Laborde, on his journey to Petra, determined to visit the Island of Graia, upon which no European had set foot since the time of the Crusades. He and his companions constructed a rude raft, for the people possessed no vessel on those waters by which they could reach it. They landed in safety; reached the ruins of the Fortress on the Island; made a survey, and walked round the Island, which they found to have a circumference of about 1800 English feet. De Laborde found a large excavation, intended for a reservoir, and a finely-constructed cistern, which from its structure appeared to be of a date anterior to the Fortress. His sketch of the history of Graia is very short;— after having been a kind of suburb to Elath, from the earliest period of the navigation of this Gulf, and its defence against tribes which it was difficult to subdue; it became the theatre of Christian valour in the time of the Crusades; but was wholly abandoned about the fourteenth century.

The forms of the Island and its ruins, backed by the distant range of mountains, and the effect under which they are represented, give great beauty to this highly picturesque subject.

[1] Roberts's Journal.   [2] 2 Kings, viii. 20-22   [3] 2 Kings, xvi. 5.

David Roberts R.A.

Plate 105: Island of Graia, Gulf of Akabah (Eilat)

PLATE 105: ISLAND OF GRAIA, GULF OF AKABAH (EILAT)

David Roberts R.A

Convent of St. Catherine, Mount Sinai

THIS Convent has been built in the form of a square fortress of hewn granite, and flanked with towers, of which one or two have cannon. Thus situated, in a country where, from the general helplessness of the Monks, it would not remain unmolested by the Arabs for a single day, its strength forms the chief security of the inhabitants; for it is accessible only by a projecting trap-door, guarded by another of iron, about thirty feet above the ground. The means of access are a capstan and rope, with a loop at the end, to which travellers fasten themselves, and are thus drawn up. The Convent is large, and resembles a small town, containing many buildings, several courts, and storehouses, a Mosque, with a minaret[1] and a Chapel celebrated as the richest in the land. It has an inexhaustible supply of pure water, from a well, which the Brethren point out to the traveller as that of Jethro, the father-in-law of Moses, to which the great lawgiver led his flocks,[2] while he was yet living in obscurity in Midian.

The convent has been built upon the spot where, according to tradition, the Almighty first manifested Himself to Moses, and spake to him out of the burning bush, "Cast off thy shoes, for the spot whereon thou standest is holy ground."

From the sacred character of the spot, many ascetics and anchorites established themselves in recesses in these Mountains as early as the fourth century; but tradition relates, that the Convent was established by Justinian, A.D. 527, on the site where a small Church had been built by the Empress Helena.

[1] The Mosque, a singular object in a Christian Convent, is said to have been built by Mahomet, who gave the Monks a letter of protection, a copy of which is still shown. The Mountain is visited, and highly venerated, by the Mahometans.
[2] Exodus, iii. 1.

From the Journal

5th May, 1839

This morning I was informed by my servant that my mules had been seized by the government to carry corn for the troops. I lost no time in waiting on the governor, whom I found seated in his divan, surrounded by one of the most picturesque groups I have ever seen. I was placed on his left hand; my servant filled my chabouk, and coffee was served round, after which I produced my firman. To my surprise no one could read it, as it was in the Turkish language. The signature of Abbas Pasha was recognised, and the governor apologised for our mules having been carried off, and gave orders for them immediately to be returned. I told him I was desirous to visit Damascus, from which I was within two days' journey, when he kindly offered to send a guard with me, and gave me a letter to the governor.

PLATE 107: ROCK OF MOSES, WADY-EL-LEJA, MOUNT HO

Rock of Moses,
Wady-El-Leja, Mount Horeb

WADY-EL-LEJA is a narrow Valley running up into the Mountains, and containing the deserted Convent of El-Arbain. It lies parallel to the valley containing the Convent of St. Catherine, and is West of Horeb. The view from the entrance gives one of the finest aspects of the granite range, the front of Horeb rising perpendicularly to the height of nearly fifteen hundred feet.[1]

The "Rock of Moses" is, from its size, a remarkable object: it rests isolated where it has fallen from the eastern Mountain above. It is of red granite, hard enough to account for the expression, "a rock of flint."[2] According to recent measurement, it is fifteen feet long, ten feet wide, and twelve feet high.[3] Down the front of this Rock, in an oblique direction, runs a seam, twelve or fourteen inches broad, of apparently a softer material; the Rock, also, has ten or twelve deep horizontal crevices, at nearly equal distances from each other. "On close examination," says the Artist, "I felt convinced that they were not artificial, from the nature of the Rock. I think it must have formed the vault of a cave or recess, through which water had oozed for ages, and left the present appearance."[4]

The reverence with which every object associated with Scripture is regarded in these regions by pilgrims and travellers, is strikingly observable here. This mass of stone is believed to be the actual Rock which was struck by Moses at the command of the Lord, when water gushed forth to supply the Israelites in the Desert. "Behold I will stand before thee there, upon the rock in Horeb; and thou shalt smite the rock, and there shall come water out of it, that the people may drink. And Moses did so in the sight of the elders of Israel."[5] The Arabs also call it the Rock of Moses; and the reverence of the Bedouins for the relic is scarcely less than that of the Christians.

From the Journal

(Continued)

I wish my friend Wilkie had witnessed this scene. No two of the party were dressed alike, and it was impossible to say which was the most pictureque. Two Bedouin chiefs were the finest specimens of men I had ever seen. The walls were hung round with rich habiliments and accoutrements, and the hosts of attendants bustling about gave a vitality to the whole strangely at variance with the dreariness and desolation around.

8th May, 1839

Having completed a number of drawings, I left Baalbec this morning, and, having given up the idea of visiting Damascus, owing to the unsettled state of the country, I travelled through the chain of Lebanon to Beyrout. We halted for the night at Zalileh, which we left the following morning at 7 o'clock, and in eight hours reached a sort of caravansary in the mountains, where we pitched our tents. On our way we saw several hamlets, some with chapels and belfries. The road led to Damascus, and there were numerous strings of mules laden with food for the army, the troops of the Sultan and of the Pasha being within fifteen hours of each other.

[1] Bibl. Res. i. 130.   [2] Carne's Travels.   [3] Deut. viii. 15.   [4] Roberts's Journal.
[5] Exodus, xvii. 6.

Interior of the Chapel of St. Catherine

"THIS view," says the artist, "represents the interior of probably the oldest and the richest of all the Eastern churches; its remote and sacred situation, its strength of structure and position, and the deep veneration in which it is held by Mahometans as well as Christians, have favoured its preservation, and secured it in the possession of its riches and relics. From its foundation in the sixth century, down to our day, it has been protected from plunder, though the country in which it is situated has been invaded by lawless conquerors, and it has always been surrounded by tribes of marauders. Its wealth is very great in all that belongs to its Chapel, which is guarded with much jealousy. This, probably, was the reason why so many difficulties were thrown in my way when I attempted to make a sketch of the interior of the Chapel. The brotherhood, though kind in the extreme, and though they allowed me to draw in every other part of the Convent, and themselves sat for sketches and studies, yet always found some excuse, whenever I proposed to make a drawing of the Chapel; they had mislaid the key, or some such frivolous reason. At length, I fairly took out my sketch-book during service; they could not interrupt me while engaged in their sacred duties; and I thus effected my object."

The present Convent was built in the sixth century by the Emperor Justinian, and some of the enrichments and decorations are of that period. Like other Greek churches, it possesses a rich and gilded screen, and contains pictures of the saints of the Greek calendar. Moses and Aaron, of course, hold conspicuous places in a spot made sacred by the eventful history of the great Lawgiver. The Screen separates the Altar from the congregation, and conceals the Patriarch from the people when he reads the service to which they respond. Its separation may be intended to represent that of the Jewish Holy Place. Though the pictures of saints and Scriptural subjects are profuse, there are no images, as in the Latin churches. The floor of the Chapel is beautifully inlaid with variegated marble; and on the right is seen a magnificent throne for the Patriarch, or Bishop. The Altar is inlaid with ebony and mother-of-pearl, of the most elaborate and beautiful designs, and is probably, as well as many of the pictures, the work of Byzantine artists. It is covered with costly and ancient votive offerings, most of them enriched with precious stones. Yet the riches of this Altar sink into insignificance when compared with those of the Chapel behind it, raised on the spot on which it is believed that Moses saw the burning bush. "Through this sacred place we were hurried, after we had been requested to uncover our feet, 'for the place whereon thou standest is holy ground.' We were, therefore, not allowed leisure for the examination of the Altar; but the walls, and even the roof, were covered with the gifts and offerings of Emperors, Kings, and Princes, from the period of its foundation. The floor was covered with the richest and most costly Persian carpets. On the left, as we entered, we saw the tomb containing the relics of St. Catherine, which were said to have been transported by angels, after her martyrdom at Alexandria, to the summit of Mount Sinai, whence they were brought down by the Monks to their present resting-place, and where they have ever since been held in the most profound veneration."[1]

[1] Roberts's Journal.

Plate 108: Interior of the Chapel of St. Catherine

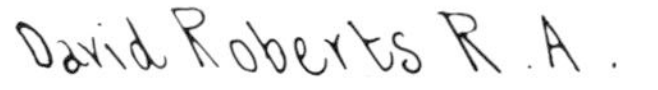

David Roberts R.A.

Above: The Artist's Signature.

The text on the opposite page describes the following double-spread Plate.

Encampment of the Aulad-Sa'id

THIS scene represents the arrival of the caravan of the Artist and his companions, in the country, and at the tents of the Aulad-Sa'id. They were friendly with the Beni-Sa'id, under whose guidance and protection he travelled.[1] The Aulad-Sa'id were encamped close to the base of Mount Serbal. The Mountain is red granite, without a trace of vegetation; and rises majestically to the height of five thousand feet. The powerful tribe which finds its home in this district has been the guardian of the Convent of St. Catherine, from perhaps the period of its foundation. One of the travellers on this occasion thus describes the general appearance of the Arab community.

"At five o'clock we arrived at the encampment of the Aulad-Sa'id. Our painted pavilions looked a litte out of place beside the black Arab tents, which were more in character with the dark and wild mountains which formed the back-ground of the picture, and the wild figures who were moving about. The whole scene was quite patriarchal in its character, and carried the mind back to the times when men were hunters, and shepherds in the field, and dwellers in tents. A kid had been killed for us, and our servants were busy, cooking it at a fire in the open air: before one of the tents, two women, seated on the ground, were grinding at a small hand-mill, one turning the stone, while the other poured in the corn: at another, a girl was baking the Arab bread for us. The camels, relieved from their burdens, were cropping the scanty herbage around the tents: troops of boys and girls were driving home the goats from their pasture in the neighbouring valleys; and although some of the highest peaks were still lighted by the setting sun, the moon was beginning to shed a sweet silvery light over the valley."[2]

"Here," says Robinson, "was a fine view of Mount Serbal: as thus seen it presents the appearance of a long, thin, lofty ridge of granite, with numerous points or peaks, of which there are reckoned five principal ones, the whole being strictly what the Germans call a *Kämm*. We saw it now in the bright beams of a morning sun, a grand and noble object, as its ragged peaks were defined upon the deep azure beyond... Here the interior peaks of the great circle of Sinai began to open upon us — black, rugged, desolate summits; and as we advanced, the dark and frowning front of Sinai itself (the present Horeb of the Monks) began to appear. We were still gradually ascending, and the valley gradually opening; but as yet all was a naked desert. Afterwards, a few shrubs were sprinkled round, and a small encampment of black tents

was seen on our right, with camels and goats browsing, and some asses belonging to the Convent. The scenery through which we now passed, reminded me strongly of the Mountains around the Mer de Glace, in Switzerland. I had never seen a spot more wild and desolate."[3]

But it is to be recollected that, although in these Sketches the customary names of the Mountains have been adopted, their claims as the sites of the Delivery of the Law have excited much learned discussion. Jebel Mousa, the Sinai of the Monks, exhibits features incompatible with the Sacred History; Jebel Katerin, the loftier peak of Horeb (which is now regarded as the original name of the range), seems scarcely less incompatible. It has been strongly argued,[4] that the true Mountain of the Law was Mount Serbal, anciently named Paran; the most conspicuous, and the first, object in the entrance to the Wilderness; a Mountain, wholly separate, of sublime elevation, and of the most striking form and magnitude.

To a people whose entire living generation had seen only the level lands of Egypt, the Israelite march into this region of mountain magnificence, with its sharp and splintered peaks and profound valleys, must have been a perpetual source of astonishment and awe. No nobler school could have been conceived, for training a nation of slaves into a nation of freemen, or weaning a people from the grossness of idolatry to a sense of the grandeur and power of the God alike of Nature and Mind.

[1] Roberts's Journal.   [2] Kinnear's Cairo, Petra, and Damascus.
[3] Biblical Researches, i. 125, 130.   [4] Note in the Pictorial Bible.

Christian & Mahomedan Chapels on the Summit of Sinai   Feby 20th 1839

David Roberts R.A.

Summit of Mount Sinai
(The Chapels)

THOSE Chapels are placed on what is traditionally regarded as the summit of Sinai, but the peak distinguished as Mount St. Catherine has a greater elevation. The ascent from the Convent employs about two hours, and the spectator is rewarded by a scene of the most striking magnificence. Around, beneath, and above, all is grandeur; he stands as in the Alps, in the midst of a region of Mountains; but with a feature of beauty wanting in the Alps—the expanse of a brilliant sea, a part of the Gulf of Akabah being in sight. The Chapels on the summit are in singular juxtaposition (Christian and Mahometan); but both in a state of ruin from neglect and exposure to the storm.

The Mountain is held sacred by the Mahometans; for the legend tells, that when the Prophet rode on the sacred Camel to Ararat and back in one night, he rested, in passing, on Sinai, and the mark of the Burack, or Camel's foot, where it touched the mountain, is still shown by his followers. The Artist, having heard this tradition, asked his guide from the Convent to point it out to him; but the holy brother of St. Catherine did his bidding very reluctantly.[1] It is a few yards below, and beyond, the Chapel to the right. It has the exact form, and is not larger than the impression which the foot of a camel would make. Marks, thus connected with fable, are not infrequent in religious legend. On the summit of a Ceylonese mountain, the shape of a gigantic foot is an object of native homage, as exhibiting the parting step of Adam! The freaks of Nature are easily seized by fancy or modified by art; and the Mahometan is as much entitled to the exercise of his imagination as the Monk.

[1] Roberts's Journal.

From the Journal

10th May, 1839

The weather was delicious this morning when we started. The road is bad, and renders access to the mountains difficult. Every cranny and overhanging crag has its patch of green corn; the loose stones being carefully piled together, forming a support for the soil. Terraces rise in endless succession, and the whole rock seems overspread with hanging gardens. On our descent we found all the country thickly studded with villages, very clean and comfortable, each with its little church and modest belfry, always so pleasant to the eyes of European travellers.

Beyrout is one of the prettiest towns in Syria. Its climate and situation are delightful, and it is in the centre of the Maronites and the Druses, the most industrious people in the country. It is the residence of the various consuls, and a number of merchants. I called on the English Consul, Mr. Moore, who received me very kindly; and I met there my old companions of the Wady Mousa, Mr. Kinnear and Mr. Robertson.

Ascent of the Lower Range of Sinai

THE whole career of the Israelites, from the passage of the Red Sea to their entrance into Palestine, was a display of Miracle. Yet, such is the Divine adherence to the great law of free agency, that even Miracle was regulated by its action. The Divine Will might, obviously, at a word have transformed the native stiff-neckedness of the Israelite into perfect obedience, have extinguished his recollections alike of Egyptian enjoyment and Egyptian idolatry, and sent him at once into Palestine as its consecrated possessor. But those essential results, instead of being the work of Miracle, were left to be the work of Time. The nation was retained in the Wilderness until all the elder race had disappeared in the course of nature; until the recollections of their house, at once of temptation and bondage, had sunk with them into the grave; and until a new people had been formed, knowing no God but Jehovah; trained only by His law, guided only by His presence, and prepared to triumph only in His name. The Desert then remained a limit to them no more. The same resistless Power which had bound up a whole nation in this sterile and awful place of discipline, threw open its barrier, and the Israelite marched forth invigorated in his frame by the simple life of the Wilderness, and enlightened in his heart by its religion: a new and noble nature, prepared not only to conquer, but to govern; not only to be the lord of Palestine, but to stand forth the model to the world.

This Sketch gives a portion of the Israelite march to Sinai. The scene is thus graphically described:— "The black and frowning mountains before us, the outworks as it were of Sinai, rose abrupt and rugged from their very base, eight hundred to a thousand feet in height, as if forbidding all approach to the sanctuary within. On the west of the Pass, the cliffs bear the name of Jebel-el-Haweit . . . At 12¾ o'clock, we began gradually to ascend towards the foot of the Pass before us, called by our Arabs Nukb Hâwy (Windy Pass), and by Burckhardt Nukb er-Râhah, from the tract above it. We reached the foot at a quarter past one o'clock, and dismounting, commenced the slow and toilsome ascent along the narrow defile, about S. by E., between blackened, shattered cliffs of granite, some eight hundred feet high, and not more than two hundred and fifty yards apart, which every moment threaten to send down their ruins on the head of the traveller. Nor is this at all times an empty threat; for the whole Pass is filled with large stones and rocks, the débris of those cliffs. The bottom is a deep and narrow water-course, where the wintry torrent sweeps down with fearful violence. A path has been made for camels along the shelving piles of rocks, partly by removing the topmost blocks, and sometimes by laying down large stones side by side, somewhat in the manner of a Swiss mountain-road. But although I had crossed the most rugged passes of the Alps, and made from Chamouny the whole circuit of Mont Blanc, I never found a path so rude and difficult as that which we were now ascending. The camels toiled slowly and painfully along, stopping frequently; so that though it took them two hours and a quarter to reach the top of the Pass, the distance cannot be reckoned at more than one hour."[1]

The Artist says, "After winding through this terrific Pass for about three hours, night closed around us, before reaching the Plain, at the extremity of which stands the Convent. The effect of the setting sun upon the high peaks which overhung the Pass, whilst the ravine below was enveloped in shadow, was a sight of remarkable beauty. The pathway which wound up the face of the Mountain, the work of a remote age, and which must have been one of prodigious labour, was now neglected and broken by the mountain-torrents. Other parts were overgrown, and displaced by the roots of the wild plants, which everywhere projected from the cliffs and hollows of the rocks. Huge fragments, which had been loosened by the rains of winter, had rolled down, and choked the narrow pathway, rendering it difficult for our small caravan to thread its course, especially when darkness overtook us."[2]

[1] Biblical Researches, i. 129.   [2] Roberts's Journal.

Plate 111: Ascent to the lower range of Sinai

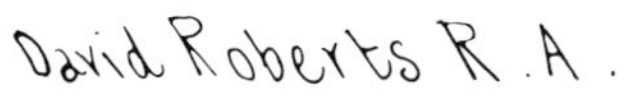

David Roberts R.A.

Above: The Artist's Signature.

The text on the opposite page describes the following double-spread Plate.

Ascent of the lower range of Sinai
February 16 1839

Ascent to the Summit of Sinai. Sep 24th 1844.

Ascent to the Summit of Sinai

LABORDE describes his course, towards the summit of Sinai, as lying through a ravine to the south-west. The Monks had originally arranged a series of slabs in tolerably regular order, which once formed a convenient staircase to the top of the Mountain. The rains, however, disturbed them, and as no repairs have for a long time been attended to, the stairs are in many places in ruins. On approachig the foot of Sinai, and immediately before quitting Horeb, the traveller sees a door built in the form of an arch; on the key-stone of the arch, a cross has been carved. An affecting custom used to take place near this door; one of the Monks of the Convent stationed himself there in prayer, and heard the confessions of the pilgrims, who, when thus nearly at the end of their pilgrimage, were not in the habit of accomplishing it until after they had obtained absolution. Laborde passed a similar door before arriving at the spot whence he discovered the summit of Sinai, and the two edifices which surmount it.[1]

The condition of the staircase appears since to have grown more ruinous, for the Artist, twenty years afterwards, observes, "In many places the steps have given way, and rolled down, and at the time when we ascended, the snow lay deep in the places sheltered from the sun, and the way was so slippery from the ice, as to render the ascent not only a work of great difficulty, but of some danger."[2] Those steps are of great antiquity, and appear to have been constructed at least as early as the time of the first devotees who established themselves in the Mountains of the Wilderness.

[1] Journey to Mount Sinai. [2] Roberts's Journal.

From the Journal

11th May, 1839

Occupied all day arranging for my voyage to Alexandria.

12th May, 1839

Dined with Mr. Kinnear and other friends; and on the morning of the 13th took leave of Palestine, and embarked on board the 'Majorca' for Alexandria, where we landed after a voyage of three days. During my stay here I was presented by Colonel Campbell to Mehemet Ali, who, at the request of his son, Said Bey, sat to me for his portrait. Leaving Alexandria, we reached Malta in six days, and were kept in quarantine for three weeks, after which I left in the 'Volcano' for Gibraltar. Keeping close to the coast of Africa, we had an excellent view of Algiers, and in about five days we reached the rock. Thence I proceeded to Cadiz, where I stayed a week with the consul, my old friend Mr. Brackenbury, and again left, in the 'Braganza,' for England, staying by the way two days at Lisbon, and landed safely, thank God, in London, on the 21st July, having been eleven months absent.

Convent of St. Catherine, Mount Sinai
(Looking towards the Plain of the Encampment)

IN this title, the traditional name of the Mountain is adopted, without deciding the question of reality. The Artist has taken the Sketch about due South of the Convent, looking upon the track which he pursued from the presumed Plain of the Israelite Encampment.

The general aspects of both the Plain and Mountain unquestionably give a strong sense of fitness for that great transaction, of which the direct purpose was to impress a nation of slaves, Egyptian-born, with homage for the God of Nature and of Revelation. The primitive wildness, the abrupt majesty, and the almost inaccessible height of the pinnacles, seem made for the Throne of Him who "maketh the clouds His chariot, and walketh upon the wings of the wind." Here, superior as the actual Presence must have been to all Imagination, the traveller can still imagine the "cloud, the lightning, and the trumpet." The scene amply filled the mind of a Prophet almost a thousand years after. Habakkuk, in one of the most renowned bursts of Hebrew poetry, thus records the Descent on Sinai: "God came from Teman, and the Holy One from Mount Paran. His brightness was as the light; He had horns coming out of His hand; and there was the hiding of His power. Before Him went the pestilence, and burning coals went forth at His feet. He stood, and measured the earth; He beheld, and drove asunder the nations, and the everlasting mountains were scattered, the perpetual hills did bow; His ways are everlasting."[1]

The author of the Biblical Researches, when he entered upon the Plain, observes,— "As we advanced, the valley opened still wider and wider, with a gentle ascent, and became full of shrubs and tufts of herbs, shut in on each side by lofty granite ridges, with rugged, shattered peaks, a thousand feet high, while the face of Horeb rose directly before us. Both my companion and myself involuntarily exclaimed, 'Here is room enough for a large encampment!' As we crossed the Plain our feelings were strongly affected, at finding here so unexpectedly a spot so entirely adapted to the Scriptural account of the Giving of the Law.[2] No traveller has described this Plain, or even mentioned it, except in a slight and general manner; probably because most of them have reached the Convent by another route. . . As we approached the Mountain, our head Arab, Beshârah, became evidently quite excited. He prayed that our pilgrimage might be accepted, and bring rain; and with great earnestness besought, that when we ascended the Mountain, we should open a cetain window in the Chapel there towards the South, which, he said, would certainly cause rain to fall. He also entreated, almost with tears, that we should induce the Monks to have compassion on the people, and say prayers, as they ought to do, for rain. When told that God alone could send rain, and that they should look to Him for it, he replied, 'Yes, but the Monks have the book of prayer for it; do persuade them to use it as they ought.' There was an earnestness in his manner which was very affecting, but cannot be described." The Arab's solicitation was trivial; but it was evidently connected with the holiness of the ground.

Having, with his companion, obtained admission to the Convent, the traveller says,— "I was affected by the strangeness and overpowering grandeur of the scenes around us; and it was for some time difficult to realise the consciousness that we were now actually within the very precincts of that Sinai, on which from the earliest childhood I had thought and read with so much wonder. Yet, when at length the impression came with its full force upon my mind, although not given to the melting mood, I could not refrain from bursting into tears."

[1] Habakuk, iii. 3.   [2] Exodus, xix. 20   [3] Biblical Researches, i. 130-134.

General View of the Convent of St. Catherine

THE whole scene of the sojourning of the Israelites lies in a Peninsula, between the forks of the upper portion of the Red Sea. The Peninsula is of a triangular form, and from about half way down to its point at the South is a mass of mountains, intersected with deep valleys, and exhibiting a few barren plains.

The geographical position of the convent is in Lat. 28° and Long. 31° from Paris. The elevation above the sea is about 4966 Paris feet.

Allusion has been already made to the differences of learned opinion on the site of the Giving of the Law. It appears that Jebel-Mûsa (the Mount of Moses) exhibits no features corresponding to the Sacred History. Robinson, to whose judgment and diligence much respect is due, regards the Plain Er-Râhah, with the Mount now named Horeb immediately in its front, as the most probable locality. but he admits that he had not visited Jebel-Serbal. He also regards Horeb as anciently the name of the whole range, and Sinai as that of a particular pinnacle; arguing from the narrative, which, before and after the Giving of the Law, speaks only of Horeb; while during that great transaction Sinai (with one exception) alone is named. "As we advanced," he says, "the dark and frowning front of Sinai itself (the present Horeb of the Monks) began to appear. It was a scene of solemn grandeur wholly unexpected, and such as we had never before seen; and the associations which at the moment rested upon our minds were almost overwhelming. . . Still advancing, the front of Horeb rose like a wall before us, and one can approach quite to the foot, and touch the Mount."[1]

He narrates a visit which he and his companion made to many of the peaks of Sinai; but not satisfied that the view from those agreed with the Scripture account, they decided upon scaling the almost inaccessible peak of Es-Sufsâfeh, the pinnacle of Horeb above the Convent. "We first attempted," he says, "to climb the side in a direct course, but found the rock so smooth and precipitous, that after some falls, we were obliged to give it up, and clamber upwards along a steep ravine by a more circuitous course. . . The extreme difficulty, and even danger of the ascent, was well rewarded by the prospect that opened before us. The whole plain Er-Râhah lay spread out beneath our feet, with the adjacent Wadys and Mountains; while Wady Esh-Sheikh on the right, and the recess on the left, both connected with and opening broadly from Er-Râhah, presented an area which seems nearly double that of the plain. Our conviction was strengthened, that here or on some one of the adjacent cliffs, was the spot where the Lord 'descended in fire' and proclaimed the Law. Here lay the plain where the whole congregation might be assembled; here was the mount that could be approached and 'touched;' and here the mountain-brow, where alone the lightnings and the thick cloud would be visible to the Camp, when the Lord 'came down in the sight of all the people upon Mount Sinai.' [2]

The primary purpose of the Law was to establish the morality of mankind. It was the first instance, from the days of Noah, in which peculiar sins were marked by Divine condemnation. The general impulse of natural justice had already prohibited crimes palpably injurious to society. But the Law not simply strengthened that original impulse, but gave it a new distinctness, a new force, and a new authority. It was revealed, as the Apostle declares, "on account of transgressions." And, as fear of punishment is the natural guard against the commission of crime, the "terrors of the Lord" were displayed to the eyes of the people. All, hitherto, had been preparative to Divine awe. The miraculous passage of the Red Sea, the miraculous support in the Wilderness, the surrounding scene of utter desolation, the daily rescue from famine; were all combined in creating a sense of total dependence. But the Giving of the Law presented a new character of Jehovah. The people had, till then, seen Him only as their Protector. They were now to see Him as their Judge. Death was to be proclaimed against national and individual crime; and the wild hills, the continual thunders, the cloudy throne, and the angelic trumpet, were only accessories to that sacred terror, which was to be consummated by the voice of God Himself, pronouncing the principles of moral government for all the generations of man.

Plate 114: General View of the Convent of St. Catherine

David Roberts R.A.

Above: The Artist's Signature.

The text on the opposite page describes the following double-spread Plate.

PLATE 114: GENERAL VIEW OF THE CONVENT OF ST. CATHERINE

Chapel of Elijah, Mount Sinai

AFTER passing the second portal in the ascent by the steps or stairs in the ravine, the traveller reaches a little plain or basin, in the ridge which divides the valley of the Convent from that of El-Leja, and here he first perceives the loftier peaks of the range; that of Jebel Mûsa on the left, and that of St. Catherine on the south-west beyond the valley of El-Leja. In this plain is a cypress-tree, near a deep well; and on a rock near it are several Arabic inscriptions, records of pilgrimage.[1] Not far from the well, and where the ascent commences, is a rude, low building, which contains the "Chapel of Elijah." It is raised on the spot to which he is presumed, by tradition, to have retired, when he fled into the wilderness from Jezebel, the wife of Ahab, in the general oppression of the Church of Israel. Within the Chapel, and on one side of the altar, is seem (on the left of the Sketch) a small cave, in which the Prophet is said to have remained. "And he came thither unto a cave, and lodged there; and, behold, the word of the Lord came to him, and said, What doest thou here, Elijah?"[2]

This little Greek Chapel is interesting, though in a state of ruin, placed as it is in front of a spot thus venerated. Pictures of saints, with lighted tapers, and other decorations of the Eastern Church, are, even in this wild place, displayed.

The Greek Church draws a broad distinction between statues and pictures in its places of worship. The former it anathematizes, while the latter it consecrates, assigning as the reason, the language of the Apostle (1 Cor. viii. 4); and pronouncing the image to be "a work of man's invention, while the picture is an adumbration of some true event, or actual existence;" their chief dependence for this opinion being the authority of the fourth General Council. The use of tapers and torches in the service in daylight is regarded by them as a memorial of the primitive and persecuted Church, when the Christians met before daylight for security, or in subterranean cells for concealment.

[1] Biblical Researches, i. 152   [2] I Kings, xix.9.

From the Journal

(Continued)

Previously to my leaving for the East I had promised to give the Messrs. Finden the refusal of the work, and on my return, after having arranged the form in which it was to be brought out, these gentlemen promised to let me know what terms they would give me for the copyright and use of the drawings. After having waited four months without having received any offer from them, I applied to Mr. Murray, who at first agreed to my proposal; but after calculating the outlay (£10,000), told me the risk was too great. I have been applied to by Mr. Moon, whom I made acquainted with all these circumstances, and he at once agreed to bring out the work in the manner I had proposed — viz. two volumes on Syria, containing 120 subjects, price £21; two volumes on Egypt, containing 120 subjects, price £21; and one volume on Modern Cairo, containing 60 subjects, price £10: 10s — in all, £52:10s. I was to be paid £3000 for the use of the drawings. This was a great risk on the publisher's part; but by exhibiting the drawings in London and other principal towns, his subscription-list in May 1841 was nearly double Murray's estimate of cost.

An Ancient Egyptian Temple on Gebel Garabe

THIS title has been given, as the one adopted in the country; although there exists some doubt of the propriety of its application.[1] A wilder spot cannot be imagined. The ruins lie in the Desert, on the summit of a mountain, of no great elevation, but of difficult access. These extraordinary relics of an unknown period were discovered by Niebuhr in 1761; and though often visited since, the inscriptions have defied every attempt made to apply to them our growing knowledge of the Egyptian hieroglyphic character. No real approach has yet been obtained to the origin, or the purport, of these erections. One of the later conjectures is, that it was an ancient place of pilgrimage, and that the upright stones covered with inscriptions were votive rather than sepulchral monuments.[2]

The Artist made several exact copies of the inscriptions, but none of them have yet been deciphered. "They lie within a small enclosure on the mountain, 160 feet long by 70 feet broad. Within this space are about fifteen upright stones, like tombstones, and several fallen ones, covered with hieroglyphics, and also the remains of a small Temple, whose columns are decorated with the head of Isis for a capital." The whole summit is covered with upright and fallen stones, some of them evidently fragments of structures. Several of the stones and the inscriptions are remarkably well preserved; others are worn away and decayed. "What could have been the intent of these temples and memorial stones in the midst of solitude and silence, in this lone and distant land with which they would seem to have no possible connexion? This is a point wrapped in the darkness of time, and which the hand of modern science has not yet unveiled."[3]

[1] Roberts's Journal.   [2] Lord Prudhoe.   [3] Bib. Res. i. 116.

From the Journal

(Continued)

What gratified me, perhaps, more than anything else, was that the subscription in my native town amounted to £1200; a much larger sum in proportion to its wealth and population than was subscribed in London. Before the drawings were shown to the public they were submitted to the Queen, to the Archbishops of York and Canterbury, and to the Bishop of London, who all subscribed for the work, the Queen graciously allowing it to be dedicated to her. It was at one time agreed that Mr. Harding and Mr. Louis Haghe were to have lithographed the drawings, but it was ultimately arranged that they should all be done by Mr. Haghe, and there can be only one opinion as to the masterly manner in which he executed his work. The notices given by the public journals, wherever these drawings were exhibited, were highly laudatory; the work, when completed, was equally favourably noticed; and the success of the publication was all that could be desired.

Principal Court of the Convent of St. Catherine

THE Artist, in this View, introduces the costume of the Monks of St. Catherine. The Superior is distinguished by a black cloak; the rest of the Brotherhood wear robes of the striped brown cloth spun from the hair of camels and goats, such as are in use among the Bedouins. The Monks, who do not exceed twenty in number, are the tailors, shoemakers, bakers, brewers, carpenters, and other handicraftsmen, of the Convent. The Superior, at this period, was an intelligent and courteous person; he had travelled long, and in the chief countries of Europe; his visit to England was a subject on which he was eloquent.[1]

Most of the Monks are natives of the Greek Islands. In general, they do not remain in the Convent more than from four to five years; when they return to their country, proud of their having been "sufferers among the Bedouins;" some, however, have been here forty years. Their rules are strict with regard to food and prayer; they are obliged to attend mass twice a-day and twice in the night, and they taste no flesh all the year round; four days a week they live on bread and vegetables; the latter they cultivate in a pleasant garden adjoining the building, into which there is a subterraneous passage. The soil is strong, but in this climate, wherever water is in plenty, almost the very rocks will produce vegetation. Their fruits are oranges, lemons, almonds, mulberries, apricots, peaches, pears, apples, and olives and all of the finest quality. Nebek trees, and a few cypresses, overshade the beds in which melons, cucumbers, and various kinds of culinary and sweet-scented herbs, are grown. The garden is, however, seldom visited by the Monks, except the few whose business it is to keep it in order, for although surrounded by high walls, it is not inaccessible to the Bedouins, who steal the fruit, and sell it to the Monks; but they leave untouched the other productions of the garden.[2] The Convent contains eight or ten small court-yards, some of which are neatly laid out in beds of flowers and vegetables, with dates and many vines. Its apparent space within and the variety of its appropriation surprise every traveller. The number of small rooms in the lower and upper stories formerly exceeded three hundred. It contains also storerooms for provisions, bakehouses, &c., and besides the Great Church, it has Chapels for the separate worship of the Syrian, Coptic, Armenian, and Latin Christians, and, what naturally still more excites surprise, a Mosque; which, as has been already mentioned, was built by a species of compact, in the sixteenth century, to preserve the Convent from destruction by the Arabs.

[1] Roberts's Journal.   [2] Burckhardt's Travels.

Wells of Moses Wilderness of Tyh. February 12th 1839.   David Roberts. R.A.

Eyun Musa,
The Wells of Moses

THESE Fountains lie on the East side of the Gulf of Suez, near the shore; and are close to the spot where the Israelites (traditionally) reached the coast, after the miraculous passage of the Red Sea. The Wells vary in number, in the accounts of travellers; generally from seven to ten, or even up to fifteen; they are probably subject to change; from some the waters escape, or they are filled up, and others are again excavated. The water is brackish, a taste to which habit or necessity can alone reconcile the traveller. About twenty stunted palm-trees, or palm-bushes, grow around in the sand. A little barley is irrigated from some of the Fountains, which gives the spot a peculiar value in the eyes of Suez; it being the only effort of cultivation in the neighbourhood. Near the Fountains is a low mound of fragments of tiles and pottery with some foundations, indicating the site of a former village.[1]

But the true interest in the whole shore arises from its having been traversed by the host of Israel. At every halt of the multitude, water must have been of the first importance. Its supply in such an exigency must have been wholly miraculous. The natural supply is utterly impossible. A single caravan, perhaps a single camel, would now exhaust the Fountains, which, under the rod of Moses, supplied, from day to day, the thirst of millions!

[1] Biblical Researches, i.99.

Enfield, 6th March, 1840.

My Dear Roberts,— Although so long a time has elapsed without my being able to see you until the other day, I did not even then mention the principal object of my visit to you, for in company is not the best way to transact private business. It was merely to say, that if in consequence of your long and expensive trip in the East, and recent change of residence, you should require some ready funds for your present purposes, you would not, I hope, stand upon any ceremony in making such wants known to me, as I might assist you, as you must clearly understand, without any other interest than the satisfaction of serving a friend. I trust our friendship will justify me in your eyes for taking this liberty, for unless I felt so you may be sure I would not have said a word about it.

Let me know if I can be useful to you; and believe me now, as I have always been, yours faithfully,

Wm. Mark

Approach to Mount Sinai

THIS View is taken from the Encampment of the Artist and his party: and exhibits the first aspect of the Chain of Sinai to the traveller approaching from Suez.

The Sketches of Sinai have been variously given in this work; for the purpose of rendering the untravelled inquirer master of the characteristic scenery of events associated with the noblest recollections, and the most stupendous interests of mankind.

The Views of Jerusalem and the surrounding countries had been presented, from all their leading points, and in all their varieties of aspect, with the same purpose; that of giving a complete conception of localities sacred to every feeling of religious homage. Thus, to those who contemplate a journey to Palestine, this work will contribute valuable knowledge: to those who have travelled there, the revival of recollections which none would willingly suffer to pass away: and to the larger class, who from circumstances remain at home, faithful representations, not only of the country, but of the habits of the people, and the companionship of the "Children of the Desert."

To the observer of Nature, the peninsula of Sinai is one of the most singular anomalies on the globe. It is an immense mass of mountains, without any of the discoverable purposes for which mountains seem to have been formed. It marks no boundary between nations; its summits collect no waters to fertilise the surrounding region; and, so far as research has hitherto gone, the Sinaitic range has not exhibited any of those mineral treasures, either metal or marble, which constitute mountains a source of wealth to man. Thus, standing in the midst of a Desert which almost prohibits human possession, pouring no river from its pinnacles on the plain, and barren alike of mineral and vegetable production, its existence remains a great physical problem.

Yet are we not entitled to regard the problem as solved by Scripture, and by Scripture alone? If it was the purpose of Divine Providence to draw the most visible line of distinction between the slavery of the Egyptian serf and the discipline of the Israelite; between a race accustomed to the grossness of Egyptian idolatry, and a nation designed as the especial depositories of the true worship; between the languor of frames exhausted by an African climate, or oppressed by the labours of the brick-kiln and the manufactory, and the temperate and hardy habits of the traveller and the mountaineer; or even to teach that sense of the sublime, and that breadth and boldness of thought, which are unconsciously inspired by scenes of natural grandeur; no spot on Earth could have been found fitter to make all those powerful and essential impressions than the mountain mass of Sinai. When we recollect the greatness of the purpose, can we be surprised at the majesty of the means? Can we contemplate the majesty of the means, without a new homage to the power of Providence? or can we rationally doubt that this purpose was designed, from the hour when the Deluge went down, the Globe was again prepared for the uses of mankind, and its divisions marked for the future dwelling of nations? No territory of the Earth ever accomplished objects of such holiness, might, and magnitude. It witnessed a succession of miracles, on the scale of a people, and with a duration of forty years; it trained the most memorable of all nations to Law, Government, and Religion. Its purpose was then done; Sinai became a wilderness once more: and it has never been repeopled, to this hour. Its purpose was fulfilled, — amply, once, and For Ever!

Quay at Suez February 11th 1834

David Roberts R.A

Scene on the Quay of Suez

IT may still be too early to predict the future importance of the comparatively quiet Quay of Suez; although the failure of the attempt to improve our intercourse with India by the navigation of the Euphrates has hitherto left the direct passage between Europe and Asia by the Red Sea without a rival. A point which unites two quarters of the globe, and by which two oceans have their nearest connexion, would naturally, with the increasing activity of commerce, increase in value; notwithstanding the want of fresh water, of every kind of verdure, and the utter absence of cultivation. The date of Suez does not go farther back than the earlier period of the sixteenth century, when it became the place of transit for Eastern merchandise, and even fitted out naval armaments. The discovery of the passage by the Cape of Good Hope gradually reduced its value; and it existed only as a place for provisioning the caravans to Mecca; but now, the employment of steam navigation, and the British intercourse with the East, promise to remove the wretched establishments on the Quay of Suez. Yet, even this contingency depends on others. The shallowness of the Gulf at this part is already felt as a serious obstruction; and a Railway directed to any more favourable point of the shore would consign the Town to immediate decay. The project of a Ship Canal would be equally fatal; and although this has hitherto been only a matter of theory, it would be difficult to limit the enterprise of a Government which in six months completed the Mahmoodieh Canal forty miles long!

From the Letters

The other letter, from Roberts's countryman Allan Cunningham, proffering his assistance in the literary portion of the work. Roberts often regretted afterwards that Cunningham's offer was not accepted.

26th March, 1840

My dear Roberts,—I have been able to think of nothing else save your drawings since I saw you last night. They are equally interesting and peculiar, and I am glad that you are about to make the world better acquainted with their merits.

I told you that the person who penned the letterpress should be familiar with Scripture and with Eastern History. I may now add, on reflecting on the character of the drawings, that he should also have a taste in art, and a knowledge both of sculpture and architecture. It is easy to write a few graceful sentences, but they must be to the point, must illustrate not encumber the engravings, else they will be worse than vain. Now I know not but I might be tempted to offer you the use of my pen if you are not already engaged to some other writer. I have not travelled, it is true, but the subject is familiar to my mind, and I have taste enough in art, and knowledge enough in architecture, to induce me to think that, with the aid of your own recollections and notes, I should acquit myself without blame but with honour. My admiration of your drawings and of the subject has driven me to make this offer, which, till I looked over your portfolio, I did not dream of.—I remain, my dear Roberts, yours always,

Allan Cunningham

General View of Suez

SUEZ (in Arabic, Suweis) stands on a corner of land projecting into the head of the Arabian Gulf, distant from Cairo about sixty four geographical, or seventy-five English statute miles. The site of Kolsum (Tell Kolsum) is still traceable, a third of a mile from Suez. The names of Arsinoe, Cleopatris, and Clysma, are given to imaginary sites in the neighbourhood; all of which were probably only elder forms of Kolsum.

"Even among the miserable cities of Turkey and Egypt, few present so wretched an appearance as Suez. Standing on the borders of the Desert and on the shore of the Sea, with bad and unwholesome water, and not a blade of grass growing around it, and depending upon Cairo for the food which supports its inhabitants, it sustains a poor existence by the trade of the great caravan for Mecca, and the small commerce between the ports of Cosseir, Djiddeh, and Mocha. A new project has lately been attempted here, which, it might be supposed, would have a tendency to regenerate the fallen city. The route to India by the Red Sea is in the full tide of successful experiment; the English flag is often seen waving in the harbour; and about once in two months an English Steamer arrives from Bombay: but even the clatter of a steam-boat is unable to infuse life into its sluggish population."[1]

It is only eight years since this description was written, on the spot; and now there are not only arrivals and departures of the English steam-packets, twice in the month, for England and Bombay, but steam communications even to China. The rapid and valuable intercourse now established between Europe and our Asiatic possessions across the African Isthmus, has, in spite of every disadvantage of climate and infertility, already raised Suez to an importance which no town on the Gulf ever possessed before.

The place of the Passage of the Israelites has excited much learned inquiry. It has been generally supposed to commence from the mouth of the Wady Tawarik, south of Ras Atakah. But this hypothesis seems untenable, from the breadth of the Sea, which there is twelve geographical miles.

The more probable conception is, that the passage was made across the small arm of the Sea, which runs up by Suez, a breadth of less than four miles. From the Sacred Narrative, a North (or N.E.) wind blew "all night" (uncovering the shoals above the site of Suez). And in the "morning watch" (at two in the morning) the Sea returned. Thus not more than two or three hours seem to have been allotted for the passage of three millions of people. Within this time they might have hastened over the narrow arm, while to march the greater distance would have been impossible. The miracle consisted, not in the march of the people, but in the Divine direction of the wind; and the return of the waters at the command of Moses.[2]

[1] Stephens's Incidents of Travel.　[2] Biblical Researches, i.83.

Convent of Ukbah (Wadi Feiran) Feby 24th 1839

David Roberts, R.A

Fortress of Akabah

THIS Fortress is situated at the head of the Gulf of Akabah, on the Red Sea, and lies in the usual route of travellers who visit Petra from Egypt, taking Mount Sinai and other places of Biblical interest on their way.

The present Fortress was built in the sixteenth century, by the Sultan el Ghoury of Egypt. It is square, with strong angular towers, and contains a garrison of thirty men. It stands near the sea-shore, from which it is separated only by a grove of date trees. The chief advantage of its position is derived from its wells of tolerably good water, both within and without the Fort. It is a depôt for the supply of provisions to the pilgrims who accompany the great caravans to and from Mecca. The Artist made careful researches, and even examination of the wells, in search of evidence, from sculptured remains or inscriptions, of its history before the sixteenth century, but without success;[1] though there is little doubt that it occupies the site of Elath-Ailah, or Ælana; from this name was probably derived that of the Ælanitic Gulf, given to this arm of the sea. Ælana was probably a city near the port of the Edomites, who were conquered by David. After him Solomon made here an important port, when he so much extended maritime commerce in the East.

There are many tumuli near Akabah; heaps formed by the ruins of ancient structures. The water on the coast is very shallow, and sharp shelving rocks forbid the idea that the ancient port was at Akabah; near it, on the other side of the Bay, lies the Island of Graia, offering a most favourable position for a naval station. The Artist thinks, with great probability, that this was the Ezion-Geber of Scripture, while Elath was the entrepot of its commerce.

[1] Roberts's Journal.

Arabs of the Tribe of the Benisaid Feby 7th 1834

Arabs of the Desert

THE principal figure is Besharah, an intelligent native of the Beni Said tribe, who accompanied Mr. Roberts from Egypt to Mount Sinai and Akabah.[1]

The dress of all the Arab tribes who were met with on the route to Petra is nearly the same. Where the person is of rank, as in the present instance, the turban is worn; but in general, a kerchief of gay colours, folded diagonally, is bound round the head by a fillet of dark worsted, or a cord, leaving the corners to fall over the neck and shoulders. A coarse shirt, with loose sleeves, hanging to the knee, is gathered round the waist by a leathern girdle; over this is worn a large mantle of woolen stuff, striped in bands of white and brown. The legs and feet are generally without covering, but some wear sandals of fish-skin. They are all armed with a broad, crooked knife, about eighteen inches long, and a matchlock gun of the rudest construction.

[1] Roberts's Journal.

Facsimile pages from David Roberts' Private Journal to the East.

Courtesy of the National Library of Scotland, Edinburgh.

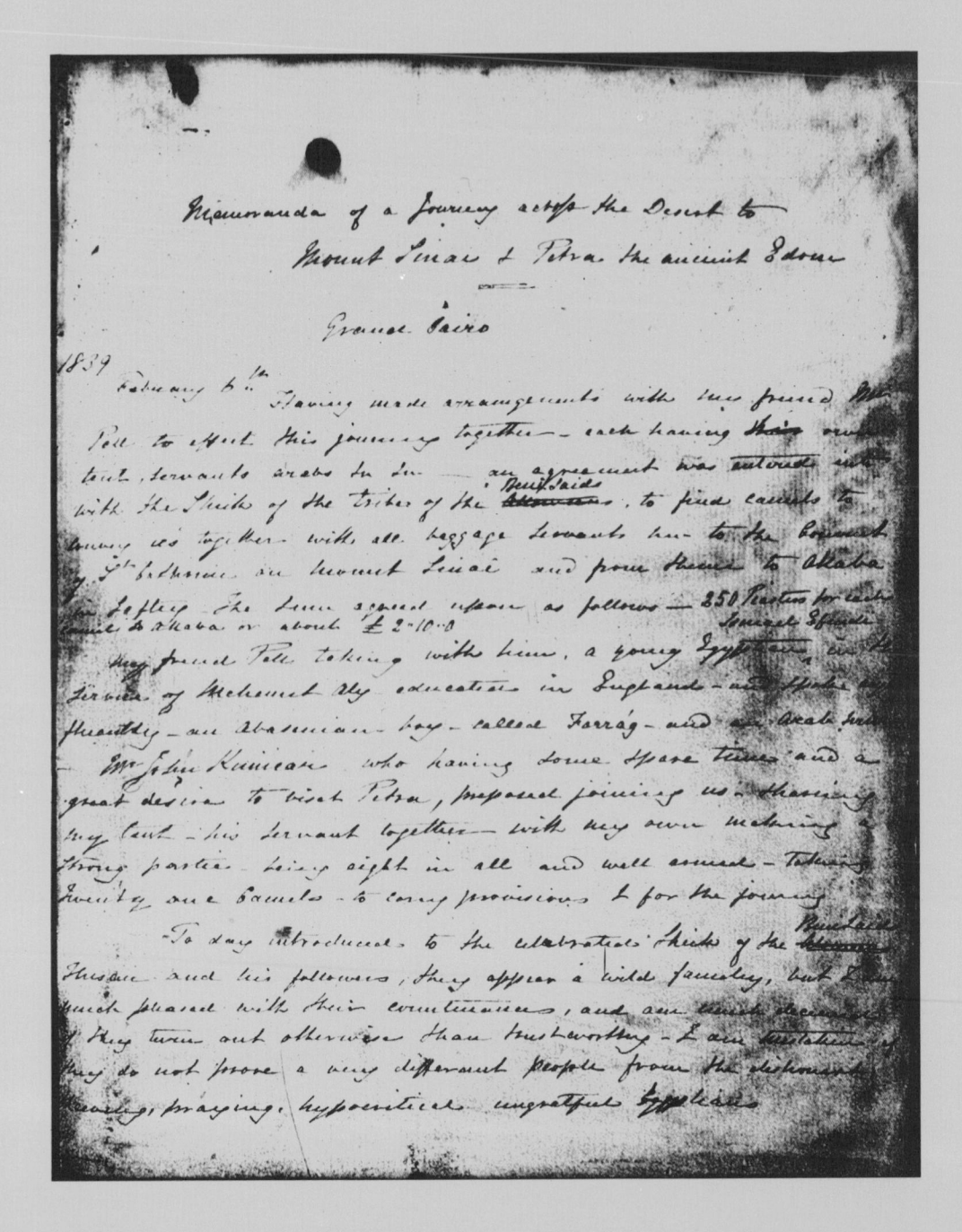

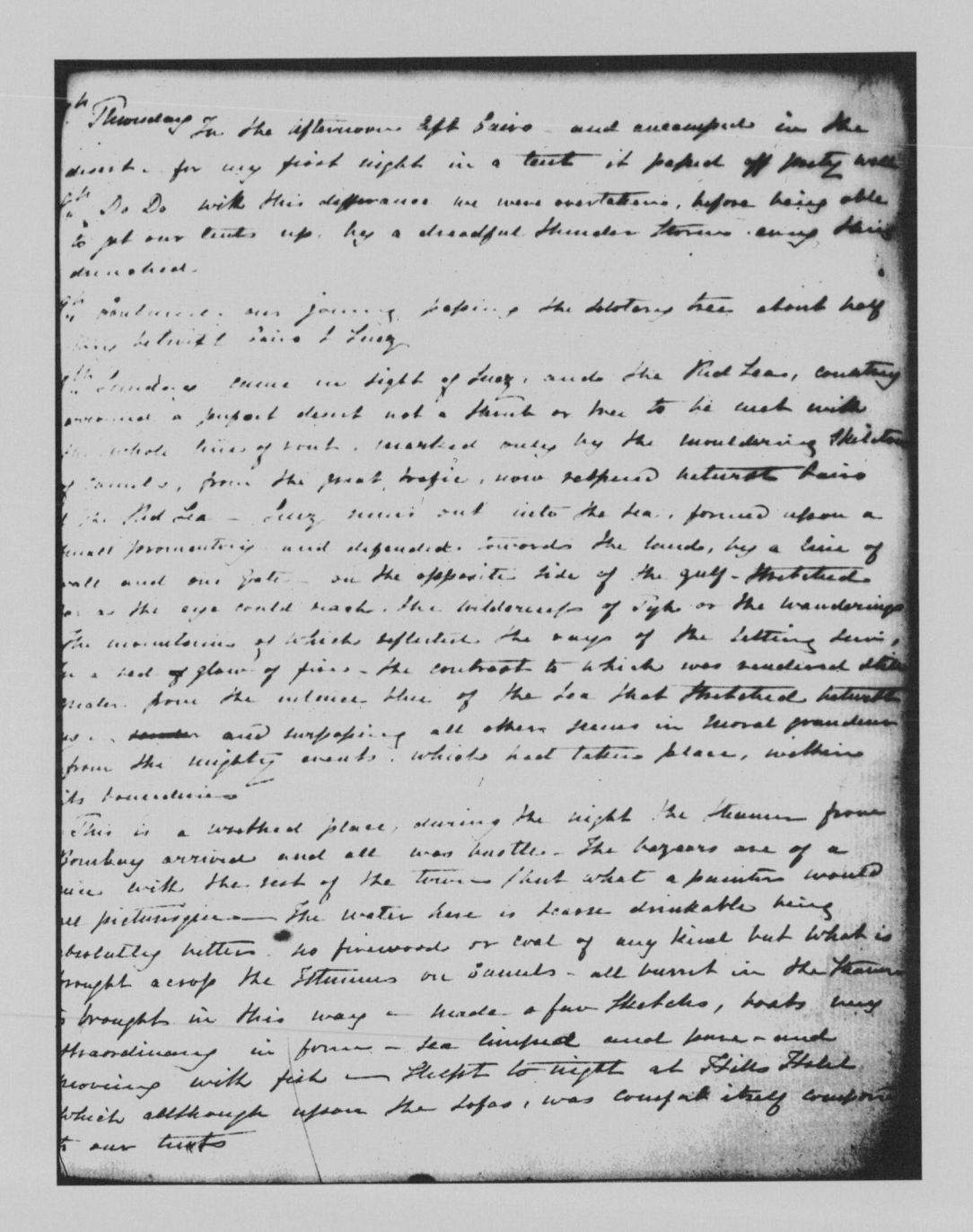

The most undoubted part of this enclosure is facing the West... the approach to it is difficult and can only be found by those well acquainted with the locality. There are two entrances to the enclosure on which stands the mosque of Omar, on the West side and this part which is held most sacred is about one hundred feet to the South of the most southern of the two entrances and is partly hidden by houses. Here the stones are of equal magnitude with those of the East & South sides, but from being partly concealed by the houses are probably in better preservation. The Jews still resort here at stated periods... to their brethren... the sons of Levi... from the Temple... that the feast of the passover was about to commence. I was taken to this part by one of the young Jewish converts who have just taken up their abode here. He informed me, that this part of the Temple facing the hill of Zion, is the part still held in the greatest veneration and even when he himself beheld it a Polish Jew & christian, his eyes were so filled with tears that he could distinguish nothing around him. The unfortunate Jews cannot even here pray in peace but are pelted with stones which in the very act and every insult is heaped upon the unfortunate remnant that still... the city of David.

Examining closely the stones of which the wall is constructed I found it to

a compact lime stone. I observed many Hebrew characters written in ink upon the stones, which my young friend translated for me, and in a small chink I found a leaf printed in Hebrew. It contained a prayer beginning 'Blessed are they that praise the God of Israel. May also the sons of Jacob scattered over the face of the earth be gathered again under the walls of his temple again in prayer to his name.' A tear glistened in his eye as he read & responded to the prayer & carefully... it... where he... placed it... found it in.

There are five of these young men, all Polish Jews, who are doctors as well as missionaries which not only affords them a means of support but gives them great influence over the people as they look upon every European as a Doctor & place implicit faith in their prescriptions. I, myself have been extremely fortunate in the cases that have been referred to me, through my remedies seldom went beyond a colonel pill in most cases it has brought relief to the patient and many times when I did not even apply it myself. —

The Mosque of Omar was described to me by Ismael Effendi after... not having seen Burkhardt's

Facsimile pages of the List of Subscribers — published in the First Edition (1842), London.

LIST OF SUBSCRIBERS.

THE QUEEN'S MOST EXCELLENT MAJESTY.

HER MAJESTY ADELAIDE, THE QUEEN DOWAGER.

HIS IMPERIAL MAJESTY THE EMPEROR OF ALL THE RUSSIAS.

HIS IMPERIAL MAJESTY THE EMPEROR OF AUSTRIA.

HIS MAJESTY THE KING OF THE FRENCH.

HIS MAJESTY THE KING OF PRUSSIA.

HIS MAJESTY THE KING OF BAVARIA.

HIS HIGHNESS MEHEMET ALI, PASHA OF EGYPT.

HIS GRACE THE LORD ARCHBISHOP OF CANTERBURY.

HIS GRACE THE LORD ARCHBISHOP OF YORK.

THE RIGHT HONOURABLE LORD WHARNCLIFFE, LORD PRESIDENT OF THE COUNCIL.

HIS SERENE HIGHNESS PRINCE ESTERHAZY.

HIS GRACE THE DUKE OF WELLINGTON, CHANCELLOR OF THE UNIVERSITY OF OXFORD.

HIS GRACE THE DUKE OF NORTHUMBERLAND, CHANCELLOR OF THE UNIVERSITY OF CAMBRIDGE.

THE RIGHT HONOURABLE SIR ROBERT PEEL, BART., M.P., FIRST LORD OF THE TREASURY.

THE HONOURABLE THE EAST INDIA COMPANY.

The Most Noble the Marquis of Lothian.
The Most Noble the Marquis of Lansdowne.
The Most Noble the Marquis of Abercorn.
The Most Noble the Marquis of Ely.
The Most Noble the Marquis of Northampton.
The Most Noble the Marquis of Bristol.
The Most Noble the Marquis of Blandford.
The Most Noble the Marquis of Titchfield.
The Right Honourable the Earl of Derby.
The Right Honourable the Earl of Essex.
The Right Honourable the Earl of Athlone.
The Right Honourable the Earl of Westmoreland.
The Right Honourable Countess of Jersey.
The Right Honourable Countess Dowager of Ashburnham.
The Right Honourable the Earl of Dartmouth.
The Right Honourable Earl Grey.
The Right Honourable Countess of Mount Edgecumbe.
The Right Honourable Countess of Gainsborough.
The Right Honourable Lord Viscount Kenmure.
The Right Honourable Lord Viscount Powerscourt.

The Right Honourable Lord Viscount Melville.
The Right Honourable Lord Viscount Canning.
The Right Honourable Lord Viscount Acheson.
The Right Honourable Viscountess Milton.
The Right Honourable and Right Rev. Lord Bishop of London.
The Right Reverend Lord Bishop of Llandaff.
The Right Honourable Lord Arundel.
The Right Honourable Lord Ward.
The Right Honourable Lord Gray.
The Right Honourable Lord Monson.
The Right Honourable Lady Langford.
The Right Honourable Lord Ravensworth.
The Right Honourable Lord Wenlock.
The Right Honourable Lord Ashley, M.P.
The Right Honourable Lord Walpole.
The Right Honourable Lord Francis Egerton, M P.
The Right Honourable Lord Claude Hamilton, M.P.
The Right Hon. Sir G. H. Rose, M.P., G.C.H.
Monsieur le Baron Köller.
Monsieur le Baron Taylor.

List of Subscribers

A.

Joseph Ablett, Esq.
Mr. T. Agnew.
P. B. Ainslie, Esq.
Miss Alderson.
Henry Alexander, Esq.
Andrew Allen, Esq.
Samuel Angell, Esq.
E. E. Antrobus, Esq.
Mrs. Applebee.
W. Archer, Esq.
W. Armston, Esq.
Messrs. Artaria and Fontaine.
Messrs. Asher and Co.
Wm. Astell, Esq., M.P.
Mr. B. Atkinson.
Charles B. Auber, Esq.
Col. Austin.

B.

Lady A. C. Baird-Preston.
J. Bailey, Esq.
Sir E. B. Baker, Bart.
Geo. Bankes, Esq., M.P.
W. Barber, Esq.
David Barclay, Esq., M.P.
R. Barclay, Esq.
G. R. Barclay, Esq.
Lieut.-Gen. Sir Andrew Barnard, G.C.B.
J. R. Barker, Esq.
Sir Thos. Baring, Bart.
G. H. Barnett, Esq.
R. C. Barston, Esq.
John Horatio Bastard, Esq.
W. Butterworth Bayley, Esq.
R. Beauchamp, Esq.
C. Beckett, Esq.
Rev. C. Beckford.
William Bell, Esq.
W. Bellamy, Esq.
W. Bennett, Esq.
J. C. G. Bennett, Esq.
J. W. Bennett, Esq.
Hon. and Rev. H. Bertie.
R. Bethell, Esq.
R. Bevan, Esq.
Elhanan Bicknell, Esq.
J. T. Bigge, Esq
E. Bilke, Esq.
Miss Birch.
W. Bissett, Esq.

Mrs. John Blake, Jun.
W. Blanshard, Esq.
Thos. Blaydes, Esq.
S. Boddington, Esq.
F. Bode, Esq.
Mr. L. Booth.
W. S. Booth, Esq.
James Bourdillon, Jun., Esq.
J. Bourke, Esq.
E. C. Boville, Esq.
G. Bowes, Esq.
R. Bowley, Esq.
Mrs. Alfred Bowman.
R. Bowman, Esq.
John Bradbury, Esq.
J. R. G. Braddyll, Esq.
R. W. Brandling, Esq.
George Brooke, Jun., Esq.
J. Brown, Esq.
Messrs. J. G. and T. C. Brown.
Col. Sir J. Bryant, C.B.
David Bryce, Esq.
W. Bumstead, Esq.
Mr. Burland.
Geo. Burnand, Esq.
Burton Archer Burton, Esq.
John Bustard, Esq.
Thos. Butler, Esq.

C.

B. B. Cabbell, Esq.
J. H. Calcraft, Esq.
Thos. Calverley, Esq.
Sir Robert Campbell, Bart.
A. F. Campbell, Esq.
Archibald Campbell, Esq.
Arthur Cane, Esq.
Mr. J. Carr.
J. J. Cavan, Esq.
Hon. R. Cavendish.
H. Cazenove, Esq.
Elias Chadwick, Esq.
Edward Chance, Esq.
W. R. Chapman, Esq.
Wm. Chapman, Esq.
Joseph Chater, Esq.
George Chater, Esq.
Miss C. Cheap.
Alex. Chisholm, Esq.
The Misses Christie.
W. Stanley Clarke, Esq.

H. B. Clarke, Esq.
Mrs. E. Clayton.
J. Clements, Esq.
Geo. Coates, Esq.
Sir C. B. Codrington.
S. Collins, Esq.
Mrs. Colley.
Messrs. Colnaghi, Son, and Co.
R. Copland, Esq.
R. Corbett, Esq.
Rev. T. Cornthwaite.
Capt. Alexander Cotton, R.N.
Wm. Cotton, Esq.
Thos. Lane Coulson, Esq.
Miss Burdett Coutts.
R. S. Cox, Esq.
W. C. Crane, Esq.
A. J. B. Cresswell, Esq., M.P.
Mr. A. Crichton.
Rev. George Croly, LL.D.
A. Crookenden, Esq.
Sir R. H. Cunliffe, Bart.
J. W. Cunningham, Esq.
Miss Currer.
Messrs. Currie and Co.

D.

Thomas Danger, Esq.
E. T. Daniel, Esq.
Miss Daniel.
H. Davidson, Esq.
Mr. G. Davey.
Mr. R. Davies.
H. De Castro, Esq.
J. E. Denison, Esq., M.P.
Thos. Devas, Jun., Esq.
Mrs. Deverill.
M. De Vitré, Esq.
David Dias, Esq.
Charles Dickens, Esq.
Francis Dickens, Esq.
John Dickinson, Esq.
Mr. J. Dickinson.
Mr. J. Dimmock.
W. F. Donkin, Esq.
John Dowell, Esq.
R. S. Drayton, Esq.
W. Drysdale, Esq.
L. Duckworth, Esq.
James Duncan, Esq.
Wedderburn Dundas, Esq.

E.

Thomas Edge, Esq.
Neil B. Edmonstone, Esq.
James Egan, Esq.
Russell Ellice, Esq.
Richard Ellison, Esq.
Lieut.-Gen. Sir W. Eustace, K.C.H.
W. C. Eustace, Esq.
Rev. R. W. Evans.
John Evans, Esq.
J. W. Evans, Esq.
Mr. E. Everitt.
Walter Ewer, Esq.
W. H. Exley, Esq.

F.

Rev. F. W. Faber.
R. W. Fenning, Esq.
Henry Fenwick, Esq.
George Ferrer, Esq.
T. F. Field, Esq.
J. Fielden, Esq., M.P.
Charles Finch, Esq.
Mr. J. Finlay.
Samuel Flemming, Esq.
William Flint, Esq.
G. Folliott, Esq.
R. Forbes, Esq.
Antoine Forrer, Esq.
John Forster, Esq.
C. Forster, Jun., Esq.
H. Hawes Fox, Esq.
William Fox, Esq.
J. W. Fraser, Esq.
Mr. Freeman.
James Fripp, Esq.
J. S. Froude, Esq.
D. W. Fry, Esq.
Joseph Fry, Esq.
Mr. E. Fry.

G.

H. Gaitskell, Esq.
Col. Archibald Galloway, C.B.
Rev. E. Gardiner.
Thomas Garrard, Esq.
James Garstang, Esq.
Sir William Geary, Bart.
John R. Gee, Esq.
Mr. R. Gell.

List of Subscribers

Richard Gilbert, Esq.
Mr. J. Gilbert.
William Gillham, Esq.
Robert Gillman, Esq.
Rev. B. Goodrich.
W. H. Goore, Esq.
James Gillispie Grahame, Esq.
Rev. Walker Gray.
Alexander Green, Esq.
George Greenwell, Esq.
R. H. Gregg, Esq.
Thomas Greig, Esq.
Rev. T. S. Grimshawe.
Miss Grindlay.
Capt. Grindlay.
John Grindrod, Esq., M.D.
Mr. J. C. Grundy.
Arthur Guiness, Esq.
Sir John Guise, Bart., K.C.B.
Hudson Gurney, Esq.
Joseph J. Gurney, Esq.
Frederick Gye, Jun., Esq.

H.

Moses Hadfield, Esq.
James S. Hamilton, Esq.
— Harding, Esq.
John Hardy, Esq., M.P.
J. S. Harford, Esq.
Mr. Harraden.
Charles Harris, Esq.
J. Harrison, Esq.
Sir J. Dalrymple Hay, Bart.
D. R. Hay, Esq.
B. R. Haydon, Esq.
Stephen Heelis, Esq.
Samuel Hemmings, Esq.
Hon. and Rev. V. C. Henniker.
Mr. H. Hering.
B. Hick, Esq.
H. B. Hickman, Esq.
— Hill, Esq.
D. O. Hill, Esq.
Miss Hill.
Mr. A. Hill.
Charles Hindley, Esq., M.P.
Capt. John Hine.
C. H. Hodgson, Esq.
Mr. Hogarth.
James Weir Hogg, Esq., M.P.
John Hog, Esq.

Mrs. Holcombe.
Lieut. Col. Gwynne Holford.
Marcus H. Holmes, Esq.
S. Hooper, Esq.
Rev. Thos. H. Horne.
Admiral Sir W. Hotham, G.C.B.
Miss Houghton.
John Houseman, Esq.
G. F. Howe, Esq.
John Howell, Esq.
Rev. Thomas Hubbard.
William Hulton, Esq.
S. B. Hunt, Esq.
John Hurst, Esq.
F. Hurst, Esq.
Rev. Robert Hussey.

I.

Rev. L. H. Irving.

J.

W. B. James, Esq.
Sir W. Jardine.
Sir R. Jenkins, M.P., G.C.B.
Mrs. Jenkins.
Mr. R. Jennings.
George Jervis, Esq.
Gaskell Johnson, Esq.
Mrs. Johnson.
J. J. Hope Johnstone, Esq., M.P.
S. H. Jonas, Esq.
Mr. E. Jones.

K.

Monsieur De Kalergi.
Mrs. Thomas M. Keith.
Thomas R. Kemp, Esq.
J. J. Kent, Esq.
R. T. King, Esq.
John George Kinnear, Esq.
Arthur J. Knapp, Esq.
Mrs. Knibb.
Mr. Thomas Knibb.
H. Gally Knight, Esq., M.P.
George Knott, Esq.
George A. Kollman, Esq.

L.

James Lamb, Esq.

J. M. Leake, Esq.
W. Leatham, Esq.
Henry Ledgetter, Esq.
Miss Leifchild.
Miss Leigh.
Rev. F. K. Leighton.
Robert Leonard, Esq.
C. P. Leslie, Esq.
Colonel Lewis.
R. G. Leycester, Esq.
B. Lindo, Esq.
Hon. Hugh Lindsey.
R. G. Lingee, Esq.
Mr. G. Linnecar.
Edward Lloyd, Esq.
George Lock, Esq.
E. Loder, Esq.
Mrs. Long.
Killet Longe, Esq.
R. W. Lopez, Esq.
Mr. G. Lovejoy.
Major-Gen. Sir J. L. Lushington, G.C.B.
Miss Lushington.
George Lyall, Esq. M.P.
V. S. Lyne, Esq.
Mr. H. Lacy.

M.

E. A. Mackenzie, Esq.
Charles Maclaren, Esq.
John Macvicar, Esq.
W. McClure, Esq.
Peter McLagan, Esq.
George Magnay, Esq.
Rev. J. Mainwaring.
Sir John Marjoribanks, Bart.
Henry Man, Esq.
Mrs. Mansion.
Mr. T. K. Margetts.
Edward Marr, Esq.
J. Markwell, Esq.
R. C. Marsden, Esq.
F. Marshall, Esq.
— Marshall, Esq.
H. C. Marshall, Esq.
W. Martin, Esq.
Algernon L. Massingberd, Esq.
John Masterman, Esq., M.P.
John Masterman, Jun., Esq.
Joseph Mayer, Esq.

James Meadows, Esq.
William Meyer, Esq.
Capt. H. Meynell, R.N., M.P.
Rev. Dr. Mill.
P. J. Mills, Esq.
W. Miller, Esq.
Messrs. Miller and Field.
Mr. A. Milliken.
Lady Milner.
David Mitchell, Esq.
Mr. J. A. Molteno.
Alex. Moneypenny, Esq.
C. J. Monkhouse, Esq.
Hugh Montgommery, Esq.
R. C. Moody, Esq.
P. M. Moorhouse, Esq.
Sir John Mordaunt, Bart., M.P.
William Morris, Esq.
James Morrison, Esq., M.P.
Joseph Morton, Esq.
Charles Moss, Esq.
John Moxon, Esq.
John Murray, Esq.
W. H. Murray, Esq.
John Petty Muspratt, Esq.

N.

J. W. Neate, Esq.
John Needham, Esq.
W. Noble, Esq., M.D.
John North, Esq.
G. B. Northcote, Esq.
Mr. J. L. Norton.

O.

Thomas C. Oldham, Esq.
O. Ommanney, Esq.

P.

C. W. Packe, Esq., M.P.
Messrs. Parbury, Allan, and Co.
M. E. N. Parker, Esq.
C. Parker, Esq.
C. S. Paris, Esq.
Sir J. D. Paul, Bart.
G. R. Paul, Esq.
Robert Peake, Esq.
Mrs. Elizabeth Pease.
George Peel, Esq.
C. Peers, Esq.

List of Subscribers

E. O. Pemberton, Esq.
Hon. W. H. Percy.
Hugh Perkins, Esq.
W. Peters, Esq.
N. Philips, Esq.
Philographic Society of Plymouth.
Edw. Piper, Esq.
W. H. Playfair, Esq.
Rev. J. J. Plumer.
R. H. Podmore, Esq.
R. H. Pollen, Esq.
Mrs. E. Popillon.
J. Porter, Esq.
Henry Potts, Esq.
Charles Potts, Esq.
B. E. Potz, Esq.
R. C. Powles, Esq.
John Poynder, Esq.
E..Poynder, Esq.
E. R. Pratt, Esq.
Mr. Purchase.

R.

Rev. H. Raikes, Chancellor of the Diocese of
   Chester.
A. Rainy, Esq.
A. Randall, Esq.
Col. John Dawson Rawdon.
John Rawson, Esq.
T. S. Rawson, Esq.
S. Rendall, Esq.
Foster Reynolds, Esq.
Miss J. Richardson.
C. J. Richardson, Esq.
Mr. J. M. Richardson.
Legh Richmond, Esq.
Joseph Ridgway, Esq.
W. Rivington, Esq.
H. C. Robarts, Esq.
W. Robertson, Esq.
Thomas Robinson, Esq.
W. G. Romaine, Esq.
Edmund Roper, Esq.
Rickman Ross, Esq.
— Ross, Esq.
John Ruskin, Esq.
H. T. Ryall, Esq.
Mr. J. Ryman.

Rev. J. Salter.
Rev. Hugh Salvin.
W. T. Salvin, Esq.
Joseph Sandiford, Esq.
G. F. Sargent, Esq.
J. J. Saunders, Esq.
J. Schneider, Esq.
Mrs. Schinomelpenninck.
M. Schunck, Esq.
William Scott, Esq.
Mr. J. Seacome.
Thomas Seddon, Esq.
H. K. Seymer, Esq.
H. H. Seymour, Esq.
R. C. Sewell, Esq., D.C.L.
Rev. W. Sewell.
W. Shackell, Esq.
Mr. W. Sharland.
C. Sharp, Esq.
Miss Sharpe.
William Shaw, Esq.
John Sheppard, Esq.
Mr. R. Sheppard.
Henry Shield, Esq.
Mrs. Sidebotham.
H. Sievier, Esq.
G. P. Simcox, Esq.
Messrs. Simms and Son.
George Simson, Esq.
W. J. J. Sinclair, Esq.
Rev. J. Slade.
James Slater, Esq.
Messrs. Slocombe and Simms.
Mrs. Sloper.
John Smart, Esq.
T. C. Smith, Esq.
Joseph Grace Smith, Esq.
Martin Tucker Smith, Esq.
David Smith, Esq.
Messrs. Smith, Elder, and Co.
Dr. G. Smyttan.
E. V. Southerne, Esq.
John B. Sparke, Esq.
C. Spicer, Esq.
Mr. Sprent.
W. R. C. Stansfield, Esq., M.P.
Rev. Henry Stebbing, D.D.
Thomas Stillwell, Jun., Esq.
William Stirling, Esq.
William Stone, Esq.
Charles Stone, Esq.
J. Sundius, Esq.

Mr. R. Sunter.
Rev. Dr. Swete.
Sir John Swinburne, Bart.
Lieut.-Col. William Sykes.
Lady Sykes.

T.

C. M. Taylor, Esq.
Edw. Clough Taylor, Esq.
Thomas Taylor, Esq.
Colonel Tempest.
Rev. W. Tennant.
F. W. Tetley, Esq.
S. P. Thomas, Esq.
Samuel Thomas, Esq.
Mrs. M. Thompson.
H. S. Thompson, Esq.
Thomas Thorby, Esq.
Venerable Archdeacon Thorp.
Reymes Thurell, Esq.
Mr. C. Thurnham.
B. Tipper, Esq.
W. Tipping, Esq.
Rev. W. W. Tireman.
Mrs. Todhunter.
John Tollemache, Esq., M.P.
C. Tottie, Esq.
J. Townsend, Esq.
Sir John Trevelyan, Bart.
James Tripp, Esq.
G. S. Trower, Esq.
C. Trueman, Esq.
Capt. Harvey Tuckett.
E. R. Tunno, Esq.
Charles Hampden Turner, Esq.

U.

Joseph Unwin, Esq.
Richard Urwick, Esq.
E. V. Utterson, Esq.

V.

Mr. W. H. Vale.
R. H. Valpy, Esq.
Lieut.-Col. Patrick Vans Agnew, C.B.
Rev. Kerr Vaughan.
Rev. James Veitch.
W. A. Vere, Esq.
John Vere, Esq.

W.

Thomas Waghorne, Esq.
C. E. Wagstaff, Esq.
J. B. Walbancke, Esq.
J. T. Walker, Esq.
Miss Walker.
Samuel Walters, Esq.
F. Warden, Esq.
Mr. J. Watson.
Major-Gen. Welsh.
Rev. H. Wheeler.
G. White, Esq.
Mr. J. D. White.
Alfred Whitmore.
W. Wigram, Esq.
Sir David Wilkie, R.A., dec.
W. Willmott, Esq.
Sir H. Willock, K.S.L.
R. P. Willock, Esq.
John Wilson, Esq.
Miss Wollaston.
Rev. R. W. K. Wood.
G. Woodfall, Esq.
J. Woodhouse, Esq.
John Woods, Esq.
C. M. Woodyer, Esq.
P. Wraighton, Esq.
J. Wrexford, Esq.
R. Wright, Esq.
Rev. C. Wright.

Y.

Sir W. Young, Bart., M.P.

Z.

Mr. J. Zanetti.

List of Pictures Painted by David Roberts*

Year	No.	Subject of Picture	Buyer	Price £	Exhibited
1821	1	New Abbey, Dumfriesshire	A dealer	Never paid for	
	2	Old House, Cowgate, Edinburgh	Baron Clerk-Rattray	2 10	Edinburgh.
	3	The Nether Bow, Edinburgh	James Stewart	2 10	Edinburgh.
1824	4	New Abbey, Dumfriesshire	Mrs. H. Bicknell	...	Edinburgh.
	5	Dryburgh Abbey—given to	Gosden	...	British Institn.
	6	East Front, Melrose Abbey	Sir Felix Booth	26 5	British Artists.
	7	South Transept, Melrose Abbey	Sir Felix Booth	26 5	British Artists.
1825	8	West Front, Notre Dame, Rouen	Sir Felix Booth	84 0	British Artists.
	9	Entrance to the Church of St. Maclou, Rouen	M.A. Taylor, M.P.	26 5	British Artists.
	10	South Transept of Notre Dame, Rouen	M.A. Taylor, M.P.	26 5	British Artists.
	11	Part of the Church of St. Jacques, Dieppe	W. Robins	12 12	British Artists.
1826	12	Chancel of Church of St. Jacques, Dieppe	Lord Northwick	200 0	British Institn.
	13	Exterior of Rouen Cathedral	Lord Northwick	200 0	Royal Academy.
	14	Interior of the Pantheon, or Church of St. Genevieve, Paris	Marquis of Stafford	84 0	British Artists.
	15	Rue du Change, Rouen	A dealer	30 0	British Artists.
	16	Exterior of St. Jacques, Dieppe	William Beckford	52 10	British Artists.
1827	17	Entrance to St. Genevieve, Amiens	Colnaghi	...	R.A.
	18	Interior of Choir of York Minster	Colnaghi	...	
	19	Marché au Blé, Abbeville	Robert Vernon	63 0	British Institn.
	20	Part of Hotel de Ville, Louvain	Sir Francis Freeling	42 0	British Institn.
	21	Interior of St. Gudule, with the Oak Pulpit, Brussels	...	...	British Institn.
	22	West End of Roslin Castle	Lord Carysfort	52 10	British Artists.
	23	Shrine of Edward the Confessor, Westminster Abbey	Lord Northwick	84 0	British Artists.
	24	Exterior of Cathedral of Notre Dame, Antwerp	Lord Northwick	157 10	British Artists.
	25	Alloway Kirk—the scene of Burns' 'Tam o' Shanter'	Lord Northwick	...	British Artists.
1828	26	Chancel of St. Rombould, Tirlemont	Lord Northwick	31 10	British Institn.
	27	Tower of St. Rombauld, Mechlin	Duke of Bedord	26 5	British Artists.
	28	Entrance to a Church—composition	E.M. Westmacott	8 8	British Artists.
	29	Exterior of St. Wulfran, Abbeville	Buchan	40 0	British Artists.
	30	View in Abbeville	Marquis of Lansdowne	26 5	British Artists.
	31	The Bargate, Southampton	Buchan	15 15	British Artists.
1828	32	Exterior of Town Hall, Louvain	William Wells	21 0	...
	33	Tower of St. Rombauld, Mechlin—a replica	William Wells	26 5	...
	34	Chapel of the Virgin, St. Pierre, Caen	Lord Northwick	84 0	British Institn.
1829	35	Exterior of Church of St. Remy, Amiens	Scarnel	15 0	British Institn.
	36	Interior of St. Jacques, Dieppe—a replica	W. Trotter	...	Edinburgh.
	37	Exterior of Antwerp Cathedral—a replica	Gritten	...	Edinburgh.
	38	Exterior of Town-Hall, Ghent	J.P. Ord	31 10	Edinburgh.
	39	Exterior of St. Maclou, Rouen	J.P. Ord	31 10	Edinburgh.
	40	Interior of St. Rombauld, Tirlemont	Lord Farnborough	52 10	British Artists.
	41	Departure of the Israelites out of Egypt— a composition	Lord Northwick	...	British Artist.
1830	42	Choir of the Church of St. Pierre, Caen	William Wells	84 0	British Artists.
	43	Exterior of the Chapel of the Virgin, St. Pierre, Caen	J.P. Ord	84 0	British Artists.
	44	Ruins of the Monastery of the Black Friars, St. Andrews	Walker	21 0	British Artists.
	45	Ruins of Cathedral of St. Regulus, St. Andrews	Redfern	26 5	British Artists.
	46	Composition of Hindoo Architecture	Captain Grindlay	21 0	British Artists.
	47	Exterior of St. Pierre, Caen—given to	E. Childe	...	...
	48	Exterior of South Transept, Rouen Cathedral—given to	E. Childe	...	...
	49	Exterior of Church of St. Lawrence, Rotterdam—given to	D. R. Hay	...	...
	50	The Castle of Nuremberg, on the Rhine—given to	John Jackson	...	...
	51	The Shrine—a composition	Marquis of Lansdowne	...	R.A.
1831	52	Exterior of Great Entrance to Rouen Cathedral	D.R. Hay	105 0	British Artists.
	53	Interior of Church of St. Sauveur, Caen	Marquis of Lansdowne	...	British Institn.
	54	Ruins—a composition	Robert Vernon	36 15	...
	55	Interior of a Church—a composition	Earl of Essex	21 0	...
	56	Ruins of Cathedral of St. Rule, St. Andrews	Duke of Bedford	26 5	British Artists.
	57	Part of the South Front of the Courtyard of Falkland Palace	...	...	British Artists.
	58	Interior of a Churc, a composition given to	John Fawcet	...	British Artists.
1832	59	Grand Staircase, Stafford House	Marquis of Stafford	200 0	British Artists.
	60	View on the Rhine	Charles Farley	14 0	British Artists.
	61	Ruins—a composition	...	105 0	British Artists.
	62	Exterior of St. Lawrence, Rotterdam—a replica	...	26 5	British Artists.
	63	Interior of Lady Chapel, St. Pierre, Caen	James Stewart	26 5	British Artists.
	64	The Fallen Tower, Heidelberg	...	...	British Artists.
	65	Edinburgh Castle from the Grassmarket	Lord Wharncliffe	63 0	British Artists.
1834	66	Interior of Seville Cathedral	D.R. Hay	300 0	British Institn.
	67	Exterior of the Tower of the Giralda— Painted at Seville	G.G. Barrett	115 10	British Artists.
	68	Interior of a Flemish Church	General Phipps	36 15	British Artists.
1832	69	Interior of a Church	J. Fairley	52 10	British Artists.
	70	Tower of Church of St. Nicholas, Cordova	Cawston	14 0	British Artists.
	71	The Tower of the Giralda, Seville	T. Dyson	25 0	British Artists.
	72	View on the Rhine	Charles Farley	10 10	R.A.
1835	73	Old Houses on the Durro, Granada	J. Sheepskins	54 10	
1835	74	Exterior of Cathedral, Burgos	Captain Barrett	150 0	R.A.
	75	Fortress of the Alhambra, Granada	Lord Northwick	52 10	
	76	Interior of Chapel in the Cathedral, Bayonne	Gritten	20 0	R.A.
	77	Exterior of Lady Chapel, Bordeaux Cathedral	Grittrn	20 0	...
	78	Moorish Tower and Bridge, Cordova	...	52 10	British Artists
	79	Part of Exterior of Cathedral, Burgos	Duke of Sutherland	50 0	

* As published by J. Ballantine, Edinburgh, 1866.

List of Pictures

Year	No.	Subject of Picture	Buyer	Price £	Exhibited
	80	Court of the Lions, Alhambra	Count Jenison	31 10	
	81	Old Houses on the Darro, Granada	Artaria	26 5	...
	82	Gate of St. Jean, Bordeaux	Hastings	21 0	...
	83	Part of the Castle of Marchinella, Andalusia given to	Bright	...	...
	84	Interior of the Cathedral, Burgos	Robert Vernon	38 10	...
	85	Interior of Chapel in Bayonne Cathedral	Wadmore	37 15	...
	86	Gateway of Monastery of the Carmelites, Burgos—given to	J. Clarke	...	...
1836	87	Interior of Cahpel of Ferinand and Isabella, Granada	William Beckford	262 10	R.A.
1837	88	St. Paul's from Ludgate Hill, with the Lord Mayor's Procession	E. Goodall	42 0	...
	89	Exterior of St. Paul's Cathedral, with the Lord Mayor's Procession	J. Clarke	...	...
	90	Ruins of an Abbey—given to	Alexander Perie	...	...
	91	Edinburgh Castle—given to	J.M'Gregor	...	...
	92	General View of the Alhambra, Granada	Marquis of Lansdowne	315 0	R.A.
	93	General View of the Alhambra—a small replica	Thomas Miller	...	...
	94	Interior of the Mosque of Cordova	F.Hall Standish	105 0	...
	95	Tomb of the Percy Family, Beverley Minster given to	Mrs. H. Bicknell	...	...
	96	Tower of the Church of St. Mark, Seville	...	...	...
	97	Part of the Alhambra	Count Jenison	...	...
1838	98	High Altar of Cathedral at Seville	F. Hall Standish	105 0	...
	99	Exterior of Church of Ferdinand and Isabella Granada—given to	E. Bicknell		
1840	100	Interior of the Greek church of the Nativity, Bethlehem	F. Hall Standish	200 0	R.A.
	101	Outer Court of the Temple of Edfou, Egypt	F. Hall Standish	200 0	R.A.
	102	Gate of Metwalis, Cairo	H.M. The Queen	105 0	R.A.
	103	Remains of the Portico of the Lesser Temple of Baalbec	E. Bicknell	250 0	R.A.
	104	Statue of the Vocal Menon, Thebes—Sunrise	...	100 0	R.A.
1841	105	Bazaar of the Coppersmiths, Cairo	G. Knott	210 0	British Institn.
	106	Ruins of Baalbec—Lebanon in the distance	G, Knott	420 0	R.A.
	107	Bridge of Toledo	H.M. The Queen	52 10	R.A.
	108	Fountain on the Prado, Madrid	H.M. The Queen	52 10	R.A.
	109	Portico of the Great Temple, Dendera, Upper Egypt	D. Barclay, M.P.	330 0	R.A.
	110	Do.—a replica	Rev. W. Hurnard	100 0	R.A.
	111	Jerusalem from the Mount of Olives	Lord Monson	330 0	R.A.
1842	112	Interior of the Church of St. Miguel, Xerez	E. Bicknell	105 0	R.A.
	113	Thebes, looking across the Great Hall, Karnac	Llewellen	200 0	R.A.
	114	Termination of the Ravine leading to Petra—given to	E. Bicknell jun.	...	R.A.
	115	Interior of Church of St. Helena, Mount Sinai	D. Barclay, M.P.	210 0	R.A.
	116	Ruins of Temple of Kom Ombo—given to	Mrs. H. Bicknell		
	117	Gateway of Temple of Baalbec— diploma picture	Royal Academy	...	R.A.
1843	118	Ruins on the Island of Philæ, Nubia	J.Pell	100 0	R.A.
	119	Interior of Roslin Chapel	J. Sheepshanks	105 0	R.A.
	120	The Gate of the Mosque of Metwalis, Cairo	J. Sheeoshanks	105 0	R.A.
	121	Entrance to the Crypt, Roslin Chapel	G. Knott	157 10	R.A.
	122	Interior of Church of Stanford-on-Avon	Baroness Braye	126 0	R.A.
1844	123	The Pyramids of Ghezeh—Sunset	Baroness Braye	126 0	R.A.
	124	The Temple called Pharaoh's Bed, Philæ	Grundy		
	125	Interior of Chapel in the Church of St. Jean, Caen	Bacon	210 0	R.A.
	126	Interior of Chapel of the virgin, St. Pierre, Caen	Bacon	84 0	R.A.
	127	Interior of Roslin Chapel	J. Feilden	100 0	
	128	Ruins of the Temple at Baalbec	T. Dyson	31 10	...
	129	Ruins of Temple of Erment	T. Dyson	31 10	...
1845	130	Ruins of the Great Temple of Karnac	J. Arden	400 0	R.A.
	131	Jerusalem from the South-East	Lord Fras.Egerton	315 0	...
	132	Porch of Roslin Chapel—given to	T. M'Kinlay	...	...
	133	Interior of Roslin Chapel—given to	P.S. Fraser	...	...
	134	Street in St. Lo, Normandy	W.Wethered	50 0	...
	135	Interior of Melrose Abbey	E. Bicknell	40 0	...
	136	Interior of Church of St. Pierre, Caen	W.Wethered	20 0	...
1846	137	Ruins of the Temple of the Sun, Baalbec	G. Yong	105 0	British Institn.
	138	Grand Cairo from the high ground to the East of the City	...	...	R.A.
	139	Tombs of the Caliphs, Cairo	G. Young	105 0	R.A.
	140	Ruins of the Temple of the Sun, Baalbec	James Foster	210 0	R.A.
	141	Street in Grand Cairo	E. Bicknell	52 10	R.A.
	142	High Altar of St. Antoine, Ghent	Art Union	200 0	R.A.
1847	143	Edinburgh from the Castle	S. Jones Loyd, M.P.	525 0	R.A.
	144	Interior, a Recollection of Spain— Composition	J. Arden	110 0	R.A.
	145	West Front of Antwerp Cathedral	R. Newsham	210 0	R.A.
	146	Baalbec, Surprise of a Caravan—given to	The Garrick Club	...	...
	147	Craigmillar Castle—given to	J. Mereweather	...	...
	148	Ruins of Baalbec	A. Fraser	...	...
1848	149	Chancel of the Collegiate Church of St. Paul, Antwerp	Robert Vernon	350 0	R.A.
	150	Ruins of Temple of Hermonthes, Upper Egypt	...	...	R.A.
	151	Mount of St. Michael, Coast of Normandy	James Foster	250 0	R.A.
	152	Mount St. Michael, from the Sands— given to	Mrs. H. Bicknell	...	...
	153	Interior of a Church, composition—given to	Mrs. H. Bicknell	...	...
1849	154	Destruction of Jerusalem by Titus	Llewellen	500 0	R.A.

List of Pictures

Year	No.	Subject of Picture	Buyer	Price £		Exhibited
	155	Roberts' Interview with the				
		Pacha of Egypt	...	...		...
1850	156	Interior of St. Gomar, Lierre	E. Bicknell	315	0	R.A.
1851	157	Interior of St. Jacques, Antwerp	S. Rucker	315	0	R.A.
	158	Shrine of St. Gomar, Lierre	R. Newsham	105	0	R.A.
	159	The Sanctuary of the Koran,				
		Mosque of Cordova	T.G. Fonnereau	52	10	R.A.
	160	Entrance to the Great Temple of				
		Aboosimbel in Nubia	T.G. Fonnereau	52	10	R.A.
	161	Remains of the Eastern Portico of the				
		Temple of the Sun at Baalbec, Mount				
		Lebanon in the distance	S. Rucker	157	10	R.A.
	162	View looking from under the Portico of the				
		Great Temple of Edfou, Upper Egypt	Gambart	80	0	R.A.
	163	Ruins, Egypt—given to	F. Rogers	...		...
	164	The Sea of Galilee—given to	Mrs. H. Bicknell	...		...
	165	The Simoom—given to	Charles Dickens	...		...
	166	Portico of the Temple of Philæ	...	...		British Instit n.
	167	Donaldson's Hospital, Edinburgh	W.H. Playfair	200	0	...
	168	High Altar of St. Jacques, Bruges	...	...		R.A.
	169	Entrance to the North Transept,				
		Crystal Palace	H.M. The Queen			
	170	Surprise of the Caravan—Scene in Syria	James David	500	0	
	171	Interior of St. Ann's, Bruges	T. Jackson	400	0	R.A.
1852	172	Interior of St. Stephen's Cathedral, Vienna	T. Cubitt	500	0	R.A.
	173	Venice—the Piazzetta and Ducal Palace	T. Cubitt	400	0	0
	174	Exterior of Antwerp Cathedral	T. Cubitt	300	0	R.A.
	175	Lucerne—given to	Mrs. H. Bicknell	...		...
1853	176	Proposed restoration of the				
		Temp of the Sun at Tivoli on a rock				
		called Dunsapie, near Edinburgh	S. Christie, M.P.	84	0	R.A.
	177	Gibraltar and the African Coast—given to	Mrs. H. Bicknell	...		...
	178	Entrance to Carmona—given to	J. Mereweather	...		...
	179	Elgin Cathedral, from the Lossie	Gambart	50	0	...
	180	Dunblane Cathedral	Gambart	50	0	...
	181	Ruins of the Temple of Kom Ombo, Morning	Gambart	125	0	...
	182	Ruins of the Temple of Kom Ombo, Evening	Gambart	125	0	...
	183	Caerlaverock Castle	Gambart	125	0	...
	184	Church of the Jesuits, Grand Canal, Venice	Gambart	125	0	...
	185	Venice, the Ducal Palace	Lord Londesborough	525	0	R.A.
	186	Rome from Mount Onofrio—Finished				
		Sketch for the Edinburgh picture	Mrs. H. Bicknell	...		...
	187	Inauguration of the International Exhibi-				
		tion, May 1851	H.M. The Queen	630	0	R.A.
	188	Interior of Cathedral of St. Stephen, Vienna	J. Davis	525	0	R.A.

Year	No.	Subject of Picture	Buyer	Price £		Exhibited
	189	Street in Verona	J. H. Turner	136	10	R.A.
	190	Bethlehem, looking towards the Dead Sea	W. Bashall	165	0	R.A.
1854	191	View on the Canal of the Guidecca, Venice	A. Brooks	250	0	R.A.
	192	Town of Tiberias, Mount Hermon in the				
		distance	A. Brooks	150	0	Winter Exhib.
	193	Saida, looking towards the range of Le-				
		banon	A. Brooks	150	0	Winter Exhib.
	194	The Dogana and St. Maria della Salute,				
		Venice—given to	Mrs. H. Bicknell	...		...
	195	Interior of St. Peter's, Rome—Christmas				
		Day, 1853	T. Cubitt	1050	0	R.A.
	196	Rome from the Convent of St. Onofrio—				
		given to	R. Scottish Academy	...		...
1855	197	Ruins of Temple at Pæstum	R. Newsham	157	10	
	198	Ruins of Temple of Pæstum—different view	W. Williams	157	0	
	199	Façade of the Temple of Neptune, Pæstum	Llewellen	200	0	
	200	Approach to the Grand Canal, Venice	Jos. Miller	150	0	R.A.
	201	St. Peter, Rome, from the Villa Madama				
		given to	Mrs. J. Arden	...		R.A.
	202	Interior of St. Stephen's Cathedral, Vienna				
		—small replica	W. Wethered	157	10	...
	203	The Opening of the Crystal Palace, Syden-				
		ham, finished Sketch—given to	Sir J. Paxton, M.P.	...		...
1856	204	Tower of Santa Fosca, Torcello—given to	Mrs. H. Bicknell	...		...
	205	Roslin Castle—given to	Rev. James White	...		...
	206	Interior of St. Jacques, Bruges	Thos. Miller	210	0	
	207	Monuments of the Scaligeri, Verona	Rollins	210	0	R.A.
	208	Monument to Bartolomeo Colleoni, S.S.				
		Giovanni e Paolo, Venice	...	...		R.A.
	209	Mount St. Michael, Normandy	James T. Caird	210	0	R.A.
	210	Interior of Church of St. Gomar, Lierre	T. Baring, M.P.	600	0	R.A.
	211	The Basilica of San Lorenzo, Rome—				
		Interior	Aldn. Salomons, M.P.	525	0	...
	212	The Piazza Navona, Rome	...	...		R.A.
1857	213	Tyre	E. Bicknell	157	10	R.A.
	214	Sidon	...	...		R.A.
	215	Interior of the Duomo, Milan	J. Holdsorth	650	0	R.A.
	216	San Giorgio Maggiore, Venice				R.A.
1858	217	Ruins of Baalbec—given to	Mrs. E. Berry	...		R.A.
	218	Distant View of Edinburgh	Mrs. H. Bicknell	...		R.A.
	219	The Ducal Palace, Venice	...	...		R.A.
	220	The High Altar in the Church of S.S.				
		Giovanni e Paolo, Venice	James T. Caird	630	0	...
	221	Edinburgh from the Calton Hill	Robert Napier	525	0	...
1859	222	Ruins of the Forum Romanum	William Herbert	220	0	...

Year	No.	Subject of Picture	Buyer	Price £		Exhibited
	223	Entrance to Pisa	Gambart	200	0	...
	224	Exterior of St. Maria della Salute, Venice	James T. Caird	...		...
	225	View on the Via Appia, Rome—given to	Mrs. H. Bicknell	420	0	R.A.
	226	Market Place, Verona	Gambart	200	0	R.A.
	227	Interior of Mark's Cathedral, Venice	H.W. Eaton	630	0	...
	228	Interior of St. Mark's Venice—another view	Theophilus Burnand	262	10	
	229	Interior of Cathedral, Pisa	B. Preston	525	0	R.A.
	230	The Forum, Rome	W. Wethered	52	10	...
	231	Forum and Temple of Jupiter, Rome	W. Wethered	52	10	...
	232	Arch of Titus, Rome—given to	Mrs. H. Bicknell	•	...	...
	233	Ruins of Kom Ombo, Nile	Rev. James White	...		...
	234	Ruins of Temple of Neptune, Pozzuolo	Rev. Jamrs White	...		...
	235	Temple of Pallas, Rome	Gambart	100	0	...
	236	Ruins of the Forum of Nerva, Rome	Gambart	100	0	...
1860	237	Great Square of St. Mark, Venice	Gambart	525	0	R.A.
	238	Street in Antwerp	J.B. Bunning	150	0	R.A.
	239	Approach to the Forum, Rome	R. Ravenhill	210	0	R.A.
	240	The Collosseum, Rome—Evening	R. Ravenhill	210	0	R.A.
	241	The Cathedral and Piazza, Brescia	Flateau	157	10	
	242	Jerusalem from the Mount of Olives— painted on a Proof of his umpub- lished Plate	Flateau	105	0	
1860	243	On the Grand Canal, Venice—given to	James Mereweather	...		...
	244	Piazza of St. Mark, Venice, looking towards the Canal	Gambart	200	0	R.A.
	245	Piazza of St. Mark, Venice, from the Canal	Gambart	200	0	R.A.
	246	Jerusalem looking south	Gambart	400	0	...
	247	Castle and Bridge of St. Angelo, Rome— given to	Mrs. H. Bicknell	...		...
	248	A Fête-Day at St. Peter's, Rome—Interior	Robert Napier	840	0	R.A.
	249	Interior of Collegiate Church of St. Paul, Antwerp—given to	Mrs. J.T. Caird	...		...
1861	250	Interior of Church of S.S. Giovanni e Paolo, Venice	Mrs. H. Bicknell	...		...
	251	Temple of the Sun, Baalbec	D. Dunbar	700	0	R.A.
	252	Interior of Chancel, St. Paul's, Antwerp	A. Burnand	525	0	R.A.
	253	The Houses of Parliament from Millbank	C. Lucas	210	0	R.A.
	254	Somerset House and the Adelphi from Hungerford	C. Lucas	210	0	R.A.
	255	St. Paul's from Waterloo's Bridge	C. Lucas	210	0	R.A.
	256	Houses of Parliament and Westminster Abbey	C. Lucas	210	0	R.A.
	257	The New Palace of Westminster from the Thames	C. Lucas	525	0	R.A.
	258	Greenwich Hospital from the River	C. Lucas	525	0	R.A.
	259	St. Paul's Cathedral from Blackfriars	C. Lucas	525	0	R.A.

Year	No.	Subject of Picture	Buyer	Price £		Exhibited
	260	Interior of Chapel in the Cathedral of Notre Dame, Bruges	Lancaster	420	0	R.A.
1862	261	Egyptian Temple and Pyramids, a com- position—given to	Mrs. H. Bicknell	...		...
	262	Egyptian composition—given to	Dr. Bence Jones	...		...
	263	The Ducal Palace from the Grand Canal, Venice	Gambart	210	0	French Gallery
	264	The Doganan and Santa Maria, Venice	Gambart	210	0	R.A.
1863	265	Edinburgh from Calton Hill, looking west	Gambart	105	0	
	266	Edinburgh from Calton Hill, looking east	Gambart	105	0	
	267	The Brig o'Doon, Ayr—given to	James Ballantine	...		...
	268	Interior of St. Stephen's Cathedral, Vienna	J.B. Bunning	210	0	R.A.
	269	Interior of Milan Cathedral	T. Burnand	525	0	R.A.
	270	St. Paul's from the River, looking east	C. Lucas	210	0	R.A.
	271	St. Paul's from the Thames, looking west —sunset	C. Lucas	...		...
	272	Site of the Capitol from the Tiber, Rome	Gambart	262	10	
	273	Interior of Church of St. Jacques, Bruges	Gambart	262	10	
	274	Rome, View on the Tiber looking towards Mounts Palatine and Aventine	Gambart	262	10	
	275	Interior of Church of St. Jean, Caen	Gambart	262	10	
	276	View of the Mausoleum of Hadiran, better known as the Castle of St. Angelo, from the Villa Barberini, Rome	T.J. Miller, M.P.	630	0	R.A.
	277	Interior of Chapel in the Church of Dixmude	J. Pender, M.P.	630	0	R.A.
	278	Interior of Basilica of St. Peter, Rome— small replica of Mr. Napier's	Gambart	525	0	
	279	St. Andrews from the Sea—given to	Mrs. H. Bicknell	...		...

David Roberts contributed illustrations to many publications, of which the following are the most important:—

Bulwer's *Pilgrims of the Rhine,* 1834.

The *Landscape Annual* for four years, 1835 to 1838.

Roberts' *Picturesque Views in Spain,* published 1837.

The publication of Roberts' great work, *Sketches in the Holy Land, Syria, and Egypt,* commenced in 1842 and was completed in 1849. The large plates measured 19 inches by 13, the vignettes 13 by 9.

He also furnished a number of drawings for *Scotland Delineated,* published in 1847.

His 'Departure of the Israelites from Egypt' was engraved in mezzotint by Quilley— size 28 inches by 18.

MAP

to Illustrate

THE ROUTE OF

DAVID ROBERTS, ESQ; R.A.

IN

THE HOLY LAND, PETREA & SYRIA.

NOTE—*The Route is indicated thus* ▬▬▬

Arca Erek

TRIPOLIS

Theuprosopon Pr.

Botrys

Ebden

Bvidus Gebal

Baalbek or *HELIOPOLIS*

BEIRUT OR BERYTUS   Zalileh

Sidon   Jezzin   DAMASCUS

Sarepta   Mt. Hermon

Tyre   Banias or *CAESAREA PHILIPPI*

Kedesh

Lake Meram

ACRE OR ACO PTOLEMAS   Safed   Bethsaida or *IULIAS*   Neve

Mt. Carmel   Lake of Tiberias

Tiberias

Nazareth   Gadara

CAESAREA PALAESTINA   Zerin or Jezreel   Bethshean *SCYTHOPOLIS*

Jenin or Ginaea

SEBASTE OR SAMARIA   *Jerash or GERASA*

Apollonia   Nabulus or *SHECHEM*

Mt. Gilead

Shiloh

RABBATH AMMON PHILADELPHIA

JAFFA

Ludd or Lydda   Bethel   *JERICHO*

Ramleh   Ramah Gibeon

JERUSALEM

Asdod   Bethany

Bethlehem   St. Saba

Askalon

Beit Jebrin or *ELEUTEROPOLIS*   El Khulil or *HEBRON*   LAND OF MOAB

GAZA   Ain Jidy

DEAD SEA

RABBATH MOAB AREPOLIS

Kerak

Beersheba

MOUTHS OF THE NILE

ROSETTA   *DAMIETTA*

ALEXANDRIA   D E L T A   Khulasah

MAREOTIS   El Arish

Arabs Tower   Tineho   *Tafileh*

Tantah   Katieh   Bahrdoal

Abdeh

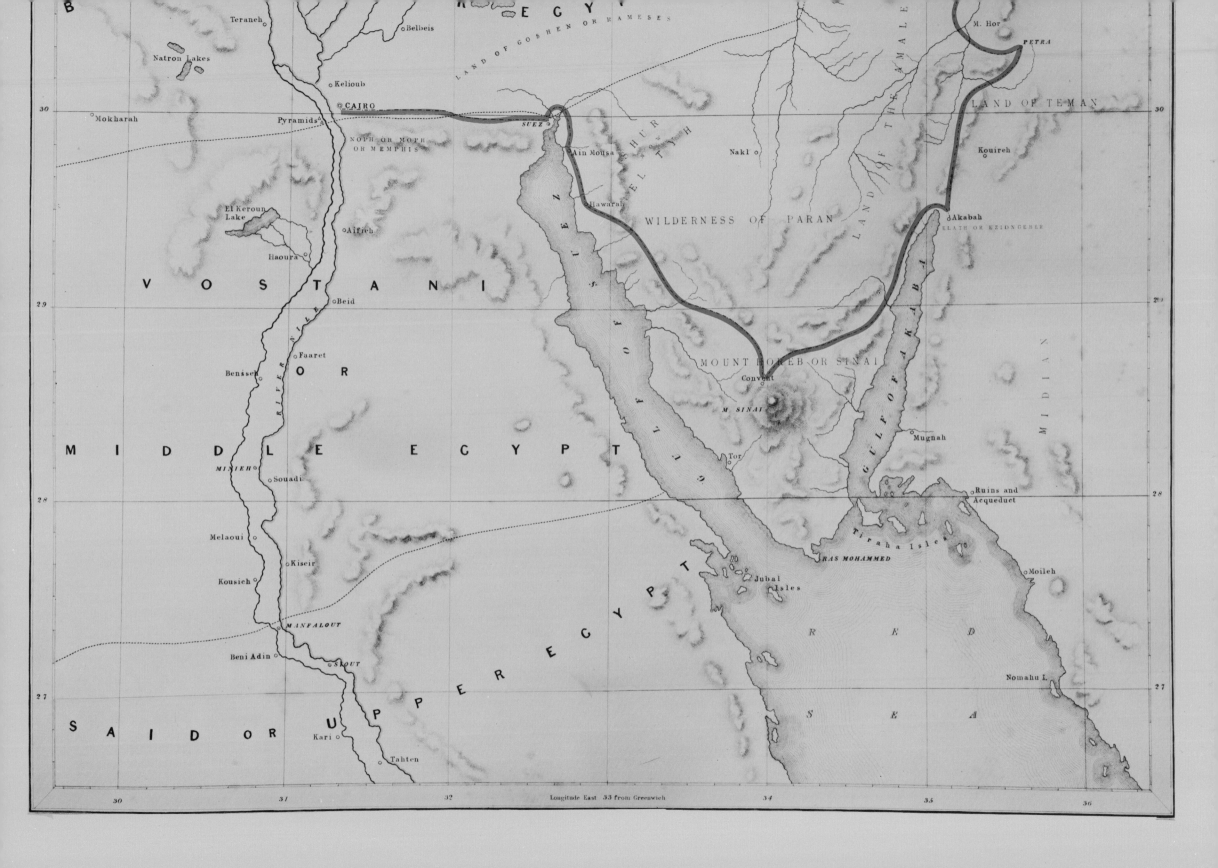

LIST OF LITHOGRAPHS IN THE SERIES OF DAVID ROBERTS "THE HOLY LAND"

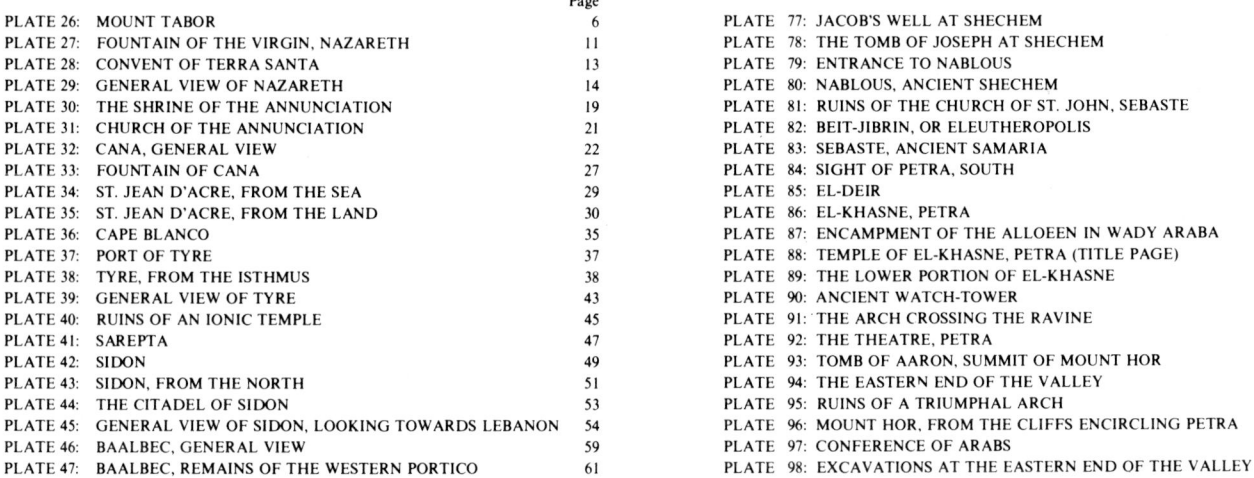

Note: The sequence of the Plates slightly differs from the First Edition, due to technical limitations.

SEPTENTRIO. h

IERVSALEM, et suburbia eius, sic ut tempore Christi floruit, cū locis in quib'
Christ'paff'est, quæ religiofe a Christianis obseruat, etiam nū Venerationi habent. Chrifti de
scripta per Christianum Adrichom Del phum.

Castra Romanorum 259.

Erebinthonices 261.

Stagnum Serpentū 268.

Fanum Chamos 193.

Vicus Jerusalem 270.

Alexand. Mag. 266. Castra Chaldeorum 258.

Castra Pompey 264. *Silu frugifera 267.*

Horti et prædia 262. Mausoleum Helenæ Reginæ 263.

Mons Septentrionalis 264.

Porta Turrium multi Ephraim 164. *Porta Ephraim 157.* *Turris Furnorum 172.* *Collis Gareb 260.* *Monumentum Herodis 265.*

IERVSALEM

255. *251.* *250.*

Turris Pfephma, chias Neb Iofa 175.

Murus tertius, 150.

NOVA CIVITAS 147. Platea BEZETHA 147. lata. Flor 150.

Castrum Affyrior. 149.

Turris Angularis 169.

Porta Anguli et Beniamin 135.

Monumentum Fullonis 194.

Mons scandali 193.

Mons Caluariæ 235.

Christus se tibi, Tu te Chrifto.

Turris Ulippus 141.

Via in Anathot. et Bethel 208.

Sepulchrum Domini 239.

249.

Murus fecun dus 136. qui et medius 136.

Mons Calaariæ 235.

Midas Tur ris 155. *Porta Vetula 138.* *Monumentum Aloxādri 174.*

Berg tha mons 148.

Porta Ge nath 159.

Euri fi 125. *Monumentum Joan Pont. 155.*

Porta Ephraim 156.

Structura Jacotea 140.

Locus 132.

Do Nem Maria 121. *Habeate no fardoates 151.*

VAL

Villa Mariam. *Strai topte don 139.* *256.*

Palatium Herodis.

Amygdale stagni 126.

SECUNDA CIVITAS 153.

Porta Ephraim 156.

Xenodochium 145.

Torrens Cedro.

248.

Regia 137.

Turris Pha feius 143. *Porta ferra 137.* *Turris me 142.*

Porta Vetus Iudiciaria 160.

Porta Prior.

Murus Primus 34. qui et anti quus 54.

FILIA SION

Palatium Pilati Præsidis Romani 172.

Monumentum Anani pontificis 237.

Regis Ma nobata 74. *Porta Ster quiling 163.*

Fons Drusini.

Piscina interior 61.

QVA

Baris pharaon 230.

Amphitheatru 28.

Forum scru tarium 48.

201. Stephanus 202.

Mons

Regia Grupte 62.

Christum 120.

Capnaculū 33.

Hortus Oliueti 188.

Rupes eminens 167.

Domus Simonis Phary 43.

Piscina interior 61.

Anto nia ark 29.

Turris Strutonis 116. *Piscina Probatica 36.*

Oli ue

Geth fema ni.

192.

Castra Herodis 231.

For. magnū 46.

Crypta 34.

Domus Nathinæorum 40. *Ophel. 55.*

210.

Villa 187.

211.

Gi

Salomon 236.

Acia mons 17.

Archiuum 30.

212.

on.

Turris et Habitacula.

Porta 64. *Porta Ster 66.* *facerdotum 50.*

CCIDENS.

ORIENS